ALCOHOLISM
AND AGING

ALCOHOLISM AND AGING

An Annotated Bibliography and Review

Compiled by
Nancy J. Osgood,
Helen E. Wood, and
Iris A. Parham

Bibliographies and Indexes in Gerontology, Number 24
Erdman B. Palmore, Series Adviser

GREENWOOD PRESS
Westport, Connecticut • London

Library of Congress Cataloging-in-Publication Data

Osgood, Nancy J.
    Alcoholism and aging : an annotated bibliography and review /
compiled by Nancy J. Osgood, Helen E. Wood, and Iris A. Parham.
        p. cm.—(Bibliographies and indexes in gerontology, ISSN
0743–7560 ; no. 24)
    Includes indexes.
    ISBN 0–313–28398–2 (alk. paper)
    1. Aged—Alcohol use—Bibliography.   2. Alcoholism—Bibliography.
I. Wood, Helen E.   II. Parham, Iris A.   III. Title.   IV. Series.
Z7721.083   1995
[HV5138]
016.3629′2′0846—dc20   94–41371

British Library Cataloguing in Publication Data is available.

Library of Congress Catalog Card Number: 94–41371
ISBN: 0–313–28398–2
ISSN: 0743–7560

First published in 1995

Greenwood Press, 88 Post Road West, Westport, CT 06881
An imprint of Greenwood Publishing Group, Inc.

Printed in the United States of America

The paper used in this book complies with the
Permanent Paper Standard issued by the National
Information Standards Organization (Z39.48–1984).

10 9 8 7 6 5 4 3 2 1

Contents

Series Foreword

The annotated bibliographies in this series provide answers to the fundamental question, "What is known?" Their purpose is simple, yet profound: to provide comprehensive reviews and references for the work done in various fields of gerontology. They are based on the fact that it is no longer possible for anyone to comprehend the vast body of research and writing in even one sub-specialty without years of work.

This fact has become true only in recent years. When I was an undergraduate (Class of '52) I think no one at Duke had even heard of gerontology. Almost no one in the world was identified as a gerontologist. Now there are over 6,000 professional members of the Gerontological Society of America. When I was an undergraduate there were no courses in gerontology. Now there are thousands of courses offered by most major (and many minor) colleges and universities. When I was an undergraduate there was only one gerontological journal (the Journal of Gerontology, begun in 1945). Now there are over forty professional journals and several dozen books in gerontology published each year.

The reasons for this dramatic growth are well known: the dramatic increase in numbers of aged, the shift from family to public responsibility for the security and care of the elderly, the recognition of aging as a "social problem," and the growth of science in general. It is less well known that this explosive growth in knowledge has developed the need for new solutions to the old problem of comprehending and "keeping up" with a field of knowledge. The old indexes and library card catalogues have become increasingly inadequate for the job. On-line computer indexes and abstracts are one solution but make no evaluative selections nor organize sources logically as is done here. These annotated bibliographies are also more widely available than on-line computer indexes.

These bibliographies will obviously be useful for students, teachers, and researchers who need to know what research has (or has not) been done in their field. This bibliography will also be useful to health care providers, service agencies, other professionals, and concerned relatives and friends of older persons with drinking problems. The annotations contain enough information so that the researcher usually does not have to search out the original articles. This bibliography features unusually long annotations in order to maximize the information reported.

In the past, the "review of literature" has often been haphazard and was rarely comprehensive, because of the large investment of time (and money) that would be required by a truly comprehensive review. Now, using these bibliographies, researchers and others concerned with this topic can be more confident that they are not missing important previous research and other reports; they can be more confident that they are not duplicating past efforts and "reinventing the wheel." It may well become standard and expected practice for researchers to consult such bibliographies, even before they start their research.

The research and writing relevant to alcoholism and aging has become a large and rapidly growing field. This is attested to by the 301 references annotated in this bibliography, plus about 100 listed at the end of Chapter 1 that were not annotated because of space limitations, and by the wide variety of disciplines represented here. Thus this volume will be useful to teachers, other professionals, and researchers in many different fields.

The author and her colleagues have done an outstanding job of covering the recent literature and organizing it into easily accessible form. Not only are the entries organized into five chapters dealing with different types of references, but there is an overview chapter, an author and subject index with many cross-references.

Thus one can look for relevant material in this volume in several ways: (1) look up a given subject in the subject index; (2) look up a given author in the author index; or (3) turn to the chapter that covers the type of reference in which you are interested.

Nancy Osgood is exceptionally well-qualified to produce this bibliography. She has long been a specialist in this area, has done significant research, and has published several articles and reports on geriatric alcoholism. She has also published another annotated bibliography in this series, *Suicide and the Elderly*.

So it is with great pleasure that we add this bibliography to our series. We believe you will find this volume to be the most useful, comprehensive, and easily accessible reference work in its field. I will appreciate any comments you care to send me.

Erdman B. Palmore
Center for the Study of Aging and Human Development
Box 3003, Duke University Medical Center
Durham, NC 27710

Introduction

This book was conceived during the course of an Administration on Aging (AoA) grant (#90-AM-0389) aimed at education about and prevention of alcoholism in community elders; this project was further refined and supported by the Virginia Geriatric Education Center Grant (1991-1994, #1D31AH63020[01-03] from HRSA, DHHS). For some time alcoholism has been recognized as a significant and costly health problem, but only in recent years has attention been paid to alcohol use and abuse in older adults. The literatures of gerontology and substance abuse are rapidly expanding and comprise diverse topics directed toward a variety of disciplines. Designing an adequate education and prevention program, therefore, required considerable investigative effort. Although the excellent bibliography by Barnes, Abel and Ernst (1980) provided numerous leads, virtually no published works containing concentrated bibliographic information on alcoholism and aging could be found for the last 12-15 years - a period that has witnessed a burgeoning of research interest in this topic. The goal of this book, then, is to fill the gap by bringing together in one volume a wide variety of references that represent the state of our knowledge on alcoholism and aging. A broad sample of works published in English since the late 1970's is cited herein and comprises review articles, original investigations, books and book chapters, and a variety of short works and case studies. Empirical works were afforded particular attention. Since many citations cover multiple areas of interest including epidemiology, risk factors, diagnosis, and treatment, the volume is organized by type of work (overview, book chapter, empirical article, and short work) rather than by topic. A subject index is included for the reader who is interested in specific topics. In an effort to provide as much information as possible to the reader, we composed annotations that are somewhat longer than usual (up to a page), particularly in the case of books and empirical works. This necessitated our confining the number of annotations to approximately three hundred in order to meet book length requirements. We regret, therefore, that not all works by all authors could be included; however, a representative sample from major authors in the field is included. Dissertations, unpublished papers, and conference presentations are not covered. In addition, the topics represented are devoted almost entirely to human subjects.

The annotations offered in this book are original summaries and reflect long hours of reading and research by the authors. Certainly, we take full responsibility for all information appearing here and apologize for any errors or oversights. References were obtained via computer searches, book and journal article reference lists, and personal searches of indexes, abstract sources, and journal issue contents. Listed below are the index and abstract sources that were consulted in compiling this book:

Ageline

CINL Cumulative Index to Nursing Literature

Current Contents, Social and Behavioral Sciences

ERIC index to education materials

Excerpta Medica

Gerontological Abstracts

Index Medicus

MEDLINE medical journal index

Nursing and Allied Health Literature Index

Psychology Abstracts

PSYCinfo index to psychological literature

Social Sciences Index

Sociology Abstracts

Although this book will undoubtedly appeal most to practitioners and researchers in the fields of aging and substance abuse, we hope that a wide variety of professionals - ministers, general practitioners, and mental health and social workers -,and professionals-to-be will find it useful and informative. It is our further hope that the information presented in this volume will stimulate a continued interest in detection, prevention, and treatment of alcoholism in older adults, as well as intensified and improved research efforts.

This project would not have been completed without a number of individuals and organizations. In particular, we would like to thank Pam MacIntyre for her excellent editing skills and library work, and our secretary, Debra Wood, for the many hours spent in formatting this text and making corrections. Barbara Fitzgerald provided an invaluable service by running computer searches and patiently checking for missing publication dates and volume numbers. Kay Lentz and Margaret Flannagan provided word processing assistance throughout the project, and students Michele Sykes, Suzanne Sherman, Amy Sharpe, and Cathy Churcher offered additional library help and editorial assistance when not studying for their gerontology classes. We offer a special thanks to consultants on the AoA project who provided additional resources: Drs. Marcia Lawton and Demetrios Julius, and the Geriatric Education Center at Virginia Commonwealth University. Colleagues who suggested books and articles to annotate include Drs. Frederick Blow, Anthony La Greca, and Larry Dupree. Certainly, this project could not have proceeded without excellent library services, and we would like to thank all the librarians of the reference and interlibrary loan offices at the Tompkins-McCaw and James Branch Cabell libraries, Virginia Commonwealth University/Medical College of Virginia. Last, but certainly not least, we thank our spouses, Ray Jordan, Mark Wood, and Ed Swarbrick, for their patience and loving support throughout this endeavor.

Alcoholism and Aging: An Overview

The field of alcoholism and aging is a relatively new area of scientific inquiry. Compared to what we know about the problem of alcoholism in teenagers, young adults, and middle-aged adults, our current state of knowledge about the problem of alcohol abuse and alcoholism in the elderly is meager. Until very recently, researchers were not particularly interested in alcohol problems among the elderly. However, with the dramatic increase in the numbers of older adults and the recent realization that many older people do have drinking problems, the field has expanded rapidly in recent years. In this chapter we will examine our current state of knowledge regarding alcoholism and aging, problems with existing data, and future research agendas that should be implemented.

PREVALENCE

Three types of studies have been conducted to examine the relationship between alcoholism and aging. Results from community surveys, longitudinal studies, and clinical studies provide very different findings. Surveys of drinking practices in community populations have provided strong evidence that older persons drink less than younger people and that, compared to other age groups, those 60 and older are more likely to be abstainers. Studies conducted on clinical populations have revealed much higher rates of alcoholism and heavy drinking among those 60 and older than rates reported in community surveys. Some longitudinal studies offer strong evidence for stability in drinking patterns over the lifecourse. Several explanations have been offered to account for the lower prevalence rates found for the community-dwelling elderly. Findings from these studies will be reviewed and discussed below.

Available data indicate that some older adults are more likely than others to drink heavily. A review of existing literature also reveals different types of older alcoholics. This section includes a discussion of types of older alcoholics and characteristics of older alcohol abusers and alcoholics.

Findings from Community Surveys

Estimates of prevalence rates of alcoholism and problem drinking in older adults, based on community surveys, have ranged from 2-10%. In one of the first large-scale community surveys (cross-sectional) Knupfer and Room (1964) conducted a household survey in 1962 of 1,268 persons in San Francisco. They collected data on the extent of heavy drinking using a complicated classification scheme, which utilized frequency and quantity of drinking behavior, as well as type of beverage consumed. They found that the proportion of abstainers was higher for those 60 and over than for any other age group. Only 14% of those 21 to 29 years of age were abstainers, compared to 41% in the age group 60+. They also found that the proportion of heavy drinkers steadily decreased by decades from 26% in the 21-29 age group to only 9% in the 60 and over age group. A large national probability sample survey yielding 2,746 interviews conducted in 1964-1965 by Cahalan, Cisin, and Crossley (1969), which utilized the same measures as Knupfer and Room (1964), also found higher percentages of abstainers in the older age groups. In the 21-29-year-old age group 24% were abstainers, compared to 47% in the over 60 age group. Cahalan and colleagues also found the incidence of heavy drinking was less in the oldest age cohort with only 6% classified as heavy drinkers, compared to 15% for those in the age groups 30-39 and 40-49. Thirty percent of their sample over 60 claimed they had drank more in the past.

Five other cross-sectional community surveys conducted in the 1970's revealed lower rates of heavy drinking and higher rates of abstention among older adults. Based on a survey of 169 working class people 65 and older living on the Upper East Side of Manhattan, Johnson and Goodrich (1974) reported that 86 (51%) older adults were abstainers. The prevalence of heavy drinking was approximately 1.2%. Rathbone-McCuan, Lohn, Levenson, and Hsu (1976) surveyed 695 persons 55 and older in Baltimore, Maryland, using the Michigan Alcoholism Screening Test (MAST). They found that 55% were non-drinkers. Barnes (1979) conducted a household survey of drinking patterns in Erie and Niagara Counties in Western New York State interviewing 1,041 individuals 18 years and older. Responses were used to establish a Quantity-Frequency-Variability (QFV) index of drinking behavior. Five categories of drinkers were derived: heavy, moderate, light, infrequent drinkers, and abstainers. Findings revealed a lower proportion of heavy drinkers and a higher proportion of abstainers in the older age group. Heavy drinking was almost nonexistent among older females (1). About a quarter of the males 60+ were heavy drinkers. About one-third of those 60+ were abstainers, compared to only 8% in the under 50 group and 13% in the 50-59 group. Older adults also reported significantly fewer alcohol-related problems such as driving while drunk in the previous year than did those 50 to 59 years of age or those under 50.

Results from a community survey of drinking behaviors of 928 persons 60 and older conducted in Boston in 1977 similarly revealed high rates of abstainers among older adults. Meyers, Hingson, Mucatel, Heeren, and Goldman (1985-86) found that 53% of those 60 and over were abstainers. A household survey of the adult population aged 18 and over conducted in 1978 in Canada (Smart & Liban, 1982) produced similar findings. Based on interviews with 1,103 individuals in 1,480 households, Smart and Liban found that alcohol dependency decreased with age. A much greater proportion of the 18-25-year-olds (39.4%) than those 60 and older (10.6%) reported at least one dependency symptom. Alcohol problems also decreased with age.

More recent data gathered in a large multi-site national study conducted in five U.S. cities, namely Baltimore, Los Angeles, New Haven, Durham, and St. Louis, confirm earlier findings of lower prevalence rates for alcohol dependence in older adults. The Epidemiological Catchment Area (ECA) Program was unique because it used criteria established by the <u>Diagnostic and Statistical Manual III-R</u> to determine diagnosis. The findings of the ECA study were that for men ages 18 to 29 lifetime prevalence for alcohol dependence was 27%; for men 30 to 44, it was 28%; for men 45 to 64 it was 21%; and for men 65 and older, it was 14%. Corresponding prevalence rates for women were 7%, 6%, 3%, and 1.5% (Miller, Belkin, & Gold, 1991). Douglass, Shuster, and McClelland (1988) also reported significantly lower prevalence rates for alcoholism or alcohol dependence for older people. In another recent cross-sectional study (Molgaard, Nakamura, Stanford, Peddecord & Morton, 1990) the percent prevalences of self-reported alcohol consumption were determined in a randomly-chosen sample of residents, aged 45 years and over, from San Diego County, California. Again, total drinking (in any amount) decreased from 70.2% in the youngest age category (45-54 years) to 49.6% in the oldest age category (75 years and over). This finding held up across three ethnic groups surveyed (Whites, Blacks, and Mexican-Americans). Gender and race were important moderating variables with the highest prevalence of self-reported drinking in any amount found among white males.

Not all studies have confirmed age-associated declines in heavy drinking and alcoholism. In one early community study conducted in the Washington Heights area of Manhattan, which contained a subsample of 987 people 65 and older, Bailey, Haberman, and Alksne (1965) found two peaks in prevalence rates for problem drinking. For those 20 and over the first peak occurred in the 45-54-year-old age group, where the prevalence rate was 23 per 1,000. The prevalence decreased to 17 per 1,000 for the age group 55-65 years of age. A second peak of 22 per 1,000 occurred in the 65-74-year-old group. Elderly widowers had a rate of 105 per 1,000.

Three longitudinal studies of drinking behavior have found stability in drinking patterns over the lifecourse. In their study of drinking patterns among the elderly in rural Arizona, Christopherson, Escher, and Bainton (1984) interviewed 444 people 65 years of age and older. They measured quantity and frequency of alcohol intake and average daily intake of alcohol. The results of the statistical analysis indicate that there are four types of older drinkers: abstainers, light drinkers; moderate drinkers; and heavy drinkers. There was strong evidence for either abstaining or drinking as stable, lifelong behaviors. Glynn, Bouchard, LoCastro, and Laird (1985) reported on patterns of drinking among various age groups of males in the Normative Aging Study, a longitudinal study of aging initiated in 1963 in Boston. The study included 2,100 community dwelling men born between 1884 and 1945, who were classified into six birth cohorts each spanning nine years. Levels of alcohol consumption reported in 1973 and 1982 were compared in order to determine time, period, and cohort effects. Based on their analysis the researchers concluded that over the nine years there was no tendency for age-related declines in consumption, problems with drinking, or average daily intake. They found a slight increase in the prevalence of drinking problems over time. They concluded that decreases in consumption and drinking problems with age are due to cohort and period effects, rather than to aging. Fillmore and Midanik (1983) report data from a five-year longitudinal problem drinking study. Two independent probability samples of the general adult population were used. The first consisted of 786 white male residents of San Francisco, aged 21-59, who were interviewed in 1967-68. In 1972, 615 (78%) of these men were followed-up by interview or mail questionnaire. The analysis is based on 186 men age 21-29 and 110 men age 40-49 at Time 1, who were contacted at both measurement times and who reported drinking during each year of measurement. Various problem drinking scales developed by Cahalan, Cisin, & Crossley (1969) were used to obtain data on intake of alcohol and frequency of binge drinking and symptomatic drinking. Older men reported higher levels of a given alcohol-related problem at both points in time, and they reported more alcohol-related problems than did younger men at both Time 1 and Time 2. The data thus demonstrated that the chronicity of alcohol problems is stronger in the older cohort than in the younger as measured across time. Temple and Leino (1989) similarly examined long-term changes in drinking through a 20-year prospective follow-up study of two general population surveys of males. The first study involved interviews with 405 males 23 and older in San Francisco. The second consisted of interviews with 786 males aged 21-59 in San Francisco. Analysis of data revealed that as respondents aged 20 years, alcohol consumption remained stable. Results do not support the age-related decline in alcohol consumption noted in cross-sectional studies.

Findings From Clinical Studies

Prevalence estimates of alcohol problems in the elderly based on studies in clinical populations are much higher than those based on community samples.

Prevalence rates for alcoholism and problem drinking in clinical populations range from 10% to 56%. In some of the early studies of alcohol-related admissions to general hospitals and psychiatric facilities of individuals 60 and older prevalence rates varied. Simon, Epstein, and Reynolds (1968) found that 28% of all admissions were 60 or older. Whittier and Korenyi (1961) reported that 20% of alcohol-related admissions to a state mental health facility were 60 or older. Gaitz and Baer (1971) found that 44% of all alcohol-related admissions to a county psychiatric facility were 60 and older. Funkhouser (1977-1978) reported an alcoholism rate of 55.3% from a series of older admissions to a Veterans Administration (VA) geriatric hospital. McCusker, Cherubin, and Zimberg (1971) reported the highest rate of geriatric alcoholism in a study of male admissions over age 70 to Harlem Hospital in New York City. Fifty-six percent of the males admitted were alcoholics.

In three more recent studies conducted in clinical settings slightly lower prevalence rates were found. In a Veterans Administration Medical Center study Magruder-Habib, Saltz and Barron (1986) classified 10.2% of patients 65 years old and older (predominantly males) as alcoholics. Curtis, Geller, Stokes, Levine, and Moore (1989) in a recent study of new admissions to the Johns Hopkins Hospital reported an alcoholism rate of 21% (during a 3-month period) in patients over 60 years of age. Hurt, Finlayson, Morse, and Davis (1988) report that over a 17-year period, 10% of the population in their Alcoholism and Drug Dependence Unit was 65 years of age or older. An earlier study of psychiatric diagnosis in a large geriatric mental health outreach program revealed that substance abuse ranked third among all mental disorders, with 10% of cases, following dementia and depression (Reifler, Raskind, & Kethley, 1982).

An examination of prevalence of specific alcohol-related hospitalizations among the elderly reveals much lower rates than those reported above. However, it remains clear that alcohol-related problems are more common among older adults than previously thought. Adams, Yuan, Barboriak, and Rimm (1993) conducted a cross-sectional prevalence survey using 1989 hospital claims data from the Health Care Financing Administration (HCFA). The prevalence of alcohol-related hospitalizations among those aged 65 and older nationally was 54.7 per 10,000 for men and 14.8 per 10,000 for women. A considerable geographic variation among rates was found in this study that correlated strongly with per capita consumption of alcohol by state. The authors emphasize that rates of alcohol-related hospitalization in older persons are similar to those for myocardial infarction using similar databases.

Explanations for Decrease in Alcohol Consumption with Age

Although compared to household surveys and other studies of community-dwelling elders clinical studies have revealed higher prevalence rates of alcoholism and alcohol problems among the elderly, the generally-accepted finding based on current data available is that decrease in prevalence of alcoholism and heavy drinking is a function of the aging process. Longitudinal studies do not support this conclusion. Several hypotheses have been put forth to explain why older people living in the community exhibit a decrease in heavy drinking and alcohol problems. In his insightful review article entitled "Research Issues Concerning Alcohol Consumption Among Aging Populations" Stall (1987) discusses six of the major hypotheses offered: the mortality hypothesis, the morbidity hypothesis, the biological hypothesis, the cohort hypothesis, the maturation hypothesis, and the measurement hypothesis.

The mortality hypothesis suggests that the reason prevalence seems to be lower in the elderly is that heavy drinkers die earlier, thereby lowering the alcohol problem of the elderly as a whole through a survivor effect. Another similar hypothesis, the morbidity hypothesis, posits that because more older adults suffer from chronic disease and take medications, both of which limit their ability to safely consume alcohol, they decrease their intake of alcohol. Closely related to the morbidity hypothesis is the biological hypothesis, which suggests that biological changes associated with aging place a limit on the amount of alcohol elders can comfortably consume, resulting in a decrease in consumption.

A different explanation, the cohort hypothesis, argues that declines in prevalence with age revealed in cross-sectional studies are not related to aging per se. Rather, the lowered rates reflect "historical conditions which affected certain generations in unique ways." Elders today who were raised during the Prohibition Era may drink less than younger people, who did not experience Prohibition. Future generations of elders, who do not experience Prohibition, may drink much more heavily. Data from the few existing prospective and longitudinal studies which have been conducted and reviewed earlier in this section tend to support this hypothesis.

Another hypothesis put forth, which has received little support, the maturation hypothesis, suggests that alcoholism is a "self-limiting" disease, and as individuals age and mature heavy drinking goes into "spontaneous remission."

The final hypothesis Stall discusses, the measurement hypothesis, posits that the lower prevalence rates of alcoholism and heavy drinking among the elderly reflect problems of measurement of this condition in the aging population. Numerous researchers have noted the problem in interpreting current statistics on prevalence due to the lack of applicability of standard methods of estimating prevalence for the older population (Blazer & Pennybacker, 1984; Hartford & Thienhaus, 1984; Williams, 1984). Graham (1986) discusses several serious problems with existing instruments used to measure alcoholism and alcohol abuse in the elderly in her article entitled "Identifying and Measuring Alcohol Abuse among the Elderly: Serious Problems with Existing Instrumentation." Graham points out that self-report measures of alcohol abuse, which for many prevalence studies is the main measure, require accurate recent memory of past consumption, the ability to do mental averaging, and willingness to provide truthful information about a behavior of which peers may not approve. Graham suggests that compared to other age groups, older adults suffer more short-term memory impairment and also may have more trouble and less experience doing mental averaging. They also may be even more likely than younger individuals to deny their drinking and not truthfully report quantity and frequency of alcohol consumption. Another problem with self-report measures of alcohol consumption is the problem of setting cut-offs. Four drinks per day for a thirty-year-old and four drinks per day for an eighty-year-old are not the same.

Other measures use alcohol-related social or legal problems. Most of these measures were standardized on nonelderly males and are inappropriate for older men and women. Behaviors such as breaking the law, physical fights, and other problems are generally inappropriate for older adults. According to Graham, criteria which include alcohol-related health problems may also be less appropriate for the elderly. Many of the health conditions will naturally occur as a function of aging. Separating alcohol-related health impairments from medication effects and chronic illnesses also poses problems.

Many measures of alcohol abuse focus on symptoms of dependence and may include items on physical withdrawal and tolerance. Some symptoms of alcohol dependence may be confounded with symptoms of age-related disease. Older adults also consume small quantities of alcohol and are less likely than younger alcoholics to experience withdrawal symptoms.

For these reasons prevalence of alcoholism and alcohol problems in the elderly is probably much higher than current estimates indicate. The problem is likely to be more significant in the future. Even if prevalence rates stay the same as currently, due to the increase in the aging population, there will be significantly more older alcoholics and heavy drinkers. Currently there are 30 million individuals 60 and older. By the year 2010, when the baby boomers enter the ranks of the elderly, this figure will swell to approximately 52 million. Based on prospective and longitudinal studies, we can also expect that future generations of elders, who have not experienced Prohibition and other social and political conditions experienced by today's generation of elders, will have different values and attitudes about drinking and will be less likely than the current generation of elders to abstain and more likely to drink heavily.

Vulnerable Elders

One important question addressed by numerous researchers is: who, among the elderly, is most vulnerable to alcoholism and alcohol problems? On most characteristics, there is limited agreement on who is most vulnerable; however, one characteristic has been identified in most studies. Older alcoholics are predominately male (Barnes, 1979; Borgatta, Montgomery, & Borgatta, 1982; Cahalan, Cisin, & Crossley, 1969; Goodwin, Sanchez, Thomas, Hunt, Garry, Goodwin, 1987; Holzer, Robins, Myers, Weissman, Tischler, Leaf,

Anthony, & Bednarski, 1983; McCusker, Cherubin, & Zimberg, 1971; Meyers, Hingson, Mucatel, Heeren, & Goldman, 1985-86; Rathbone-McCuan, Lohn, Levenson, & Hsu, 1976; Simon, Epstein, & Reynolds, 1968; Smart & Liban, 1982). With respect to race, findings are contradictory. Schuckit, Morrissey, and O'Leary (1978) and Meyers, Hingson, Mucatel, Heeren, and Goldman, (1985-86) found alcoholism to be more predominant in white elders. Blazer, George, Woodbury, Manton, and Jordan (1984) on the other hand, using DSM-III-R criteria, found older Blacks in North Carolina to be more likely to experience problems than older Whites. Holzer, Robins, Myers, Weissman, Tischler, Leaf, Anthony, and Bednarski (1983) reporting on findings from the ECA studies in Baltimore, St. Louis, and New Haven, found no significant differences between racial groups. Findings regarding education are also contradictory. Cahalan, Cisin, and Crossley (1969) found that those with higher levels of education drink more; however evidence from the ECA studies reported by Holzer, Robins, Myers, Weissman, Tischler, Leaf, Anthony, and Bednarski (1983) revealed that those with lower levels of education drink more. With respect to income, Smart and Liban (1982) found that drinking was negatively associated with income; however most other reports suggest that those with higher incomes drink more (Borgatta, Montgomery, & Borgatta, 1982; Cahalan, Cisin, & Crossley, 1969; Douglass, Shuster, & McClelland, 1988; Guttmann, Sirratt, Carrigan, & Holahan, 1978; Holzer, Robins, Myers, Weissman, Tischler, Leaf, Anthony, & Bednarski, 1983; Meyers, Hingson, Mucatel, Heeren, & Goldman, 1985-86).

Early- Versus Late-Onset Alcoholism

Elderly alcoholics have been grouped into different types. The early- and late-onset dichotomy, first discussed by Droller (1964), who took the life histories of seven alcoholics in Britain, is the most popular typology found in the literature. Early-onset alcoholics, also referred to as "survivors," are individuals who began drinking earlier in life and brought their alcoholism and drinking problems into late life. Late-onset alcoholics, also called "reactive problem drinkers," first experienced alcoholism or alcohol-related problems later in life. Many studies set the demarcation of early- versus late-onset at age 40; while others suggest 50 or 60 as the distinguishing age. Simon, Epstein, and Reynolds (1968), Rosin and Glatt (1971), Gaitz and Baer (1971), Zimberg (1982), Bahr (1969), Zimering and Domeischel (1982), and Schuckit, Morrissey, and O'Leary (1978) have all identified early- and late-onset alcoholics in their studies of geriatric alcoholics. There is general agreement that approximately one-third of all older alcoholics are late-onset alcoholics and approximately two-thirds are early-onset. A recent study of 216 older adults (65+) in treatment for alcoholism at the Mayo Clinic Alcoholism and Drug Dependence Unit (Hurt, Finlayson, Morse & Davis, 1988) revealed that 41% of the group had late-onset alcoholism, compared to 56% of the patients, who were characterized as early-onset alcoholics.

Some researchers have identified other types of older alcoholics and offered more extensive typologies. Gomberg (1982) first identified a third group of alcoholics, which she labeled "intermittents." According to Gomberg, intermittents have had a history of periods of heavy drinking (often binge or weekend drinking) earlier in life; but alcoholism was not a major problem until late life when heavy drinking resurfaced under the stresses of aging. Gomberg suggests that this group of older alcoholics may be sizable. Zimberg (1978) and Blose (1978) also identified intermittents, as well as early- and late-onset alcoholics among the elderly they studied in clinical populations. Carruth, Williams, Mysak, and Boudreaux, (1973) identified a group that fits Gomberg's description, but labeled the group "late-onset exacerbation" drinkers.

Dunham (1981), in a study of 310 older (60+) lower-income persons living in government-funded, low income housing in Miami, reported seven categories of drinkers: life-long abstainers (68%), a rise-and-fall pattern (peaks in middle age) (6.8%), a rise-and-sustained pattern (after age 20) (7.7%), a light throughout life pattern (5.8%), a light with a late rise pattern (after age 60) (2%), a late starter pattern (after age 40) (3%), and a highly variable pattern (2.3%). Applying Dunham's classification to her own data, Moriarty (1989) commented on four basic types of drinking patterns: Type 1, corresponding to the "rise and sustained" variety; Type 2 corresponding to "late starter;" Type 3, similar to the "light with a late rise" pattern; and Type 4, similar to the "rise-and-fall" pattern.

Most attention has focused on a comparison of early- and late-onset alcoholics. The two groups have been described as distinctly different, with the early-onset group more closely resembling primary alcoholics in younger age groups in their personalities and family and social histories, and the late-onset group demonstrating a very different set of characteristics. In their early study of early- and late-onset alcoholics Schuckit and Pastor (1979) found that early-onset drinkers were more likely than late-onset drinkers to be widowed, to have a family history of alcoholism, and to have spent time in jail. Late-onset drinkers were more likely to have serious health problems and to be separated or divorced. Atkinson, Turner, Kofoed, and Tolson (1985) also found that the early-onset alcoholics were more likely than the late-onset group to have histories that reflect the disruption that is characteristic of chronic alcohol abuse at younger ages. Early-onset alcoholics also had more family alcoholism and more criminal-legal problems and less current psychological stability as measured by scales on the Minnesota Multiphasic Personality Inventory. In his study of early- and late-onset alcoholics, Bienenfeld (1987) found late-onset alcoholics are more likely than early-onset alcoholics to be separated or divorced, have organic mental disorder, and suffer from serious health problems. According to the literature, compared to early-onset alcoholics, late-onset alcoholics are less likely to have spent time in jail or to have a family history of alcoholism. Tobias, Lippmann, Pary, Oropilla, and Embry (1989) also compared early- and late-onset alcoholics in a clinical population. They found that, compared to late-onset alcoholics, early-onset alcoholics are more likely to have a family history of drinking, criminal arrests, and an unstable personality. In addition, they have a poor response to treatment. Late-onset alcoholics, by contrast, begin drinking at 60 or older and do not have an unstable personality, and are less likely to have a family history of alcoholism or criminal arrests. Their response to treatment is favorable.

Early- and late-onset male alcoholics (N = 107) were compared on several personality dimensions (von Knorring, von Knorring, Smigan, Lindberg, & Edholm, 1987). Compared to late-onset alcoholics, early-onset alcoholics had significantly higher scores on somatic anxiety and verbal aggression and lower scores on socialization and inhibition of aggression as measured by the Karolinska Scales of Personality. Early-onset alcoholics were much more likely to have a family history of alcoholism than were late-onset alcoholics. Compared to late-onset alcoholics, early-onset alcoholics had also more often been in trouble with the law.

In a recent study of 170 older clients admitted to a day treatment program for elderly alcoholics, Schonfeld and Dupree (1991) found that 100 were late-onset alcoholics, 48 were early-onset, and 22 were uncertain. Twenty-three early-onset alcoholics were compared with 23 late-onset alcoholics on numerous dimensions. Schonfeld and Dupree found that, compared to late-onset alcoholics, the early-onset alcoholics experienced a higher frequency of delirium tremens, severe inner shakes, and severe sweating. The early-onset alcoholics also reported being intoxicated twice as often as the late-onset subjects. Early-onset alcoholics reported higher levels of life satisfaction than late-onset alcoholics. Compared to late-onset alcoholics, early-onset alcoholics demonstrated a lower expectancy of success from treatment; and they also were less likely to complete treatment.

PRECIPITANTS

The Stress Hypothesis

Findings from research studies which examine the effects of stress on older adults and the relationship between stress and alcoholism are contradictory. Some studies suggest that the stresses of aging (e.g., widowhood, retirement, and illness) contribute to increased drinking; while others find no relationship between stress and drinking behavior in the older populations.

Numerous factors have been identified as precipitants of alcoholism in late-life. Much of the literature on late-onset alcoholism, as distinguished from early-onset alcoholism, identifies loss and stress as major precipitants. The stress hypothesis suggests that the losses and stresses of aging such as widowhood, retirement, and poor health trigger drinking or perpetuate drinking in late-life. Late-life alcoholism is described as a reaction to the stresses of aging. Older people who begin drinking heavily for the first time in late life, or who later resume heavy drinking after years of abstinence or mild drinking are viewed as attempting to adjust or cope with life changes and age-associated stresses through abusing alcohol. Late-onset alcoholics are described as having a situational substance abuse problem. They are often referred to in the literature as reactive problem drinkers, indicating that the heavy drinking is primarily a reaction to losses, changes, and stresses that accompany aging. As summarized by Dupree, Broskowski, and Schonfeld (1984).

> ...'the geriatric problem drinker'...develops an abusive use of
> alcohol to the stress of aging....[This] later-life onset abuser's
> reasons for drinking are hypothesized to be more in response
> to fairly recent age-related events rather than a reflection of
> long-term, well-defined psychological problems (p. 510).

The stress hypothesis has received support from numerous clinical studies, but has not been confirmed in general population surveys. In an early clinical study conducted in the United Kingdom, Glatt (1961) observed 200 males hospitalized for alcoholism treatment. Glatt noted that for many of the men who began drinking after age 50 "their excessive drinking followed a situation of severe stress, such as the loss of a wife" (p. 105). Another early clinical report from Droller (1964) offered further support for the stress hypothesis. Droller reported that five of seven elderly alcoholics who were late-onset alcoholics began drinking after losing a spouse or experiencing other age-related changes or losses. In 1971 Rosin and Glatt reported findings from a series of 103 older alcoholic patients. Forty-one patients were classified as late-onset alcoholics. For 29 of these individuals stressful situations such as widowhood, retirement, or declining health were listed as the precipitating cause of excessive drinking. Of the 70 early-onset alcoholics, only 16 listed stress as a precipitating cause. Hubbard, Santos, and Santos (1979) reported on 12 late-onset alcoholics referred to a mental health outreach program for older adults. Most of these individuals had experienced a major stressful event such as the loss of a job or spouse, which triggered their drinking.

Confirmation of the stress hypothesis comes from a study of elderly drunken-driving offenders (Wells-Parker, Miles, & Spencer, 1983). Ninety-two offenders and 68 non-offender men over age 60 were interviewed by trained interviewers. Fifty-two questions related to drinking problems were adapted from existing instruments, particularly the Mortimer-Filkins Interview Schedule. Subjects were also asked whether the problem had first occurred before or after age 55 and whether the problem had occurred during the past five years. The measure of psychosocial stress history was developed from two existing scales of stressful events: The Social Readjustment Rating Scale developed by Holmes and Rahe and a modified version of the Holmes and Rahe scale developed by Dohrenwend and colleagues. In addition to data obtained in interviews, extensive demographic and psychometric data on all DWI offenders were examined; and driving histories were also available for controls. Three groups of older DWI offenders were identified. One group had at least one DWI arrest prior to age 55. One group had no arrests prior to age 55 with one arrest occurring during the preceding five years. One group had no arrests prior to age 55, but had an arrest prior to the five-year period covered by the interview. The first group were long term offenders, whereas the other two groups clearly had late-onset DWI problems. Multivariate analysis of variance revealed that the DWI offenders reported significantly more stressful life events within the one year interval prior to arrest than did the control group. Five of the 29 offenders in the late-onset group of DWI offenders experienced at least one death of a significant person within the interval of arrest, compared to only one of the 64 controls ($x^2 = 5.165$, $p < .025$). These results suggest that the occurrence of a first-time DWI offense at an older age is related to the occurrence of potentially stressful events, particularly losses of significant others.

Researchers from the Mayo Clinic recently reported their findings from a study of 216 elderly patients treated for alcoholism from 1972 through 1983 (Finlayson, Hurt, Davis & Morse, 1988; Hurt, Finlayson, Morse & Davis, 1988). Persons over age 65 comprised 10% of all patients admitted to the Mayo Clinic's Alcoholism and Drug Dependence Unit during this time. The researchers claim that these patients were easily divided into early- and late-onset types, with 59% of the men and 51% of the women comprising the early-onset group, and 39% of the men and 46% of the women comprising the late-onset group. Psychiatric diagnoses and results of psychologic testing did not differ between the two groups. However, late-onset drinkers were more likely to report having experienced life events (e.g., retirement, death of spouse) associated with problem drinking.

One recent clinical study provided no support for the stress hypothesis. Adams and Waskel (1991) studied sixty men ranging in age from 61 to 79 years. These men, all of whom were in alcoholism treatment centers, were administered a modified Veterans Alcohol Screening Test to determine age of onset and the Stokes/Gordon Stress Scale to determine the presence of stressors. Data analysis revealed that only 11% met the criteria for late-onset. Many were intermittents, who developed more serious alcohol-related problems in late life. The stress scores of early- and late-onset drinkers were not significantly different. The authors suggest that we reassess the commonly-held assumption that stress causes drinking problems in the elderly.

Data from general population surveys have also cast doubt on the validity of the stress hypothesis. Borgatta, Montgomery, and Borgatta (1982) examined the relationship between life crisis events and late-onset alcoholism in the elderly using the NORC General Social Survey sample from 1978 and 1980. They explored several life events. Based on their analysis, Borgatta and colleagues concluded that there is little support for the perspective that life events cause late-life drinking.

The two major stressors of late-life identified as related to problem drinking are widowhood and retirement. Data from community studies on the relationship between marital and employment status and alcoholism have not supported the stress theory. Community studies conducted by Guttmann (1978), Meyers, Hingson, Mucatel, and Goldman, (1982), Barnes, (1979), and Christopherson (1980), revealed that those who were unmarried were no more likely to experience drinking problems than were the married. Data from community studies conducted by Meyers, Hingson, Mucatel, and Goldman, (1982), Barnes (1979), and Christopherson (1980) also revealed no significant differences in drinking behavior between retired and employed persons.

In a more recent study of the relationship between life events and alcohol behavior among older adults La Greca, Akers, and Dwyer (1988) gathered data from 1,410 adults 60 and over. Older people lived in retirement communities and in age-integrated communities. They interviewed respondents in their homes and asked questions about alcohol behavior, life events, social support available, and coping resources. Based on analysis of data the researchers concluded that "there was no association between the occurrence of life events and the frequency, quantity, or problems of drinking behavior among older adults in the sample" (p. 556). Findings from these studies cast serious doubt on the validity of the stress hypothesis.

Factors Mediating The Relationship Between Stress and Alcoholism

More recently researchers have investigated factors which could mediate the relationship between stress and alcoholism. Two mediating factors that have received attention are social support and coping responses. In the study conducted by La Greca, Akers, and Dwyer (1988) the researchers investigated the effect of social support and coping resources. They found no support for the idea that social support and coping resources provide a major buffer for the impact of life events relative to drinking. On the other hand, in a more recent study of the mediating effect of coping responses, Moos, Brennan, Fondacaro, and Moos (1990) found support for the idea that social resources and positive coping responses can mediate the stress/alcoholism relationship. They surveyed 1,884 men and women between the ages of 55 and 65 using the Drinking Problems Index and the Coping Response Inventory. The Coping Response Inventory is composed of eight dimensions, each of which is measured by six items. Based on responses to the Drinking Problems Index respondents were divided into two groups: 501 problem drinkers and 609 nonproblem drinkers. Responses to the Coping Response Inventory indicated whether individuals used approach coping or avoidance coping. The researchers also included a measure of social resources in three domains: financial; spouse/partner; and friends. Results of data analysis revealed that problem drinkers reported more negative life events than non-problem drinkers. The two groups also differed in terms of coping responses. Problem drinkers were more likely than non-problem drinkers to rely on cognitive avoidance than to seek guidance and support (approach coping). Analysis also revealed that older problem drinkers who had more social resources reported fewer alcohol problems, less depression, and more self-confidence than those with fewer social resources. Older problem drinkers with fewer social resources were also more likely than those with more resources to rely on avoidance coping rather than approach coping. These findings are supported by earlier studies (Billings & Moos, 1984; Cooper, Russell, & George, 1988; Haley, Levine, Brown, & Bartolucci, 1987) which have demonstrated that reliance on avoidance coping is related to alcohol problems. These studies suggest that factors such as coping response and social support resources may mediate the relationship between stress and alcoholism in late life.

As Finney and Moos (1984) so aptly point out, "neither the clinician-researchers nor the epidemiologically-oriented social scientists who have carried out most of the research on elderly problem drinkers have focused on the conditions under which (moderators) or the mechanisms or processes through which (mediators) life stress may lead to alcohol abuse" (p. 281). Prospective longitudinal research is needed which focuses specifically on relations among stressors, coping, social support, and alcohol abuse and alcohol problems. Future research should be designed to help answer the following types of questions: Why do some older people faced with the losses and stresses of aging develop drinking problems while others do not? What social resources protect older people who confront stress from drinking heavily? Which types of coping strategies allow older adults to deal effectively with stress and avoid alcohol abuse?

Helplessness

Another precipitant of late life alcoholism discussed in the literature is helplessness. Influenced by the early work of Seligman (1975) and his colleagues on learned helplessness and depression, Hochhauser (1978) conceptualizes the problem of alcohol abuse among the elderly within a "learned helplessness" perspective. Seligman (1975, 1976) defines helplessness as a state in which individuals experience an inability to control or predict significant life events and suggests that it is the core of all depression. He notes that "the depressed patient believes or has learned that he cannot control those elements of his life that relieve suffering, bring gratification, or provide nurture--in short, he believes that he is helpless" (1975, p. 92). The aged are the most susceptible to helplessness, according to Seligman, because they have experienced the greatest loss of control. Schulz (1976) similarly argues that the loss of job, income, physical health, work, and child-rearing roles results in increased help-lessness and depression in the aged.

In a similar vein, Hochhauser (1978) argues that older people, who have experienced a variety of uncontrollable or unpredictable events, such as loss of spouse, relocation, or diagnosis of terminal illness, may view themselves as helpless to cope with such events and may believe that they are being controlled by their environment. Increased helplessness results in depression and anxiety, confusion, lowered self-esteem, feelings of worthlessness, a belief that things will not change, and the tendency to give up. To cope with this loss of control and to re-assert control, older persons may resort to alcohol use or abuse. Alcohol may give the illusion of restoring a sense of personal control and reduce some of the distress associated with a sense of helplessness. Hochhauser discusses two outcomes of stressful events such as loss of a spouse or a job or loss of health. One response is learned mastery and successful coping. The other is learned helplessness, which results in substance abuse. Hochhauser suggests that "the extent to which the elderly believe that they can predict and/or control environmental events will similarly have important effects on their levels of substance use, misuse, and abuse, and possibly their life—and death" (1978, p.22).

Depression, Loneliness, and Isolation

Depression has been identified as a precipitant of alcoholism among the elderly. Faced with the multiple losses and stresses of aging, which engender feelings of helplessness and hopelessness, many older adults become depressed. To escape overwhelming feelings of sadness and psychic pain, older adults turn to alcohol. Zimberg (1978), Carruth (1974), Nowak (1985), and other clinicians have identified depression as a major precipitant of alcoholism in older adults.

Loneliness, dissatisfaction, isolation, and alienation have also been identified as precipitants to alcoholism in the elderly. Rosin and Glatt (1971), who studied 103 older adults with alcohol problems, noted that in addition to bereavement and widowhood, loneliness was also a precipitating factor in late-onset alcoholism. Meyers, Hingson, Mucatel, and Goldman (1985-86) in their community study conducted in Boston found that older persons with alcohol-related problems have different attitudes about themselves and their lives than do their problem-free counterparts. Those with alcohol-related problems were more lonely, alienated, and frustrated than those who were problem-free. Compared to the problem-free individuals, they were also more likely to be dissatisfied with their lives and with their close friends and family relationships. Rathbone-McCuan, Levenson, and Hsu (1976) in their community survey in the Baltimore, Maryland area, found that compared to non-alcoholic elders, older problem drinkers were much more alienated from family and friends and participated less in social groups and events. Glassock (1980) and Rathbone-McCuan and Roberds (1980) both found loneliness and emptiness to be factors in alcoholism in their clinical studies.

From existing data it is impossible to distinguish whether depression, dissatisfaction, loneliness, and alienation precipitate alcoholism in late-life, or whether heavy drinking produces these feelings and behaviors. Future studies should be conducted to clarify these relationships.

EFFECTS

Alcohol has widespread negative effects on virtually every body organ system in adults of all ages. However, older adults are particularly susceptible to the negative consequences of this drug due to age-related physiologic changes. In addition, older adults' greater use of prescription and over-the-counter (OTC) medications increases the likelihood of serious alcohol-drug interactions in the older drinker. This section briefly explores age-related changes in alcohol metabolism and then reviews potential medical sequelae of alcohol use in late-life, including associated psychological complications such as depression and suicide.

Age-Related Changes in Alcohol Metabolism

For a variety of reasons, alcohol has more devastating effects on older adults than on younger people. Older adults have a decreased tolerance to alcohol. When older adults and younger adults consume the same dosage of alcohol, a higher blood alcohol level is found in older adults. Older adults, as compared to younger individuals, have a higher level of body fat, less tissue water per body mass and a changed ratio of lean body weight to fatty tissue (Lamy, 1988; Ritschel, 1976). As a result, there is a reduction in body fluids available for the distribution of water-soluble drugs (Lamy, 1988; Novak, 1972). Vestal, McGuire, Tobin, Andres, Norris, and Mezey (1977) found that a standardized dose of alcohol given to men intravenously produced blood alcohol levels over 20% higher in men over age 60 than in men under 45. These findings have been found previously in animal studies (Wiberg, Samson, Maxwell, Coldwell, & Trenholm, 1971; Wood, 1985; Wood & Armbrecht, 1982).

Age-related changes in kidney and liver function are also responsible for increased effects of alcohol on older adults. As individuals age, renal function declines and renal blood and plasma flow decrease (Lamy, 1988). In addition, the excretory functions of the kidney to preserve the volume of body fluids and maintain proper composition of these fluids decline (Lamy, 1988). Decreased hepatic blood flow reduces the liver's ability to metabolize drugs (including alcohol) (Lamy, 1988). Consequently, older adults are vulnerable to a decrease in overall clearance and metabolism of alcohol and other drugs (Baker, 1982; Bosmann, 1984; Lamy, 1988; Zimering & Domeischel, 1982).

Increased central nervous system (CNS) sensitivity to alcohol in aging adults has been discussed by Raskind and Eisdorfer (1976), Lamy (1988), Atkinson (1984), and others. As individuals age, there is a decrease in cellular brain mass and cerebral blood flow. These age-related changes can result in a baseline impairment in cognition, memory, coordination, affective regulation, motor control, and reaction time (Lamy, 1988). The CNS effects of alcohol can compound preexisting cognitive and psychomotor deficits in marginally or poorly compensated older adults.

Medical Sequelae of Alcohol Abuse

Alcohol has widespread detrimental effects on virtually every body organ system in the older adult. Alcohol negatively affects the liver and pancreas and the gastrointestinal system, causing fatty liver, hepatitis, cirrhosis, liver cancer, cancer of the pancreas, pancreatitis and stomach cancer, ulcers, and other gastrointestinal disturbances (Gambert, Newton, & Duthie, 1984; Korsten & Lieber, 1985; Lamy, 1988; Levy, Duga, Girgis, & Gordon, 1973; Sherouse, 1982; Skog, 1984; Stock, Bode & Sarles, 1980; Van Thiel, Lipsitz, Porter, Schade, Gottlieb, & Graham, 1981; Wyngaarden & Kelley, 1972).

Alcohol has serious negative effects on the heart and cardiovascular system, being associated with cardiac enlargement, elevated blood pressure, stroke, edema, cardiomyopathy, and cardiac arrhythmias (Alexander, 1972; Bosmann, 1984; Brigden, 1972; Chafetz, 1983; Factor, 1976; Gambert, Newton, & Duthie, 1984; Gould, Zahir, De Martino, & Gomprecht, 1971; Kannel, 1986; Lamy, 1988; McDonald, Burch, & Walsh, 1971; Mendelson & Mello, 1973; Rich, Siebold, & Campion, 1985; Sherouse, 1982; Smith, 1986).

Ethanol ingestion affects the endocrine system, producing extensive metabolic changes in elders. Hypoglycemia, hyperlipidemia and altered distribution of cholesterol lipoproteins are all related to heavy drinking (Bosmann, 1984; Chafetz, 1983; Devenyi, Robinson, Kapur, & Roncari, 1981; Field, Williams, & Mortimore, 1963; Gambert, Newton, & Duthie, 1984; Lamy, 1988). Heavy doses of alcohol also suppress the testicular synthesis of testosterone and increase the rate of breakdown of testosterone in the liver (Chafetz, 1983). One of the most common manifestations of endocrine problems, especially in older males, is impaired sexual functioning and reduced sex drive.

Alcohol ingestion is a major cause of malnutrition in older people. Alcohol inhibits absorption of B vitamins and Vitamin C (Lamy, 1988; Sherouse, 1982; Weg, 1978), and causes excessive excretion of magnesium and potassium (Gambert, Newton, & Duthie, 1984; Kalbfleisch, Lindeman, Ginn, & Smith, 1963; Lamy, 1988; McDonald, 1977; Weg, 1978). Protein malnutrition, carbohydrate malabsorption, and lactase-deficiency syndromes are common in older alcoholics (Gambert, Newton, & Duthie, 1984; McDonald, 1977; Moss, 1982; Perlow, Baraona, & Lieber, 1977).

As mentioned, alcohol ingestion also affects the brain and central nervous system (CNS) of older adults. Chronic alcohol use and/or abuse may be associated with dementia in older adults (Bienenfeld, 1990; Hartford & Samorajski, 1982; Lamy, 1988; Schuckit, 1980), and can result in brain atrophy

(Freund, 1984). Heavy drinking has also been shown to impair memory in older adults (Lamy, 1988; Parker & Noble, 1980), and to impair nonverbal cognitive performance (Ellis, 1990). Alcohol abuse has been found to produce fragmentation in sleep patterns and a reduction in rapid eye movement (REM) sleep (Freund, 1984). Chronic alcohol ingestion may result in alcohol tolerance, physical addiction, and dangerous withdrawal syndrome (Lamy, 1988). Alcoholics also develop cross-tolerance to other drugs, particularly to sedative-hypnotics.

Alcoholism and Suicide

Alcohol and suicide are serious related problems among the elderly. Menninger (1938), in his classic Man Against Himself, suggested that suicide is anger turned inward, and labelled alcoholism as a kind of "chronic suicide." Both alcoholics and attempters of suicide demonstrate a lack of bodily integrity, or lack of concern and care for their own bodies. Palola, Dorpat, and Larson (1962) suggest that alcoholism is a substitute for suicide. Others who have studied alcoholism and suicide claim that both problems are effects of the same cause (i.e., depression, hopelessness, stress).

The National Institute on Alcohol Abuse and Alcoholism (NIAAA) estimates that more than one-third of all suicides in the United States are related to alcohol. Only about 0.5 to 1% of the general population die by suicide, compared to 5 to 8% of alcoholics of all ages (Murphy, 1986). The risk of completed suicides in alcoholics is 50 to 70% greater than in those in the general population.

Although the association between alcohol and suicide is high in every age-group, it is greatly increased in the elderly (Blazer, 1982). Bienenfeld (1987) reported that elderly alcoholics' risk of suicide is five times greater than that of nonalcoholic elderly. According to one study conducted in Arizona (Miller, 1976), about 20% of elderly men who had committed suicide were described by their survivors as alcoholic and another 6% as heavy drinkers.

Clinical studies conducted in various countries have confirmed that alcohol use is associated with 25 to 50% of suicides (Dorpat & Ripley, 1960; Frances, Franklin, & Flavin, 1987; Rich, Young, & Fowler, 1986; Robins, 1981).

Data from recent international studies presented at the Annual Congress of International Association for Suicide Prevention (IASP) in Hamburg, Germany, confirm the relationship between alcoholism and suicide among the elderly. Clark and Clark (1991) found that 23% of the suicides they studied met the criteria for a substance use disorder. Berguland, Bergman, and Lindberg (1991), who followed 560 alcoholics in Sweden, found that 13% of the men and 17% of the women reported at least one suicide attempt. Battle and Battle (1991), who compared 35 elderly suicide attempters who survived with a sample of patients in psychotherapy with a private practice clinician, reported that

alcoholism was more prevalent in the suicide attempters than in t
psychotherapy.

There are several explanations offered in the literal
alcoholism precipitates or contributes to suicide among the elderly
as a depressant on the central nervous system. Heavy drinl..... ,
feelings of sadness, anxiety, guilt, and remorse. Continuous heavy drinking
may produce what Mayfield and Montgomery (1972) called "a depressive
syndrome of chronic intoxication." Alcohol produces chemical changes in the
brain and may alter moods and decrease critical life-evaluating functions of the
ego, allowing unconscious self-destructive impulses to gain control. The
depressant effects of alcohol may reduce inhibitions and self-control and
contribute to the "courage" some feel is a factor in suicide. Not only does
alcohol contribute to impulsiveness, it also produces changes in the brain that
result in aggression. Aggression against the self is a major factor in suicidal
behavior.

Continued regular use of alcohol often causes important relationships,
primarily among family and friends, to deteriorate, leading to social alienation
and isolation. The anger, hostility, and belligerence associated with frequent
drinking alienate family members and close friends at a time when the depressed
elderly drinker most needs social and emotional support. Coupled with
increased isolation and alienation are intense feelings of shame, guilt,
pessimism, and lower self-esteem, all factors in suicidal behavior.

Alcohol/Drug Interactions

Drug interaction with alcohol is a serious problem for older adults.
Compared to other age groups, those 65 and older take more prescription and
over-the-counter drugs. Seventy-five percent of persons 65 and older take at
least one prescribed medication (Kasper, 1982). Even those who only drink
alcohol occasionally are at risk since many of the common drugs taken by the
elderly have adverse interactions with alcohol.

Gerbino (1982) lists the following medications, often used by older
adults, as interacting negatively with alcohol: CNS depressants (e.g.,
benzodiazepines, barbiturates, muscle relaxants, antihistamines and psychotropic
agents); analgesics (e.g., aspirin, non-steroidal anti-inflammatory agents, and
narcotics); anticoagulants (aspirin, coumadin); cardiovascular drugs (digitalis,
diuretics, antihypertensives, and antiarrythmics); and antidiabetic agents.

Heavy drinking reduces the metabolism of some prescription and over-
the-counter drugs, and increases the metabolism of others, leading to ineffective,
subtherapeutic drug levels. Alcohol ingestion increases the toxic effects of some
drugs. Alcohol, when consumed in conjunction with CNS depressants such as
benzodiazepines and barbiturates, may result in confusion or sedation that is
significantly greater than the effect for one drug alone (Lamy, 1988). Such drug
synergism can result in respiratory depression and death (Raskind & Eisdorfer,

1976; Schuckit, 1982; Seixas, 1979; Williams, 1988). Alcohol inhibits the metabolism of many drugs, including antipsychotics and antidepressants, which can lead to toxic states (Bosmann, 1984; Lamy, 1988; Raskind & Eisdorfer, 1976; Schuckit, 1982).

DIAGNOSIS

Underdiagnosis and Lack of Detection

The problem of alcoholism in older adults often goes unrecognized and untreated. Many older alcoholics are almost invisible, drinking alone at home. They do not come to the attention of police and other authorities or employers and fellow employees because they have limited contact with these individuals. Many older alcoholics are retired. Compared to younger alcoholics, older alcoholics are less likely to drive while drunk or to engage in barroom brawls, street fights, or other criminal behaviors. Many older alcoholics also have limited contact with family members. Their spouses may have died, and their children and grandchildren have often moved away and have limited contact with them. Older alcoholics, drinking at home alone and in isolation, may never come to the attention of service providers and caregivers, who could recognize their problems and help them to seek treatment. For these reasons alcoholism in older adults often remains undetected, undiagnosed and untreated.

Older alcoholics who do visit physicians and/or come in contact with social service providers often are undiagnosed. For a variety of reasons, physicians and other service providers often do not accurately recognize and diagnose alcoholism in older patients/clients. Lack of professional education and knowledge about how to recognize and treat alcoholism in older adults is a major barrier to accurate identification of elderly alcoholism. Due to a lack of education, many physicians and other service providers feel helpless and incompetent when confronted with an older alcoholic. Negative stereotypes about the aging and older adults and about alcoholics and alcoholism, denial by older adults, their family members, and their physician and other service providers, and personal issues caregivers have related to aging and alcoholism are all factors that make accurate identification and appropriate diagnosis of alcoholism in elders difficult. Alcoholism mimics depression, dementia, and other physical illnesses, further contributing to the problem. Finally, current screening instruments and other diagnostic tools developed and normed on younger populations may be inappropriate for older adults and contribute to the problem of misdiagnosis and underdiagnosis.

Although the situation is better today than in previous decades, physicians still receive very limited education about alcoholism (Glass, 1989; Haugland, 1989; Mulry, Brewer & Spencer, 1987). They are seldom taught how to recognize the signs and symptoms of alcoholism. They also receive little education about alcoholism treatment or referral. As a result they often feel incompetent to treat alcoholic elders (Willenbring & Spring, 1988). A study conducted in 1983 revealed that less than 1% of the medical school curriculum is devoted to the topic of alcoholism (Pokorny & Solomon, 1983). Unfortunately, the situation is not likely much better today. In a 1986 survey of physicians conducted by the American Medical Association (AMA), 71% of the physicians surveyed described themselves as not competent to recognize and treat alcoholism (AMERSA, 1986). Other health care professionals such as nurses, social workers, and psychologists also lack adequate education about alcoholism (Gallant, 1987; Pokorny & Solomon, 1983).

Many physicians and other caregivers have many misconceptions and stereotypes about older alcoholics, which result in underdiagnosis. There is a common belief that all older alcoholics are dirty, smelly, skid row bums and homeless derelicts living on the streets. A very small percentage of older alcoholics are skid row bums or homeless derelicts. There are also many misconceptions about the gender and race of older alcoholics. Physicians and other caregivers may also be ageist, and believe the bottle is truly the only friend many older people have (Haugland, 1989), or that older alcoholics can not be effectively treated and recover (Haugland, 1989; Morse, 1984).

The lack of physician education about alcoholism and aging is revealed in studies which indicate that physicians still do not ask about alcohol and drug use unless it is already obvious (Willenbring & Spring, 1988). In a recent study of medical inpatients at John Hopkins Hospital conducted by Curtis, Geller, Stokes, Levine, and Moore (1989) the inability of physicians to accurately diagnose alcoholism in elderly patients was revealed. Two alcoholism screening tools (the CAGE and the Short Michigan Alcohol Screening Test, which will be described in more detail in a later part of this chapter) were used to screen for alcoholism in inpatients. The prevalence of screen-positive alcoholism for patients 60 and older was 21%, compared to 27% for patients under 60 years of age. Results of the study revealed that house officers correctly identified only 37% of elderly patients as alcoholics. They correctly diagnosed 60% of the younger patients as suffering from alcoholism. The study also revealed that older patients with alcoholism who were white, female, and less educated were significantly less likely to be correctly diagnosed. One other important finding from this study was that even when correctly diagnosed, older patients were significantly less likely than younger patients to be referred for treatment. The researchers concluded that "medical education is deficient in providing physicians with the skills to detect and treat elderly patients with alcoholism" (p. 310).

Kola, Kosberg, and Joyce (1984) surveyed aging agencies in the Cleveland, Ohio area and found that elderly alcoholism was generally undetected and there were few referrals for treatment. Kosberg and McCarthy (1985) surveyed staff of 50 aging-related service agencies funded under the Older Americans Act. Nutrition programs, daycare services, and multiservice programs for the elderly in two Florida counties were included. Site managers were asked if they could identify older problem drinkers. Only 36% said they could; 38% felt they could sometimes accurately identify older alcoholics; and 18% admitted that they could not identify problem drinkers.

Alcoholism is often not properly diagnosed in older adults because it mimics other psychological and physical illnesses, and because so many of the signs of normal aging resemble signs of alcoholism (Haugland, 1989). Confusion, clouding of sensorium, memory loss, slowed thought processes, and feelings of sadness mimic dementia and depression. Changes in sleep patterns and sexual drive, slowing down, confusion, incontinence, and falling are often signs of normal aging; however, they are also symptoms of alcoholism (Haugland, 1989; Westermeyer, 1984). Physicians may pass off alcoholism as aging. For these reasons, Willenbring, Christensen, Spring, and Rasmussen (1987) label alcoholism the "great masquerader."

Many older alcohol abusers present with nonspecific symptoms such as insomnia, stomach problems, musculoskeletal pain, or anxiety rather than with specific, easily identifiable physical sequelae clearly related to alcohol abuse (Bienenfeld, 1987). Older adults and their family members also often deny alcoholism. Physicians may be reluctant to recognize alcoholism because of the stigma and embarrassment associated with the condition. These factors combined contribute to the problem of misdiagnosis and underdiagnosis. Many physicians will treat the symptoms of alcoholism such as gastrointestinal problems, liver disease, and malnutrition, yet minimize the actual drinking problem or even fail to associate medical symptoms with alcoholism. Alcoholism is very seldom a primary diagnosis (Haugland, 1989). Some physicians may mistakenly think that dealing with the symptoms will cause the drinking to subside. Physicians who have some personal problems with drinking or who have an alcoholic relative may avoid discussions of alcoholism. The same is true for nurses and other health care workers.

Another reason alcoholism is not diagnosed in older adults is that older alcoholics consume much smaller quantities of alcohol than do younger alcoholics. If the diagnosis of alcoholism is based primarily on alcohol consumption, many older alcoholics will not qualify for the diagnosis (Abrams & Alexopoulos, 1987; Beresford, Blow, Brower, Adams, & Hall, 1988; Graham, 1986; Zimberg, Lipscomb, & Davis, 1971), and others also point out that most alcohol screening measures currently available are developed and normed on younger populations and may not be valid for the elderly. Current screening tools such as the Michigan Alcoholism Screening Test (MAST) measure social, employment, and legal issues related to drinking. These items may not be appropriate for older adults, who are retired or widowed and live alone and who have limited contact with police. Measures which rely on self report also pose problems because older alcoholics are even less likely than younger alcoholics to admit they have a drinking problem (Graham, 1986).

Diagnostic Tools

Even though an accurate diagnosis of late-life alcoholism is often difficult to make, there are several tools available to physicians and other caregivers to assist them in making a proper diagnosis of alcoholism in older patients/clients. A good diagnostic interview, thorough physical examination, and detailed history taking can provide clues. In addition, there are several laboratory tests which can aid in the detection of alcoholism. The Diagnostic and Statistical Manual Third Edition Revised (DSM-III-R) and upcoming DSM-IV published by the American Psychiatric Association and other criteria developed by the National Council on Alcoholism provide valuable guidelines. There are also many rating scales and screening instruments which, in spite of some of their flaws, can help the clinician and practitioner accurately identify alcoholism in older adults.

Diagnostic Interview

In addition to the standard medical diagnostic interview, clinicians should probe for sources of stress or concern and recent losses, in particular. It is also important to determine what sources of support are available to the older adult (Osgood, 1992). Attention to symptoms such as feelings of helplessness and hopelessness, and changes in sexual interest or performance may suggest alcoholism even in the absence of overt physical signs.

History Taking

The history should include a detailed questioning about current and previous medical/psychiatric diagnoses, social standing, and education of both the patient and his/her immediate family. Questions regarding the patient's sexual history and current sexual function should be included. The medical history can reveal conditions related to alcoholism such as gastritis, stomach ulcers, cirrhosis, or pancreatitis. A family history may reveal alcoholism or depression in other family members. The psychiatric history should include questions about alcohol and other drug use (both prescription and illicit). Questions about alcohol consumption, patterns of drinking, problems related to alcohol and control of drinking should be asked. The psychiatric history will reveal information about past episodes of depression, alcoholism, psychiatric illness, or suicide attempts. A sexual history should include questions on current and past level of sexual functioning, as well as changes in sexual interest or sexual functioning. Decreased libido is often related to alcoholism. The social history may reveal past problems with spouse and family members and with employers, which might indicate a problem with alcohol in the past.

Physical Examination

A thorough physical examination will usually reveal signs of alcoholism in the afflicted. Sherouse (1982) notes the following as possible signs of alcoholism to which clinicians should be aware: bruises, signs of falls, cigarette burns, vascular spider angiomas, night blindness, and pinpoint or wide pupil size. Drew (1990) lists other possible signs: odor of alcohol on the breath; hyperpigmented, sallow, or jaundiced skin; jaundiced or blood-shot eyes; trench mouth or cracking skin at the corners of the mouth; ankle swelling; protruding abdomen; acne rosacea (dilation of vessels on the nose); cuts; and tremulousness. Haugland (1989), Bloom (1983), Olsen-Noll and Bosworth (1989), and Ticehurst (1990) all note the importance of bruises and other evidence of falls or trauma as potential signs of alcoholism in older adults. Chafetz (1983) further notes the following neurological signs: absence of superficial skin reflexes, dysarthria, transient nystagmus or lateral gaze, ataxia in gait and station, depression or absence of tendon reflexes, and constriction or dilation of pupils. Haugland (1989) and Chafetz (1983) suggest that physicians be alert to mental signs such as confusion, memory loss, sleep impairment, and depression or dementia-like symptoms, impairment of judgement, and garrulousness. Finally, Ticehurst (1990) recommends that clinicians always look for evidence of self-neglect and malnutrition.

Laboratory Tests

Laboratory tests can aid in the detection of alcoholism in older adults. The National Institute on Alcohol Abuse and Alcoholism (NIAAA) recommends a battery of tests including standard serum multi-analysis panels (SMA panels) available to most clinics and hospitals. Chafetz (1983) suggests looking for the following as clues to alcoholism: abnormal liver function tests, an elevated mean red cell corpuscular volume (MCV), a high density lipoprotein reading over 60, raised triglyceride levels, a blood alcohol level of 0.1 or above, elevated uric acid levels, decreased levels of calcium and phosphate, and the presence of anemia. Chafetz (1983) also recommends doing Computerized Tomography (CT) scans, cerebral blood flow measures, and EEG's to detect pathophysiological alterations in the central nervous system. These studies may be particularly appropriate if evidence of cognitive impairment or focal neurologic deficits are present.

NCA Criteria

The National Council on Alcoholism (NCA) published its criteria for the diagnosis of alcoholism in 1972. The Council defined alcoholism as a "pathological dependency." Two types of symptoms were described and assembled into two tracts. Tract I outlined physiological and clinical symptoms;

and Track II consisted of behavioral, psychological, and attitudinal items (Gallant, 1987). Symptoms were divided into early, middle, and late phases, and each item was graded in severity from 1 to 3 (Gallant, 1987). To summarize, the NCA criteria include: physiological dependence, alcohol tolerance, major alcohol-related illness, and continued drinking despite strong contradictions (Milhorn, 1988). The diagnosis requires only one of these criteria.

DSM-III-R Criteria

Published in 1987 by the American Psychiatric Association, the Diagnostic and Statistical Manual of Mental Disorders, Third Edition, Revised (DSM-III-R) categorizes both alcohol abuse and dependence under the broader category, Psychoactive Substance Abuse Disorders. The DSM-III-R describes substance "dependence" as a syndrome involving at least three of nine characteristic (core) symptoms, among them the physiologic phenomena of tolerance and withdrawal. Dependence is conceptualized as having varying degrees of severity. The DSM-III-R does not comment on underlying processes, and core symptoms are not described as being distinct from associated social, occupational and health problems. By contrast, "abuse" denotes a maladaptive pattern of psychoactive substance use that has not met the criteria for dependence. The maladaptive pattern may be indicated in either of two ways: continued use of the substance despite persistent or recurrent social, physical, psychological or occupational problems that are caused or exacerbated by use of the substance, or recurrent use of the substance in situations when use is physically hazardous (e.g., driving while intoxicated). Examples of pathological use include: need for daily use of alcohol for adequate functioning; repeated efforts to control or reduce one's drinking; and drinking non-beverage alcohol (e.g., mouthwash). Examples of impairment in social or occupational functioning are: violence when intoxicated, problems with work performance, inability to maintain employment, legal problems, and marital or family problems.

DSM-IV Criteria

Since 1990 field trials have been underway to study the effects of changes in diagnostic criteria proposed for the Diagnostic and Statistical Manual of Mental Disorders-Fourth Edition (DSM-IV). The DSM-III-R definition of substance abuse has been criticized as insufficiently inclusive. In an attempt to broaden this residual category, DSM-IV proposes the addition of two criteria that focus on the consequences of substance use: recurrent substance-related legal and interpersonal problems, and the relinquishment of important social, occupational, or recreational activities. The dependence category comprises eleven items that include all four substance abuse criteria as well as items related to physiological dependence. One proposed option for the diagnosis of substance dependence allows for the specification "with or without" physiological symptoms of tolerance or withdrawal (see DSM-IV Options Book: Work in Progress, 1991).

Alcohol Rating Scales

Rating scales are also available to help identify alcoholism in older adults. The most popular instrument used to determine the level of alcohol-related problems is the CAGE, an acronym that stands for the key words in each of four questions: C=Have you ever tried to cut down?; A=Do you get annoyed when people talk about your drinking?; G=Do you ever feel guilty about your drinking?; E=Do you ever have an eye opener in the morning? A positive response to two or more CAGE questions indicates a serious drinking problem. The CAGE has been shown to have a high degree of sensitivity (Bernadt, Mumford, Taylor, Smith, & Murray, 1982; Ewing, 1984).

Another screening test used quite often is the Short Michigan Alcohol Screening Test (SMAST), a 13 question version of the original Michigan Alcohol Screening Test (MAST), which consists of 24 questions. The SMAST asks questions about the effect of alcohol on the person's life, health, and behavior: Do you feel you are a normal drinker? Are you able to stop drinking when you want to? Have you ever gone to anyone for help about your drinking? Have you ever attended a meeting of Alcoholics Anonymous? The SMAST has been shown to be as effective as the MAST in picking up alcoholism (Selzer, Vinokur, & van Rooijen, 1975; Vande Creek, Zachrich, & Scherger, 1982), and has demonstrated greater than 90% sensitivity (Vande Creek, Zachrich, & Scherger, 1982). In other studies the CAGE and the SMAST have been shown to have sensitivities of 97% and 89% and specificities of 96% and 97%, respectively, when using DSM-III-R criteria for alcohol abuse and dependence (Ewing, 1984; Willenbring, Christensen, Spring, & Rasmussen, 1987). The SMAST has been validated against DSM-III-R criteria in elderly populations (Willenbring, & Spring, 1988).

The Michigan Alcoholism Screen Test--Geriatric Version (MAST-G) (Blow, 1992) is a new 24-item instrument specifically designed to detect alcoholism among older adults. The instrument was developed using a stratified sample including four groups; those currently in treatment for alcoholism, those with a previous history of alcoholism and currently in recovery, those who are social drinkers, and those who abstain from drinking. The MAST-G was validated by the Diagnostic Interview Schedule (DIS) for the diagnosis of alcohol dependence, used as the 'gold standard' because it indexes the DSM-III-R, the current standard in the field. Five underlying factors have been identified: Dependence, Loss of Control with Drinking, Loss and Loneliness, Rule-Making, and Relaxation. The psychometric properties of the MAST-G indicate that the new instrument is superior to other screening tests for identification of elderly alcoholics. The MAST-G has a sensitivity of 93.9%, specificity of 78.1%, positive predictive value of 87.2% and negative value of 88.9%. In sum, the MAST-G is the first elderly-specific alcoholism screening measure to be developed with specific items unique to older problem drinkers included (Blow, 1992).

PREVENTION AND TREATMENT

As the population over 60 continues to increase dramatically, and as more recent cohorts who were not raised under the influence of Prohibition grow older, prevention of alcoholism and alcohol treatment become increasingly important issues. Many of the problems which contribute to under-diagnosing discussed in the previous section (e.g., lack of adequate education for physicians, nurses and other health care professionals; ageism and negative stereotypes about older alcoholics; lack of valid, age-appropriate alcoholism screening tools; and limited expertise on alcoholism in personnel in aging agencies) are also barriers to effective prevention and treatment of alcoholism in older adults.

Prevention of alcoholism among vulnerable elders, particularly the recently widowed and recently retired, is important. Very few primary or secondary prevention programs have specifically targeted the elderly. Education and active outreach to lonely, isolated, depressed elders are keys to prevention. Prevention strategies and programs, which find and target older alcohol abusers before their alcoholism progresses too far, are also essential to alcohol prevention in this group.

Older alcoholics are often denied treatment because of myths and stereotypes about aging and alcoholism, and because of lack of appropriate information and referral services and limited numbers of treatment programs appropriate for older adults. The scientific literature indicates that older alcoholics are treatable, and may in fact be more treatable than younger alcoholics. Both age-segregated and age-integrated treatment programs are effective with older people. Many of the same treatment strategies that are effective with younger alcoholics, such as Alcoholics Anonymous (AA) and other social therapies, family therapy, and cognitive therapies, are also effective with older alcoholics. Although there is a significant shortage of alcohol treatment programs designed specifically for older alcoholics, many such programs have been developed and implemented across the country. Some of these programs will be described in this section.

Prevention

In an article entitled "What we know, don't know and need to know about older alcoholics and how to help them: Models of prevention and treatment" Mishara (1985) argues strongly for primary, secondary, and tertiary prevention of alcoholism among the elderly. As he notes, "primary prevention is aimed at inhibiting the development of alcohol problems before they begin" (p. 247). "Secondary prevention efforts focus upon new problem drinkers" (p. 247). "Tertiary prevention is aimed at the chronic alcoholic" (p. 251).

Primary prevention efforts need to be aimed at older individuals who are not alcoholics or alcohol abusers, but who are at risk of developing problems with alcohol. Research efforts should focus on identifying who is most at risk for alcoholism in late-life and what interventions are most effective in preventing alcoholism. Support for the stress theory would suggest that the recently widowed and recently retired should be targeted. Programs should be developed to help older people prepare for the stresses and challenges of aging, and in particular for the stresses of widowhood and retirement. Mishara (1985) calls for more programs for the recently bereaved and for more pre-retirement programs to help those who are going to retire. Wellness programs, which emphasize positive mental, physical, and emotional health, and provide education about the values of good nutrition, physical exercise, and social involvement, are another primary prevention strategy. Self-help groups and age-based support groups would aid the transition to late life.

Another prevention strategy might be to involve older people in activities that nurture self-worth and increase feelings of self-esteem. Part-time work, community activities, and volunteer opportunities in health care and other settings are all valuable. Mishara (1985) also suggests improving housing quality for elders, new career programs in later life, and aid to families with dependent older people as preventive measures which could help reduce the incidence of alcoholism in old age. Primary prevention is the most cost effective form of prevention.

Secondary prevention efforts target new problem drinkers, who have not yet become alcoholics or who have recently become alcoholics. Late-onset alcoholics, or reactive problem drinkers, are prime targets for secondary prevention efforts. These older adults need to be identified early and referred for treatment where the goal is lasting cure (Mishara, 1985). The major barrier to successful secondary prevention efforts is what Mishara calls the "tardive referral syndrome," or refusing to seek help until it is almost too late. Denial on the part of older alcoholics and their family members and caregivers is a major reason treatment is not sought earlier. Another reason intervention does not occur earlier is that older adults and their caregivers, as well as physicians and other service providers, fail to recognize the warning signs of alcoholism in older alcoholics. Education and early case identification and active outreach are essential elements of secondary prevention.

Weener (1978), Maypole (1989), Serkin (1987), Parette, Hourcade, and Parette (1990), and Dupree (1989) all advocate education about alcoholism as a key to prevention of late-life alcoholism. Education about the signs and symptoms of late-life alcoholism, physiological effects of alcoholism, and dangers of mixing drugs and alcohol should be provided to older people, family members and caregivers of older people, as well as to physicians, nurses, social workers and other helping professionals. Education of the general public is also necessary. Education about aging and age-related changes that change the way alcohol is distributed in the body is also important. Physicians and other professionals need to be educated about treatment options available for older alcoholics in their local community. Many of the treatment programs, which will be described later in this section, incorporate education as a major component of treatment. Education is effective with older adults and with caregivers and service providers. Osgood, Wood, Coogle and Pyles (1991) present results of a study of the effectiveness of one education program about alcoholism and aging, which included a training video, booklet and brochure, as well as information presented in a one-hour training session. Older adults, caregivers, and service providers received education. Findings from their study revealed significant increases in knowledge about alcoholism and aging in all groups who received education.

Because of lack of education about alcoholism and resistance and denial, older adults who were raised during the Prohibition Era when alcoholism was seen as a sin and a moral weakness will not self-refer for treatment. Traditional information and referral services have not been very successful in reaching isolated elders, particularly substance abusers. Active case identification and aggressive outreach are essential for finding older drinkers, who have just begun drinking or who are in the early stages of alcoholism before the disease progresses too far. Programs must be developed that help to find high risk elders early. More valid, age-appropriate screening measures also need to be developed; and physicians, nurses, and other helping professionals need to be educated about how to administer the instruments and how to interpret the results.

Active outreach programs described in the literature include the gatekeepers program developed by Raschko (1991) in Spokane, Washington, and the case finding strategies developed by Dupree (1989) in South Florida. The Gatekeeper Program (Raschko, 1991) is a program that is part of Elderly Services at the Community Mental Health Center in Spokane. "Gatekeepers" are meter readers, bank personnel, fuel dealers and others who are in a position to identify isolated and high risk elders, and who have been trained to recognize the signs of late life alcoholism and to refer older people for treatment. Once identified, these older people receive in-home evaluation, treatment, and clinical case management services from the Spokane Community Mental Health Center's Elderly Services. The gatekeepers are the case finding component of a comprehensive substance abuse prevention and treatment program. Overall, gatekeepers account for four out of every ten admissions to the substance abuse program.

As part of a demonstration project funded by NIAAA, Dupree (1989) developed three aggressive case-finding strategies to identify elder alcohol abusers and to link them with the Gerontology Alcohol Program (GAP). GAP is an alcohol treatment program which serves the Tampa Bay area, and is a part of the Mental Health Institute of the University of South Florida. The three case-finding strategies included: the creation of a Community Agency Referral Network (CARN); a Public Awareness Campaign (PAC); and a Community-Based Outreach (CBO). CARN and PAC were the two most successful strategies. The CARN involved on-site education about alcoholism and aging of numerous service providers in several aging and social service agencies, as well as the mailing out of information about late-life alcoholism and gerontology to physicians, clergy, counselors, and others. The PAC used the mass media to inform the public about GAP, and to encourage potential clients and their families to seek treatment for alcoholism. Phone book listings, booklets, pamphlets, posters, billboards, and television appearances were part of the information and education campaign. The CARN resulted in 247 referrals to GAP; and the PAC yielded 106 referrals. If individuals did not meet the GAP criteria for treatment, they were referred to other treatment services to receive help. The CBO was an effort to involve patients and staff of three health department clinics to identify the "hidden" alcohol abuser and to motivate them to seek treatment. This approach involved many on-site visits and consultations, educational seminars, and screening of clients. It was the least successful approach. CBO resulted in only 34 referrals, and was not a cost-effective approach.

Treatment

Although there are many myths about alcoholism treatment for elders and a shortage of elder-specific alcohol treatment programs, data from several studies confirm that older alcoholics are treatable, and may have a better chance of recovery than younger alcoholics. In one early study Linn (1978) examined all male inpatient substance abusers in treatment at a Veterans Administration Hospital in 1975 and 1976. He found that older adults (55+) were more likely than younger adults (under age 50) to stay in treatment. Another early study conducted by Blaney, Radford and MacKenzie (1975) found that in one hospital they studied over a six month follow-up period, persons over 60 had the same success rates as those 30-39 and better success rates than those under 30. In a second hospital they found the elderly had a 77% improvement rate. Those 20-29 had only a 36% improvement rate. More recently, Cartensen, Rychtarik, and Prue (1985) examined patients two to four years after discharge from an in-patient alcohol treatment program at a Mississippi VA medical center. Fifty percent of the older adults were abstaining while 13% were significantly modifying their drinking behavior.

Outpatient follow-up data from many other studies also provides evidence that elderly alcoholics have outcomes as good or better than younger alcoholics (Atkinson & Kofoed, 1982; Janik & Dunham, 1983; Rix, 1982; Wiens, Menustik, Miller, & Schmitz, 1982-1983).

There is currently a debate about whether or not older alcoholics do better in age-segregated treatment programs. Those who favor age-based treatment programs argue that older adults have unique issues, concerns, and problems, and that these are different than those shared by younger people. Supporters of age-homogeneous treatment also claim that older alcoholics require a different approach than younger alcoholics because they need a more extended period of group support and a less confrontive approach (Robertson, 1989; Zimberg, 1984).

In an early study Janik and Dunham (1983) used data from the National Alcoholism Program Information System developed by NIAAA to examine the need for specific alcoholism treatment programs for the elderly. Based on their analysis of over 6,000 subjects from 550 treatment programs they concluded that older adults fare as well as younger adults in age-integrated treatment programs. The researchers did not compare older adults in age-integrated programs with older adults in age-specific programs, however. Kofoed, Tolson, Atkinson, Toth, and Turner (1987) conducted a study of alcoholics 54-66 years old, comparing treatment outcomes of those in age-homogeneous and mixed-age treatment programs. Based on their analysis of 49 patients they concluded that the age-homogeneous group had better treatment retention, compliance, rates of treatment completion, and dealt with relapse more successfully than did those in mixed-age treatment programs. This study supports the notion that age-homogeneous treatment is superior to mixed-age treatment for older alcoholics. Dupree, Broskowski, and Schonfeld (1984) also provide strong support for age-homogeneous alcohol treatment programs. They found that 75 % of those treated in GAP, an age-homogeneous alcohol treatment program, maintained their drinking goals (in most cases, abstinence) at one year follow-up.

Intervention and treatment of late-life alcoholism is essentially similar to intervention and treatment for younger people; however the process may take longer for older people, and some treatment strategies are more effective for older adults than others. Intervention and treatment involves accurate identification of the problem, detoxification, rehabilitation, and aftercare. Identification has been discussed previously in this chapter. After identification of the older alcoholic, in most cases detoxification is necessary. Detoxification consists of nutrition and prophylaxis for withdrawal symptoms and usually takes 21 to 30 days or even longer, and is generally done in a hospital.

After detoxification alcohol rehabilitation begins. Haugland (1989) contends that the main goal in treatment is to redirect the dependency away from alcohol and onto human beings. He suggests that a sustained relationship with a new peer group whose goals are abstinence, and open, honest relationships with people, is the most important element in recovery. Haugland recommends AA and other social support groups as the cornerstone of a successful rehabilitation program. Lawson (1989), Zimberg (1985), Cohen (1976); Ruben (1986), Rains (1990), Hinrichsen (1990), Milhorn and Gardner (1990) and others all emphasize the value of AA and other social support groups for treating elderly alcoholics. Zimberg (1985) recommends creating a "therapeutic community" in which alcoholic patients communicate freely with each other and with treatment staff. They are also encouraged to take an active role in the decision-making process by participating in patient-staff meetings and creating a system of participatory patient government. Family therapy is also recommended by many clinicians who have worked with older alcoholics as an effective therapy (Amodeo, 1990; Newman-Aspel, 1990; Rathbone-McCuan & Triegaardt, 1978; Zimberg, 1985). Zimberg (1985), Snyder and Way (1979), Bienenfeld (1987), Lawson (1989), Ruben (1986), and others recommend that counseling and other rehabilitation services be delivered through existing facilities serving the elderly such as senior centers, community agencies, and medical outpatient services.

Aftercare is the final step of the treatment process. The older alcoholic must remain involved in AA or some other support group, family relationships, recreational, and social groups. Snyder and Way (1979), Sherouse (1982), Haugland (1989), Osgood (1988), and others recommend aftercare for older recovering alcoholics.

Several treatment programs developed specifically for older adults have been implemented across the country. Some of these programs will be briefly described below.

The Gerontology Alcohol Project (GAP) was a demonstration program funded by NIAAA which was developed in South Florida between 1979 to 1981 to treat late-onset elderly alcoholics (Dupree, 1989; Dupree, Broskowski, & Schonfeld, 1984; Schonfeld & Dupree, 1990). Based on a behavioral and self-management approach, Dupree and associates developed four treatment modules (groups). The first module called Analysis of Drinking Behavior (ABC's of Drinking) teaches older alcoholics how to analyze and break down their personal drinking behavior chain. They learn to identify antecedents, behavior, and consequences of drinking. The second module, Self-Management in High Risk Situations, teaches older alcoholics how to deal with the antecedents associated with their drinking. They receive information on drink refusal, peer pressure, depression, anger/frustration, tension/anxiety, cues, urges, and relapses. In the third module, Alcohol Information and Education, older alcoholics learn about medical, psychological, and other consequences of alcohol abuse. General Problem Solving Skills is the fourth module. Older alcoholics learn how to make decisions and solve their problems in constructive ways so that they do not turn to alcohol as a solution. As discussed earlier in this chapter, GAP has been a very successful program.

The Senior Alcoholism Services Project for Elderly Alcoholics was a demonstration project funded by NIAAA to develop and implement effective treatment modalities for those over 60 in Clark County, Washington (Dunlop, Skorney & Hamilton, 1982). Group work, socialization therapy, and family therapy are the cornerstones of in-patient treatment and aftercare in this program. Groups provide socialization, support, and fun for older alcoholics. Aftercare groups include: weekly support group meetings, which have an educational as well as social component, couples counseling, family group meetings, and family counseling.

Sisters of Providence Addiction Treatment Services of Oregon offers elder-specific alcoholism treatment in three hospitals in Oregon (Dunlop, 1990). The overall goal of the program, which began in March, 1988, is to "make life worth living again, to make the later years rewarding ones" (p. 29). The program provides education about alcoholism peer group support therapy, counseling, life review therapy, a family program, and an introduction to AA. The treatment program is conducted on an outpatient basis and is one year in duration. During its first year of operation the program treated 69 patients over age 55.

"The Class of 45" is a specialized elderly-oriented outpatient component of a comprehensive Alcohol and Drug Dependence Treatment Section of the Psychiatry Service at the Portland, Oregon VA Medical Center (Atkinson, 1987). The support group, patterned after Zimberg's work and the model developed in the Senior Alcohol Services Project, is open to any veteran who was on active military duty in 1945 or earlier. The program initially had 10 patients but 2 years after it was begun had grown to 30 patients. The group meets once a week for an hour and a half. Humor is a major part of the group meeting. Members also frequently reminisce and tell old war stories. Sobriety is stressed as an already-achieved or achievable goal. The "Class of 45" groups showed an 81% rate of attendance at scheduled treatment activities and an average length of stay of over 10 months. For the VA hospital outpatient population as a whole the attendance rate is 58% and the average length of stay is 5.8 months.

The Alcoholism Day Treatment Center (DTC) is part of the Alcoholism Program located in a northeast VA medical center (Burns, 1988). The program focuses on issues of aging and offers an ongoing support group for older veterans. The DTC is coordinated by a clinical specialist in psychiatric-mental health nursing. It is an outpatient clinic that meets 5 days a week for 1 1/2 to 3 hours. One meeting a week focuses on issues such as how to quit smoking, how to cook, how to be assertive, etc. Educational sessions are held twice a week providing information on aging and alcoholism. Other weekly meetings are social in nature.

DIRECTIONS FOR FUTURE RESEARCH

Until recently the subject of alcoholism and aging was a neglected topic of research, and we have a very limited and inadequate knowledge base. Compared to our knowledge about alcoholism in other age groups, there is a relative lack of research on alcohol-related behaviors among the older population. "There are no national studies of elderly drinking, alcohol problems, or alcoholism" (Douglass, 1984, p. 254). The only community data we have comes from a few national probability samples and various regional, state, or local surveys, all of which have included small numbers of older adults. Most of our knowledge about alcoholism in old age is descriptive and clinical, and is primarily based on observations of elderly males in treatment settings. Our lack of knowledge has discouraged the investigation of important questions about alcoholism and aging.

The data currently available on elderly alcoholism is plagued by numerous conceptual and methodological problems, which cast serious doubt on some of the findings. These problems will be discussed in this section. Several significant research questions about alcoholism in the elderly have not been adequately addressed. This future research agenda will be briefly outlined at the end of this section.

Problems With Existing Data

As Douglass (1984) recently pointed out: "All alcohol research in the socioepidemiological domain is plagued with a semantic variability at the conceptual and operational levels, the unraveling of which has kept alcohologists busy for decades" (p. 257). Two definitional problems have hindered research in this area. First, as Widner and Zeichner (1991) point out, the definition of elderly has varied from age 50 to age 55 to over age 60. Results from studies that define elderly in different ways are not comparable. The other major definitional problem discussed by Schuckit and Pastor, (1978), Blazer and Pennybacker (1984) and others concerns the definition of alcoholism or problem drinking. Different researchers and clinicians have used widely different criteria to define alcoholism or problem drinking. Some of these criteria are also not particularly valid for picking up alcoholism in older adults. Some define alcoholism using DSM-III-R criteria. Others use consumption level or symptoms of dependence or withdrawal as their criteria for alcoholism. Some employ social problems criteria, focusing on family, social, and legal problems which result from alcohol abuse. All of these criteria were developed and normed on younger populations, and may not be valid criteria for diagnosing alcoholism in the elderly. Older alcoholics consume less alcohol than younger alcoholics. They are also less likely than younger alcoholics to experience withdrawal. Many alcoholic elders are not married or working and they have less contact than younger alcoholics with the police, which calls into question the social problems measures. The results of studies using different criteria to define alcoholism are not comparable.

In addition to the definitional problems just discussed, epidemiological and community studies of alcoholism and aging suffer from other serious methodological problems. Sampling inadequacies and measurement problems have resulted in flawed studies. In their article entitled "Epidemiology of Alcoholism in the Elderly" Blazer and Pennybacker (1984) discuss the problem of case finding. As they point out, cases of elderly alcoholics are often hidden and do not get included in epidemiological studies and household surveys. Older alcoholics are isolated in the community. Unlike younger alcoholics, they usually do not use alcohol detoxification centers or attend programs designed for alcoholics. These sources are used to find cases of alcoholics for epidemiological studies. As Blazer and Pennybacker (1984) point out, community surveys also often fail to identify elderly alcoholics because of underreporting of symptoms. Due to memory problems and denial, older alcoholics are even less likely than younger alcoholics to accurately and honestly self report their alcoholism. Another problem, which hampers accurate case identification of alcoholic elders, is the use of diagnostic screening tools such as the MAST, which have been developed and normed on younger populations and which are not valid for screening alcoholism in the elderly. Blazer and Pennybacker (1984) conclude that "In sum, people seen in treatment may differ substantially from untreated cases in the population, and the methods of case finding employed by many studies, combined with strict case definitions, may miss a substantial number of older alcoholics" (p. 27). As a result of these problems, it is impossible to estimate accurately the number of elderly alcoholics, and our current estimates of incidence and prevalence of alcoholism in the elderly are probably underestimates of the actual problem.

Another serious shortcoming in existing studies is that the vast majority of them have used cross-sectional research designs and suffer from all the major problems of cross-sectional studies. Few long-term prospective and longitudinal studies have been conducted. Due to the lack of longitudinal studies, data that would permit causal analysis is not readily available, so any speculation about causes of decline in alcoholism in old age are inconclusive and suspect. Questions such as how much change is due to historical influences are impossible to answer. We also can not accurately project the extent of the problem of alcoholism in the future because we do not know enough about cohort effects.

Most research on alcoholism and aging is descriptive and clinical. Clinical studies also suffer from serious methodological problems. Many of the studies are no more than anecdotes of descriptive case reports. Findings are often based on samples under ten. These studies lack random assignment to treatment groups, and also lack control or comparison groups. Clinicians define alcoholism using different criteria. All of the clinical studies suffer from a bias of selection as defined by Campbell and Stanley (1966). As Douglass (1984) points out: "alcoholics in these studies essentially selected themselves into the research process by virtue of their treatment status and facility of medical care" (p. 253). The major limitation of clinical studies is the lack of generalizability of findings to elderly living in the community, or even to elderly in various other types of treatment settings.

Need For Prevention Research

The 1981 Mini-White House Conference on Aging and Alcohol and the

Surgeon General's 1988 Workshop on Health Promotion recommended the need to prevent late-life alcoholism, and to find ways to reduce the current levels of late-life alcohol abuse. To date, few studies of alcoholism and aging have focused on prevention. Recently the National Institute on Alcohol Abuse and Alcoholism (NIAAA) issued a program announcement encouraging research on the prevention of alcohol abuse among the elderly. The program announcement called for primary and secondary prevention research. In this section we will discuss some major areas of prevention suggested by NIAAA and researchers currently working in the alcohol and aging field (NIAAA, 1988).

A key need in prevention research is the development and testing of valid measurement tools to identify older people who are vulnerable to, or in the early stages of problem drinking. These instruments must be sensitive to the unique expression of alcoholism in the elderly. The MAST-G is the first age-specific instrument available. Research needs to focus on the validity of this tool in diagnosing elderly alcoholics, and compare cases identified by the MAST-G to those identified by the MAST, CAGE, DSM-III-R, and other diagnostic criteria currently being used.

One key question that should be addressed in prevention research is what is the role of various social institutions in prevention? What is the role of the family, religious organizations, and other social organizations in alcohol prevention and intervention with the elderly? It is essential to look at the differential role of various social institutions for alcohol intervention and prevention in various subgroups of elderly such as males and females, minorities and nonminorities, lower and upper income groups, etc. The following kinds of questions, with respect to each subgroup, need to be addressed: To what extent do family relations contribute to alcoholism in the old; and what role do they play in prevention and intervention? How can the church and other religious organizations aid in prevention of alcoholism in the elderly? Also, at the social level it is important to investigate the role and impact of various prevention and intervention strategies in the general community. The media is one example of a community-level prevention and intervention strategy. The research question we must seek to answer is: What community-wide prevention and intervention strategies are most effective in detecting "at risk" elders and reducing the extent of problem drinking in the older population?

Another fruitful line of inquiry that should be pursued is the study of target populations. Recently retired elders and widowers, as well as older adults who visit physicians and other health care practitioners, and those who live in retirement communities and other age-segregated living environments are "at risk" groups that should be targeted. Investigation of the extent of problem drinking in these groups is necessary. So are studies which evaluate the effectiveness of various prevention and intervention strategies that are effective in reducing alcoholism and problem drinking in these target groups. One key question that should be addressed in prevention research in the future is: How can physicians, nurses and other care providers in key positions recognize alcohol problems in older patient/clients and intervene early to prevent abuse of alcohol? Other important research questions include: how effective is pre-retirement counseling in preventing the development of alcoholism in retirees; and what types of counseling strategies are most effective for what types of retirees? What types of interventions help to prevent alcoholism and problem drinking among widowed elders; and are these different for men versus women, for the recently widowed versus those widowed longer?

In general, we have few studies which focus on the differential effectiveness of various treatment modalities and programs for different subpopulations of elderly alcoholics. We also have few studies investigating barriers to treatment. Consequently, we do not know which types of treatment are most effective for males or females, for early-onset or late-onset drinkers, for the recently widowed, and for other subgroups of "at risk" elders. We also have few studies of the effectiveness of various case identification and outreach strategies. As a result, we do not know what are the most effective ways to identify and reach vulnerable elders. As Abrams and Alexopoulos (1987) noted, "There remains a substantial need for well-designed clinical research on the predictors, presentation, course, and outcomes of the various treatment approaches of geriatric alcoholism. Also, data distinguishing the course, outcome, and predictors of outcome for late- versus early-onset alcoholism are needed. The role of various risk factors, including family history, demographic and socioeconomic status, and life events, should be carefully elucidated" (p. 1286).

Additional Agendas For Future Research

Due to the serious limitations in epidemiological and other community studies of alcoholism in the elderly, it is essential that we conduct more, better designed epidemiological and community studies of the prevalence of alcohol use by the elderly. More studies are needed to identify the principal demographic and psychosocial factors related to alcohol usage. Future studies should use the same definitions of "elderly" and "alcoholism," and they should employ similar sampling frameworks so that results are comparable. More long-term prospective and longitudinal studies are needed to examine interactive effects of social factors, personality factors, genetic factors, and stresses on the development of alcoholism in late-life. It is essential to examine cohort effects. We must address the question: What is the role of Prohibition and other major socio-cultural events on the socialization process regarding individual drinking attitudes and behaviors? Are future cohorts of elders who will not experience Prohibition likely to have higher rates of alcoholism and alcohol problems and more liberal attitudes about drinking. Cross-sectional data also do not allow us to understand how drinking patterns change or stay the same across the life course (Stall, 1987). Stall suggests we need prospective and longitudinal studies to answer the following important research questions: what are the differences between those who bring alcohol problems into old age and those who first start drinking problematically in old age? Are there any differences between those heavy drinkers who moderate consumption with age and those who continue to drink heavily into old age? What do the life histories of elderly problem drinkers tell us about the disease concept of alcoholism? The stress hypothesis has not been adequately tested. As Finney and Moos (1984) point out, previous research attempts to identify a direct link between life stress and problem drinking, and has failed to consider possible mediating factors such as personality, social support, and coping styles. Brown and Harris (1978) called these "vulnerability factors." They emphasized that personal and environmental factors cause older adults to be vulnerable to the negative effects of stress such as alcoholism. It is important that future research identify the causal mechanisms through which stressors produce alcohol abuse in vulnerable elders (Finney & Moos, 1984). We need well designed research that will allow us to answer the following types of questions: "How do life stressors produce problem drinking among older persons? Why do some older people develop drinking problems when faced with stressful life circumstances, while others continue to function adequately? How can social resources help an older individual to overcome or adapt to stressful life situations? What coping responses do elderly people use to deal with life stressor, and how do these responses help to ameliorate distress?" (Finney & Moos, 1984, p. 281).

Future research should focus on the interrelationship between alcoholism and chronic disease among the geriatric population. Research is needed to determine how high alcohol consumption complicates diagnosis, maintenance, and treatment of various diseases, and also to determine to what extent drinking affects the progress of disease in the elderly and the role disease plays in contributing to problem drinking (Douglass, 1984). We also need more studies on the effects of alcohol on sleep, appetite, sexual function, and other aspects of normal daily function (Crook & Cohen, 1984). In future research more attention should also be devoted to the relationship between alcoholism and other mental disorders such as depression and dementia.

Finally, we currently have no good cross-cultural studies of alcoholism and aging. Cross-cultural research is necessary to determine what factors are age-related and universal and what factors are culturally determined or culturally influenced. Attempts to examine cultural influences, however, must be preceded by a more accurate general knowledge of aging and alcoholism.

REFERENCES

*Abrams, R. C., & Alexopoulos, G. (1987). Substance abuse in the elderly: Alcohol and prescription drugs. Hospital and Community Psychiatry, 38(12), 1285-1287.

*Annotated in the following chapters.

*Adams, S. L., & Waskel, S. A. (1991). Late onset alcoholism among older midwestern men in treatment. Psychological Reports, 68(2), 432-434.

*Adams, W. L., Yuan Z., Barboriak, J. J., & Rimm, A. A. (1993). Alcohol-related hospitalizations of elderly people: Prevalence and geographic variation in the United States. Journal of the American Medical Association, 270(10), 1222-1225.

Alexander, C. S. (1972, October). Cobalt-beer cardiomyopathy: A clinical pathologic study of 28 cases. American Journal of Medicine, 53, 395-417.

AMERSA news release (1986). Brown University, Providence, RI.

*Amodeo, M. (1990). Treating the late life alcoholic: Guidelines for working through denial integrating individual, family, and group approaches. Journal of Geriatric Psychiatry, 23(2), 91-105.

American Psychiatric Association. (1987). Diagnostic and statistical manual of mental disorders (3rd ed., rev.). Washington, DC: Author.

American Psychiatric Association Task Force on DSM-IV. (1991). DSM-IV options book: Work in progress. Washington, DC: American Psychiatric Association.

Atkinson, R. M. (1987). Alcohol problems of the elderly. Alcohol & Alcoholism, 22(4), 415-417.

Atkinson, R. M., & Kofoed, L. L. (1982). Alcohol and drug abuse in old age: A clinical perspective. Substance and Alcohol Actions/Misuse, 3(6), 353-368.

Atkinson, R. M. (Ed.). (1984). Alcohol and drug abuse in old age. Washington, DC: American Psychiatric Press.

Atkinson, R. M., & Schuckit, M. A. (1983). Geriatric alcohol and drug misuse and abuse. Advances in Substance Abuse, 3, 195-237.

*Atkinson, R. M., Turner, J. A., Kofoed, L. L., & Tolson, R. L. (1985). Early versus late-onset alcoholism in older persons: Preliminary findings. Alcoholism: Clinical and Experimental Research, 9(6), 513-515.

Bahr, H. M. (1969). Lifetime affiliation patterns of early and late-onset heavy drinkers on skid row. Quarterly Journal of Studies on Alcohol, 30(3-A), 645-656.

Bailey, M. B., Haberman, P. W., & Alksne, H. (1965). The epidemiology of alcoholism in an urban residential area. Quarterly Journal of Studies in Alcohol, 26(1), 19-40.

Baker, S. L. (1982). Substance abuse disorders in aging veterans. Paper presented at Sixth Annual Conference on Addiction Research and Treatment: Drugs, Alcohol, and Aging, Coatesville, PA.

*Barnes, G. M. (1979). Alcohol use among older persons: Findings from a Western New York state general population survey. Journal of the American Geriatrics Society, 27(6), 244-250.

Battle, A. O., & Battle, M. V. (1991). Insights provided by survivors of elderly suicides. Paper presented at the 16th Congress for the International Association of Suicide Prevention, Hamburg, Germany.

*Beresford, T. P., Blow, F. C., Brower, K. J., Adams, K. M., & Hall, R. C. W. (1988). Alcoholism and aging in the general hospital. Psychosomatics, 29(1), 61-72.

Berguland, M., Bergman, H., & Lindberg, S. (1991). Attempted suicide and other high-risk behaviors in alcoholics related to suicide and violent death. Paper presented at the 16th Congress for the International Association of Suicide Prevention, Hamburg, Germany.

Bernadt, M. W., Mumford, J., Taylor, C., Smith, B., & Murray, R. M. (1982, February 6). Comparison of questionnaire and laboratory tests in the detection of excessive drinking and alcoholism. Lancet, 1(8267), 325-328.

*Bienenfeld, D. (1987). Alcoholism in the elderly. American Family Physician, 36(2), 163-169.

*Bienenfeld, D. (1990). Substance abuse. In D. Bienenfeld (Ed.), Verwoerdt's clinical geropsychiatry (3rd ed., pp. 164-177). Baltimore, MD: Williams & Wilkins.

Billings, A., & Moos, R. H. (1984). Coping, stress, and social resources among adults with unipolar depression. Journal of Personality and Social Psychology, 46(4), 877-891.

Blaney, R., Radford, I. S., & MacKenzie, G. (1975). A Belfast study of the prediction of outcome in the treatment of alcoholism. British Journal of Addiction, 70(1), 41-50.

Blazer, D. G. (1982). Depression in late life. St. Louis: Mosby.

*Blazer, D. G., George, L., Woodbury, M., Manton, K., & Jordan, K. (1984). The elderly alcoholic: A profile. In G. Maddox, L. N. Robins, & N. Rosenberg (Eds.), Nature and extent of alcohol problems among the elderly, (pp. 275-298). Rockville, MD: National Institute on Alcohol Abuse and Alcoholism.

*Blazer, D. G., & Pennybacker, M. R. (1984). Epidemiology of alcoholism in the elderly. In J. T. Hartford & T. Samorajski (Eds.), Alcoholism in the elderly: Social and biomedical issues, (pp. 25-33). New York: Raven Press Publications.

*Bloom, P. (1983). Alcoholism after sixty. American Family Physician, 28(2), 111-113.

*Blose, I. L. (1978). The relationship of alcohol to aging and the elderly. Alcoholism: Clinical and Experimental Research, 2(1), 17-21.

Blow, F. C. (1992). The Michigan alcoholism screening test -- Geriatric version (MAST-G): A new elderly-specific screening instrument. Paper presented at the Annual Meeting of the American Society on Aging, San Diego, CA.

*Borgatta, E. F., Montgomery, R. J. V., & Borgatta, M. L. (1982). Alcohol use and abuse, life crisis events, and the elderly. Research on Aging, 4(3), 378-408.

*Bosmann, H. B. (1984). Pharmacology of alcoholism and aging. In J. T. Hartford & T. Samorajski (Eds.), Alcoholism in the elderly: Social and biomedical issues (pp. 161-174). New York: Raven Press.

Brigden, W. (1972). Alcoholic cardiomyopathy. Cardiovascular Clinics, 4(1), 187-201.

Brown, G. W., & Harris, T. O. (1978). Social origins of depression: A study of psychiatric disorder in women. New York: Free Press.

*Burns, B. R. (1988). Treating recovering alcoholics. Journal of Gerontological Nursing, 14(5), 18-22.

Cahalan, D., Cisin, I. H., & Crossley, H. M. (1969). American drinking practices: A national study of drinking behavior and attitudes. [Monograph]. Rutgers Center of Alcohol Studies, 6. New Brunswick, NJ: Rutgers University Press.

Campbell, D. T., & Stanley, J. C. (1966). Experimental and quasi-experimental designs for research. Chicago: Rand-McNally.

Carruth, B. (1974). Alcoholism and problem drinking among older persons: Life styles, drinking practices, and drinking problems of older Americans. Paper presented at the National Council on Alcoholism Medical/Scientific Meeting, Denver, CO.

Carruth, B., Williams, E. P., Mysak, P., & Boudreaux, L. (1973). Alcoholism and problem drinking among older persons: Community care providers and the older problem drinker. New Brunswick, NJ: Rutgers Center of Alcohol Studies.

*Cartensen, L. L., Rychtarik, R. G., & Prue, D. M. (1985). Behavioral treatment of the geriatric alcohol abuser: A long-term follow-up study. Addictive Behaviors, 10(3), 307-311.

Chafetz, M. E. (1983). The alcoholic patient: Diagnosis and management. Oradell, NJ: Medical Economics Books.

Christopherson, V. A. (1980). Alcohol usage patterns among rural aged in Arizona. Tucson, AZ: Office of Human Development and Family Research, University of Arizona.

*Christopherson, V. A., Escher, M. C., & Bainton, B. R. (1984). Reasons for drinking among the elderly in rural Arizona. Journal of Studies on Alcohol, 45(5), 417-423.

Clark, D. C., & Clark, S. H. (1991). A psychological autopsy study of elderly suicide. Paper presented at the 16th Congress for the International Association of Suicide Prevention, Hamburg, Germany.

Cohen, S. (1976). Drug use in the aging patient. Journal of Studies on Alcohol, 37, 1455.

Cooper, M. L., Russell, M., & George, W. H. (1988). Coping, expectancies, and alcohol abuse: A test of social learning formulations. Journal of Abnormal Psychology, 97(2), 218-230.

*Crook, T., & Cohen, G. (1984). Future directions for alcohol research in the elderly. In J. T. Hartford & T. Samorajski (Eds.), Alcoholism in the elderly: Social and biomedical issues (pp. 277-282). NY: Raven Press.

*Curtis, J. R., Geller, G., Stokes, E. J., Levine, D. M., & Moore, R. D. (1989). Characteristics, diagnosis, and treatment of alcoholism in elderly patients. Journal of the American Geriatrics Society, 37(4), 310-316.

Devenyi, P., Robinson, G. M., Kapur, B. M., & Roncari, D. A. K. (1981). High-density lipoprotein cholesterol in male alcoholics with and without severe liver disease. American Journal of Medicine, 71, 589-594.

Dorpat, T. L., & Ripley, H. S. (1960). A study of suicide in the Seattle area. Comprehensive Psychiatry, 1(6), 349-359.

*Douglass, R. L. (1984). Aging and alcohol problems: Opportunities for socioepidemiological research. In M. Galanter (Ed.), Recent developments in alcoholism, (pp. 251-266). NY: Plenum Press.

*Douglass, R. L., Shuster, E. O., & McClelland, S. C. (1988). Drinking patterns and abstinence among the elderly. The International Journal of the Addictions, 23(4), 399-415.

*Drew, D. (1990). Home care of the elderly alcoholic. Home Healthcare Nurse, 8(5), 26-32.

Droller, H. (1964, July 18). Some aspects of alcoholism in the elderly. Lancet, 2, 137-139.

*Dunham, R. G. (1981). Aging and changing patterns of alcohol use. Journal of Psychoactive Drugs, 13(2), 143-151.

Dunlop, J. D. (1990). Peer groups support seniors fighting alcohol and drugs. Aging, 361, 28-32.

*Dunlop, J., Skorney, B., & Hamilton, J. (1982). Group treatment for elderly alcoholics and their families. Social Work with Groups, 5(1), 87-92.

*Dupree, L. W. (1989). Comparison of three case-finding strategies relative to elderly alcohol abusers. Journal of Applied Gerontology, 8(4), 501-511.

*Dupree, L. W., Broskowski, H., & Schonfeld, L. (1984). The Gerontology Alcohol Project: A behavioral treatment program for elderly alcohol abusers. The Gerontologist, 24(5), 510-516.

*Ellis, R. J. (1990). Dichotic symmetries in aging and alcoholic subjects. Alcoholism: Clinical and Experimental Research, 14(6), 863-871.

Ewing, J. A. (1984). Detecting alcoholism. The CAGE questionnaire. Journal of the American Medical Association, 252(14), 1905-1907.

Factor, S. M. (1976). Intramyocardial small-vessel disease in chronic alcoholism. American Heart Journal, 92(5), 561-575.

Field, J. B., Williams, H. E., & Mortimore, G. E. (1963). Studies on the mechanism of ethanol-induced hypoglycemia. Journal of Clinical Investigation, 42(4), 497-506.

*Fillmore, K. M., & Midanik, L. (1983). Chronicity of drinking problems among men: A longitudinal study. Journal of Studies on Alcohol, 45(3), 228-236.

*Finlayson, R. E., Hurt, R. D., Davis, L. J., & Morse, R. M. (1988). Alcoholism in elderly persons: A study of the psychiatric and psychosocial features of 216 inpatients. Mayo Clinic Proceedings, 63(8), 761-768.

*Finney, J. W., & Moos, R. H. (1984). Life stressors and problem drinking among older adults. In M. Galanter (Ed.), Recent developments in alcoholism, (pp. 267-288). NY: Plenum Press.

Frances, R. J., Franklin, J., & Flavin, D. K. American Journal of Drug and Alcohol Abuse, 13(3), 327-341.

*Freund, G. (1984). Neurobiological relationships between aging and alcohol abuse. In M. Galanter (Ed.), Recent developments in alcoholism, (pp. 203-221). New York: Plenum Press.

Funkhouser, M. J. (1977-1978). Identifying alcohol problems among elderly hospital patients. Alcohol Health and Research World, 2(2), 27-34.

Gaitz, C. M., & Baer, P. E. (1971). Characteristics of elderly patients with alcoholism. Archives of General Psychiatry, 24(4), 372-378.

Gallant, D. M. (1987). Alcoholism: A guide to diagnosis, intervention, and treatment. NY: W.W. Norton & Co.

*Gambert, S. R., Newton, M., & Duthie, E. H. (1984). Medical issues in alcoholism in the elderly. In J. T. Hartford & T. Samorajski (Eds.), Alcoholism in the elderly: Social and biomedical issues (pp. 175-191). NY: Raven Press.

*Gerbino, P. P. (1982). Complications of alcohol use combined with drug therapy in the elderly. Journal of the American Geriatrics Society, 30 (11, suppl.), 88-93.

Glass, I.B. (1989). Undergraduate training in substance abuse in the United Kingdom. British Journal of Addiction, 84(2), 197-202.

Glassock, J.A. (1980). Alcoholism and the older woman: The displaced homemaker. Paper presented at the National Council on Alcoholism meeting, Seattle, WA.

Glatt, M. M. (1961). Drinking habits of English (middle class) alcoholics. Acta Psychiatrica Scandinavia, 37, 88-113.

*Glynn, R. J., Bouchard, G. R., LoCastro, J. S., & Laird, N. M. (1985). Aging and generational effects on drinking behavior in men: Results from the normative aging study. American Journal of Public Health, 75(12), 1413-1419.

*Gomberg, E. L. (1982). Alcohol use and alcohol problems among the elderly. [Monograph]. Alcohol and Health, 4, 263-290. Rockville, MD: US Department of Health and Human Services, Public Health Service, Alcohol, Drug Abuse, and Mental Health.

*Goodwin, J. S., Sanchez, C. J., Thomas, P., Hunt, C., Garry, P. J., & Goodwin, J. M. (1987). Alcohol intake in a healthy elderly population. American Journal of Public Health, 77(2), 173-177.

Gould, L., Zahir, M., De Martino, A., & Gomprecht, R. F. (1971). Cardiac effects of a cocktail. Journal of the American Medical Association, 218(12), 1799-1802.

*Graham, K. (1986). Identifying and measuring alcohol abuse among the elderly: Serious problems with existing instrumentation. Journal of Studies on Alcohol, 47(4), 322-326.

*Guttmann, D. (1978). Patterns of legal drug use by older Americans. Addictive Diseases, 3(3), 337-356.

Guttmann, D., Sirratt, J. D., Carrigan, Z. H., & Holahan, N. A. (1978). A study of legal drug use by older Americans. In D. E. Smith (Ed.). A multi-cultural view of drug abuse: Proceedings of the National Drug Abuse Conference, 1977, (pp. 485-495). Cambridge, MA: G. K. Hall & Co./Schenkman Publishing.

Haley, W. E., Levine, E. G., Brown, S. L., & Bartolucci, A. A. (1987). Stress, appraisal, coping and social support as predictors of adaptational outcome among dementia caregivers. Psychology and Aging, 2(4), 323-330.

*Hartford, J. T., & Samorajski, T. (1982). Alcohol in the geriatric population. Journal of the American Geriatrics Society, 30(1), 18-24.

*Hartford, J. T., & Thienhaus, O. J. (1984). Psychiatric aspects of alcoholism in geriatric patients. In J. T. Hartford & T. Samorajski (Eds.), Alcoholism in the elderly: Social and biomedical issues, 25 (pp. 253-262). NY: Raven Press.

*Haugland, S. (1989). Alcoholism and other drug dependencies. Primary Care, 16(2), 411-429.

Hinrichsen, J. J. (1990). Alcoholics Anonymous. The heart of treatment for alcoholism. Aging, 361, 13-17.

Hochhauser, M. (1978). Drugs as agents of control. Journal of Psychedelic Drugs, 10(1), 65-69.

*Holzer, C. E., Robins, L. N., Myers, J. K., Weissman, M. M., Tischler, G. L., Leaf, P. J., Anthony, J. C., & Bednarski, P. B. (1983). Antecedents and correlates of alcohol abuse and dependence in the elderly. In G. Maddox, L. Robins, & N. Rosenberg (Eds.), Nature and extent of alcohol problems among the elderly (pp. 217-244). Rockville: USDHHS.

Hubbard, R. W., Santos, J. F., & Santos, M. A. (1979). Alcohol and older adults: Overt and covert influences. Social Casework, 60(3), 166-170.

*Hurt, R. D., Finlayson, R. E., Morse, R. M., & Davis, L. J. (1988). Alcoholism in elderly persons: Medical aspects and prognosis of 216 inpatients. Mayo Clinic Proceedings, 63(8), 753-760.

*Janik, S. W., & Dunham, R. G. (1983). A nationwide examination of the need for specific alcoholism treatment programs for the elderly. Journal of Studies on Alcohol, 44(2), 307-317.

Johnson, L. A., & Goodrich, C. H. (1974). Use of alcohol by persons sixty-five and over: Upper east side of Manhattan. Report to the National Institute on Alcohol Abuse and Alcoholism from Mt. Sinai School of Medicine, City University of New York.

Kalbfleisch, J. M., Lindeman, R. D., Ginn, H. E., & Smith, W. O. (1963). Effects of ethanol administration on urinary excretion of magnesium and other electrolytes in alcoholic and normal subjects. Journal of Clinical Investigation, 42(9), 1471-1475.

Kannel, W. B. (1986). Nutritional contributors to cardiovascular disease in the elderly. Journal of the American Geriatrics Society, 34(1), 27-36.

Kasper, J. A. (1982). Prescribed medicines: Use, expenditures, and source of payment. (PHS Publication No. 82-3320). Washington, DC: United States Government Printing Office.

Knupfer, G., & Room, R. (1964). Age, sex, and social class factors in amount of drinking in a metropolitan community. Social Problems, 12, 224-240.

Kofoed, L. L., Tolson, R. L., Atkinson, R. M., Toth, R. L., & Turner, J. A. (1987). Treatment compliance of older alcoholics: An elder-specific approach is superior to "mainstreaming." Journal of Studies on Alcohol, 48(1), 47-51.

*Kola, L. A., Kosberg, J. I., & Joyce, K. (1984). The alcoholic elderly client: Assessment of policies and practices of service providers. The Gerontologist, 24(5), 517-521.

Korsten, M. A., & Lieber, C. S. (1985). Medical complications of alcoholism. In J. H. Mendelson & N. K. Mello (Eds.), The diagnosis and treatment of alcoholism (2nd ed.) (pp.21-64). New York: McGraw-Hill.

*Kosberg, J. I., & McCarthy, E. J. (1985). Problem drinking participants in programs for the elderly: Programmatic considerations. Journal of Applied Gerontology, 4(2), 20-29.

*La Greca, A. J., Akers, R. L., & Dwyer, J. W. (1988). Life events and alcohol behavior among older adults. The Gerontologist, 28(4), 552-558.

*Lamy, P. M. (1988). Actions of alcohol and drugs in older people. Generations, 12(4), 9-13.

*Lawson, A. W. (1989). Substance abuse problems of the elderly: Considerations for treatment and prevention. In G. W. Lawson & A. W. Lawson (Eds.), Alcohol and substance abuse in special populations (pp. 95-113). Rockville, MD: Aspen.

Levy, L. J., Duga, J., Girgis, M., & Gordon, E. E. (1973). Ketoacidosis associated with alcoholism and nondiabetic subjects. Annals of Internal Medicine, 78(2), 213-219.

*Linn, M. W. (1978). Attrition of older alcoholics from treatment. Addictive Diseases: An International Journal, 3(3), 437-447.

*Magruder-Habib, K., Saltz, C. C., & Barron, P. M. (1986). Age-related patterns of alcoholism among veterans in ambulatory care. Hospital and Community Psychiatry, 37(12), 1251-1255.

Mayfield, D. G., & Montgomery, D. (1972). Alcoholism, alcohol, intoxication, and suicide attempts. Archives of General Psychiatry, 27(3), 349-353.

*Maypole, D. E. (1989). Alcoholism and the elderly: Review of theories, treatment, and prevention. Activities, Adaptation and Aging, 13(4), 43-54.

McCusker, J., Cherubin, C. E., & Zimberg, S. (1971). Prevalence of alcoholism in a general municipal hospital population. New York State Journal of Medicine, 71(7), 751-754.

McDonald, C. D., Burch, G. E., & Walsh, J. J. (1971). Alcoholic cardiomyopathy managed with bed rest. Annals of Internal Medicine, 74(5), 681-691.

McDonald, J. T. (1977). Effect of ethanol on human mineral metabolism. In L. Ting-Kai, S. Schenker, & L. Lumeng (Eds.), Alcohol in nutrition (NIAA Research Monograph, #2) (pp. 191-204). Washington, DC: Department of Health, Education and Welfare.

Mendelson, J. H., & Mello, N. K. (1973). Alcohol-induced hyperlipidemia and beta lipoproteins. Science, 180(4092), 1372-1374.

Menninger, K. (1938). Man against himself. New York: Harcourt, Brace & Javanovich.

Meyers, A. R., Hingson, R., Mucatel, M., & Goldman, E. (1982). Social and psychologic correlates of problem drinking in old age. Journal of the American Geriatrics Society, 30(7), 452-456.

*Meyers, A. R., Hingson, R., Mucatel, M., Heeren, T., & Goldman, E. (1985-86). The social epidemiology of alcohol use by urban older adults. International Journal of Aging and Human Development, 21(1), 49-59.

Milhorn, H. T. (1988). The diagnosis of alcoholism. American Family Physician, 37(6), 175-183.

*Milhorn, H. T., & Gardner, L. C. (1990). When to suspect alcoholism: How to help when you do. Senior Patient, 2(7), 41-46.

Miller, M. (1976). Suicide among older men. Dissertation Abstracts International, 37(6-B), 3156.

*Miller, N. S., Belkin, B. M., & Gold, M. S. (1991). Alcohol and drug dependence among the elderly: Epidemiology, diagnosis, and treatment. Comprehensive Psychiatry, 32(2), 153-165.

*Mishara, B. L. (1985). What we know, don't know, and need to know about older alcoholics and how to help them: Models of prevention and treatment. In E. Gottheil, K. A. Druley, T. E. Skoloda, & H. M. Waxman (Eds.), The combined problems of alcoholism, drug addiction and aging (pp. 243-261). Springfield, IL: Charles C. Thomas.

*Molgaard, C. A., Nakamura, C. M., Stanford, E. P., Peddecord, K. M., & Morton, D. J. (1990). Prevalence of alcohol consumption among older persons. Journal of Community Health, 15 (4), 239-251.

Moriarty, H. J. (1989). Problems in the taxonomy of alcoholism. Journal of the American Geriatrics Society, 37(5), 488.

*Moos, R. H., Brennan, P. L., Fondacaro, M. R., & Moos, B. S. (1990). Approach and avoidance coping responses among older problem and nonproblem drinkers. Psychology and Aging, 5(1), 31-40.

Morse, R. M. (1984). Alcohol and the elderly. Geriatrics, 39(12), 28-29.

Moss, G. (1982). Malabsorption associated with extreme malnutrition: Importance of replacing plasma albumin. Journal of the American College of Nutrition, 1(1), 89-92.

Mulry, J. T., Brewer, M. L. & Spencer, D. L. (1987). The effect of an inpatient chemical dependency rotation on residents' clinical behavior. Family Medicine, 19(4), 276-280.

Murphy, G. E. (1986). Suicide in alcoholism. In A. Roy (Ed.), Suicide (pp. 89-96). Baltimore, MD: Williams & Wilkins.

*Newman-Aspel, M. (1990). Two cases of late life alcoholism. Journal of Geriatric Psychiatry, 23(2), 107-116.

NIAAA. (1988). Alcohol and aging. Alcohol Alert. (DHHS Publication No. 2). Washington, DC: Government Printing Office.

Novak, L. P. (1972). Aging, total body potassium, fat free mass and cell mass in males and females between ages 18 and 85 years. Journal of Gerontology, 27(4), 438-450.

Nowak, C. A. (1985). Life events and drinking behavior in later years. In E. Gottheil, K. Druley, T. E. Skoloda, & H. M. Waxman (Eds.), The combined problems of alcoholism, drug addiction and aging (pp. 36-50). Springfield, IL: Charles C. Thomas.

*Olson-Noll, C. G., & Bosworth, M. F. (1989). Alcohol abuse in the elderly. American Family Physician, 39(4), 173-179.

*Osgood, N. J. (1988). Identifying and treating the geriatric alcoholic. Geriatric Medicine Today, 7(8), 53-57.

Osgood, N. J. (1992). Suicide in the elderly: Etiology and assessment. International Review of Psychiatry, 4(2), 217-223.

Osgood, N. J., Wood, H. E., Coogle, C. L., Pyles, M. A. (1991, August 16). Final report on the Virginia statewide model 'detection and prevention program for geriatric alcoholism'. Submitted to the Administration on Aging.

Palola, G. E., Dorpat, T. L., & Larson, W. R. (1962). Alcoholism and suicidal behavior. In D. J. Pittman, & C. R. Snyder (Eds.), Society: Culture and drinking patterns (pp. 511-546). New York: J. Wiley.

*Parette, H. P., Jr., Hourcade, J. J., & Parette, P. C. (1990). Nursing attitudes toward geriatric alcoholism. Journal of Gerontological Nursing, 16(1), 26-31.

*Parker, E. S., & Noble, E. P. (1980). Alcohol and the aging process in social drinkers. Journal of Studies on Alcohol, 41(1), 170-178.

Perlow, W., Baraona, E., & Lieber, C. S. (1977). Symptomatic intestinal disaccharidase deficiency in alcoholics. Gastroenterology, 72, 680-684.

Pokorny, A. D., & Solomon, J. (1983). A follow-up survey of drug use and alcoholism teaching in medical schools. Journal of Medical Education, 58(4), 316-321.

*Rains, V. S. (1990, October). Alcoholism in the elderly - The hidden addiction. Medical Aspects of Human Sexuality, 24, 44-47.

*Raschko, R. (1991). Gatekeepers do the casefinding in Spokane. Prevention Pipeline, 4(2), 72-74.

Raskind, M., & Eisdorfer, C. (1976). Psychopharmacology of the aged. In L. L. Simpson (Ed.), Drug treatment of mental disorders (pp. 237-266). New York: Raven Press.

Rathbone-McCuan, E., Lohn, H., Levenson, J., & Hsu, J. (1976). Community survey of aged alcoholics and problem drinkers. Washington, DC: Government Printing Office.

Rathbone-McCuan, E., & Roberds, L. A. (1980). Treatment of the older female alcoholic. Paper presented at the Western Gerontological Society Meeting, Anaheim, CA.

Rathbone-McCuan, E., & Triegaardt, J. (1978). Older alcoholic and the family. Paper presented at the NCA meeting, St. Louis, MO.

Reifler, B., Raskind, M., & Kethley, A. (1982). Psychiatric diagnosis among geriatric patients seen in outreach programs. Journal of the American Geriatrics Society, 30(8), 530-533.

Rich, C. L., Young, D., & Fowler, R. C. (1986). San Diego suicide study, I: Young vs. old subjects. Archives of General Psychiatry, 43(6), 577-582.

Rich, E. C., Siebold, C., & Campion, B. (1985). Alcohol-related acute atrial fibrillation: A case-control study and review of 40 patients. Archives of Internal Medicine, 145(5), 830-833.

Ritschel, W. A. (1976). Pharmacokinetic approach to drug dosing in the aged. Journal of the American Geriatrics Society, 24(8), 344-354.

*Rix, K. J. B. (1982). Elderly alcoholics in the Edinburgh psychiatric services. Journal of the Royal Society of Medicine, 75(3), 177-180.

*Robertson, A. (1989). Treatment issues of the older adult. Counselor, 7(2), 8-9.

Robins, E. (1981). The final months: A study of the lives of 134 persons who committed suicide. New York: Oxford University Press.

Rosin, A. J., & Glatt, M. M. (1971). Alcohol excess in the elderly. Quarterly Journal of Studies on Alcohol, 32(1-A), 53-59.

*Ruben, D. H. (1986). The elderly alcoholic: Some current dimensions. Advances in Alcohol & Substance Abuse, 5(4), 59-70.

*Schonfeld, L., & Dupree, L. W. (1990). Older problem drinkers - Long-term and late-life onset abusers: What triggers their drinking? Aging, 361, 5-8.

*Schonfeld, L., & Dupree, L. W. (1991). Antecedents of drinking for early- and late-onset elderly alcohol abusers. Journal of Studies on Alcohol, 52(6), 587-592.

*Schuckit, M. A. (1980). Alcohol and the elderly. Advances in Alcoholism, 1(16), 1-3.

*Schuckit, M. A. (1982). A clinical review of alcohol, alcoholism, and the elderly patient. Journal of Clinical Psychiatry, 43(10), 396-399.

Schuckit, M. A., Morrissey, E. R., & O'Leary, M. R. (1978). Alcohol problems in elderly men and women. Addictive Diseases: An International Journal, 3(3), 405-416.

*Schuckit, M. A., & Pastor, P. A., Jr. (1978). The elderly as a unique population: Alcoholism. Alcoholism: Clinical and Experimental Research, 2(1), 31-38.

Schuckit, M. A., & Pastor, P. A. (1979). Alcohol-related psychopathology in the aged. In O. J. Kaplan (Ed.), Psychopathology of aging (pp. 211-227). New York: Academic Press.

Schulz, R. (1976). Effects of control and predictability on the physical and psychological well-being of the institutionalized elderly. Journal of Personality and Social Psychology, 33(5), 563-573.

*Seixas, F. A. (1979). Drug/alcohol interactions: Avert potential dangers. Geriatrics, 34(10), 89-102.

Seligman, M. E. P. (1975). Helplessness: On depression, development, and death. San Francisco: Freeman.

Seligman, M. E. P. (1976). Learned helplessness and depression in animals and men. In J. T. Spence, R. C. Carsen, & J. W. Thibaut (Eds.), Behavioral approaches to therapy (pp. 111-126). Morristown, NJ: General Learning Press.

Selzer, M. L., Vinokur, A., van Rooijen, L. (1975). A self-administered short Michigan alcoholism screening test (SMAST). Journal of Studies on Alcohol, 36, 117-126.

50 Overview

*Serkin, E. (1987, September/October). Elderly alcoholics and their adult children: Stereotypes and other obstacles to treatment. Focus, (12-13), 23-25, 39.

*Sherouse, D. L. (1982). Professional's handbook on geriatric alcoholism. Springfield, IL: Charles C. Thomas.

Simon, A., Epstein, L. J., & Reynolds, L. (1968). Alcoholism in the geriatric mentally ill. Geriatrics, 23(10), 125-131.

Skog, O. J. (1984). The risk function for liver cirrhosis from lifetime alcohol consumption. Journal of Studies on Alcohol, 45(3), 199-208.

*Smart, R. G., & Liban, C. B. (1982). Predictors of problem drinking among elderly, middle-aged and youthful drinkers. In D. M. Peterson & F. J. Whittington (Eds.), Drugs, alcohol, and aging (pp. 43-53). Dubuque, IA: Kendall/Hunt.

Smith, J. W. (1977). Alcohol disorders of the heart and skeletal muscles. In N. J. Estes, & M. E. Heinemann (Eds.), Alcoholism: Development, consequences, and interventions (pp. 136-143). St. Louis: Mosby.

*Snyder, P. K., & Way, A. (1979). Alcoholism and the elderly. Aging, 291, 8-11.

*Stall, R. (1987). Research issues concerning alcohol consumption among aging populations. Drug and Alcohol Dependence, 19(3), 195-213.

Stock, C., Bode, J. C., & Sarles, H. (Eds.). (1980). Alcohol and the gastrointestinal tract (pp. 1-54). Paris: INSERM.

Temple, M. T., & Leino, E. V. (1989). Long-term outcomes of drinking: A 20-year longitudinal study of men. British Journal of Addiction, 84(8), 889-899.

*Ticehurst, S. (1990). Alcohol and the elderly. Australian and New Zealand Journal of Psychiatry, 24(2), 252-260.

*Tobias, C. R., Lippmann, S., Pary, R., Oropilla, T., & Embry, C. K. (1989). Alcoholism in the elderly: How to spot and treat a problem the patient wants to hide. Postgraduate Medicine, 86(4), 67-79.

Vande Creek, L. V., Zachrich, R. L., & Scherger, W. E. (1982). The use of standardized screening tests in family practice. Family Practice Research Journal, 2(1), 11-17.

Van Thiel, D. H., Lipsitz, H. D., Porter, L. E., Schade, R. R., Gottlieb, G. P., & Graham, T. O. (1981). Gastrointestinal and hepatic manifestations of chronic alcoholism. Gastroenterology, 81(3), 594-615.

Vestal, R. E., McGuire, E. A., Tobin, J. D., Andres, R., Norris, A. H., & Mezey, E. (1977). Aging and ethanol metabolism. Clinical Pharmacology and Therapeutics, 21(3), 343-354.

von Knorring, L., von Knorring, A. L., Smigan, L., Lindberg, U., & Edholm, M. (1987). Personality traits in subtypes of alcoholics. Journal of Studies on Alcohol, 48(6), 523-527.

Weener, J. M. (1978, June). Prevention and the elderly. State College, PA: Pennsylvania State University, Addictions Prevention Laboratory.

Weg, R. B. (1978). Drug interaction with the changing physiology of the aged: Practice and potential. In R. H. Davis & W. K. Smith (Eds.), Drugs and the elderly (pp. 71-91). Los Angeles, CA: Ethel Percy Andrus Gerontology Center, University of Southern California.

*Wells-Parker, E., Miles, S., & Spencer, B. (1983). Stress experiences and drinking histories of elderly drunken-driving offenders. Journal of Studies on Alcohol, 44(3), 429-437.

*Westermeyer, J. (1984). Cross-cultural aspects of alcoholism in the elderly. In M. Galanter (Ed.), Recent developments in alcoholism, (pp. 289-299). New York: Plenum Press.

Whittier, J. R., & Korenyi, C. (1961). Selected characteristics of aged patients: A study of mental hospital admissions. Comprehensive Psychiatry, 2(2), 113-120.

Wiberg, G. S., Samson, J. M., Maxwell, W. B., Coldwell, B. B., & Trenholm, H. L. (1971). Further studies on the acute toxicity of ethanol in young and old rats: Relative importance of pulmonary excretion and total body water. Toxicology Applied Pharmacology, 20(1), 22-29.

*Widner, S., & Zeichner, A. (1991). Alcohol abuse in the elderly: Review of epidemiology, research and treatment. Clinical Gerontologist, 11(1), 3-17.

*Wiens, A. N., Menustik, C. E., Miller, S. I., & Schmitz, R. E. (1982-1983). Medical-behavioral treatment of the older alcoholic patient. American Journal of Drug and Alcohol Abuse, 9(4), 461-475.

*Willenbring, M. L., Christensen, K. J., Spring, W. D., & Rasmussen, R. (1987). Alcoholism screening in the elderly. Journal of the American Geriatrics Society, 35(9), 864-869.

*Willenbring, M., & Spring, W. D. (1988). Evaluating alcohol use in elders. Generations, 12(4), 27-31.

Williams, E. P. (1988). Health promotion and aging: Alcohol. In F.G. Abdellah & S.R. Moore (Eds.), Surgeon general's workshop on health promotion and aging: Background papers (pp. A1-A20). Rockville, MD: U.S. Department of Health & Human Services, Public Service.

Williams, M. (1984). Alcohol and the elderly: An overview. Alcohol Health Research World, 8(3), 3-9, 52.

*Wood, W. G. (1985). Mechanisms underlying age-related differences in response to ethanol. In E. Gottheil, K. A. Druley, T. E. Skolada, & H. M. Waxman (Eds.), The combined problems of alcoholism, drug addiction and aging (pp.94-109). Springfield, IL: Charles C. Thomas.

Wood, W. G., & Armbrecht, H. J. (1982). Behavioral effects of ethanol in animals: Age differences and age changes. Alcoholism: Clinical and Experimental Research, 6(1), 3-12.

Wyngaarden, J. B., & Kelley, W. N. (1972). Gout. In J. B. Stanbury, J. B. Wyngaarden, & D. S. Frederickson (Eds.), The metabolic basis of inherited disease (3rd ed., pp. 889-968). New York: McGraw-Hill.

*Zimberg, S. (1978). Treatment of the elderly alcoholic in the community and in an institutional setting. Addictive Diseases: An International Journal, 3(3), 417-427.

Zimberg, S. (1982). Treatment of the elderly alcoholic. Paper presented at the Sixth Annual Conference on Addiction Research and Treatment: Drugs, Alcohol, and Aging, Coatesville, PA.

*Zimberg, S. (1984). Diagnosis and the management of the elderly alcoholic. In R.M. Atkinson (Ed.), [Monograph]. Alcohol and drug abuse in old age, 23-34. Washington, DC: American Psychiatric Press.

Zimberg, S. (1985). Alcoholism, drug addiction and aging. In E. Gottheil, K. Druley, T. Skoloda, & H. M. Waxman (Eds), The combined problems of alcoholism, drug addiction and aging (pp. 284-302). Springfield, IL: Charles C. Thomas.

Zimberg, S., Lipscomb, H., & Davis, E. B. (1971). Socio-psychiatric treatment of alcoholism in an urban ghetto. American Journal of Psychiatry, 127(12), 1670-1674.

*Zimering, S., & Domeischel, J. R. (1982). Is alcoholism a problem of the elderly? Journal of Drug Education, 12(2), 103-112.

Bibliographies

001   Barnes, G. M., Abel, E. L., & Ernst, C. A. S. (1980). <u>Alcohol and
        the elderly: A comprehensive bibliography</u>. Westport, CT:
        Greenwood Press.

This extensive bibliography includes over 1,200 unannotated citations arranged alphabetically by first author. References are drawn from books, articles, monographs, and reports in a variety of languages, and comprise works that link alcohol use to the older adult population (age 55 and over). Citations are dated from the 1920's through the 1970's. A brief, introductory overview and a subject index are also included.

002   Bryant, G. F. (1989). <u>Elder alcoholism: An annotated bibliography</u>.
        Oxford, OH: Miami University Press.

The author provides 107 annotated citations arranged alphabetically by first author. The majority of references are dated from the late 1970's to mid-1980's. An introductory review chapter includes brief comments on prevalence, typology, outreach and barriers to treatment, health consequences of alcoholism, and prevention. A subject index is included.

003   Ruben, D. H. (1984). <u>Drug abuse in the elderly: An annotated
        bibliography</u>. Metuchen, NJ: Scarecrow Press.

Following a brief introduction, Ruben provides eight chapters of annotations that comprise 787 bibliographic listings. Chapters are divided according to subject and include topics such as medication use and abuse, compliance, epidemiology, education/prevention, and institutionalization. Although the annotations are quite brief, they are accompanied by helpful key words. Ruben has thoughtfully included author, subject, and journal indices.

004 Rutgers University Center of Alcohol Studies. (1984-1987). <u>Library alcohol bibliography series, Addendum B070: Older persons</u>. Piscataway, NJ: Rutgers University.

The Alcohol Bibliography Series is published on an ongoing basis and includes unannotated citations of dissertations, reports, and unpublished papers as well as journal articles and books. Listings comprise both English and non-English works. The latest update of the overall series is 1991, with addenda on older persons included for the years 1984-1987.

Overview Articles

005   Atkinson, R. M.   (1990).   Aging and alcohol use disorders: Diagnostic issues in the elderly. International Psychogeriatrics, 2(1), 55-72.

This article reviews current existing literature on alcoholism in older adults. First, literature on increased biological sensitivity to alcohol in aging adults is reviewed. Next, age at onset is discussed, indicating that many adults begin problem drinking in their later years.

The author discusses prevalence studies in one section, noting that cross-sectional community studies have found lower prevalence rates in older adults, but longitudinal studies suggest that drinking patterns remain quite stable over the life course. In the next section diagnosis of late life alcoholism is the focus. DSM-III-R criteria are evaluated as are the Michigan Alcoholism Screening Test (MAST) and other instruments. The author points out that present screening and diagnostic methods for alcohol use disorder lack adequate validation for older people. The article concludes with a plea for further clinical studies to adequately specify the phenomenology of alcohol use disorders in older persons, and more research on the typology of alcohol problems in older people (i.e., primary, lifelong alcohol problems, reactive alcohol problems following loss).

006   Benshoff, J. J., & Roberto, K. A. (1987). Alcoholism in the elderly: Clinical Issues. Clinical Gerontologist, 7(2), 3-14.

This is a very straightforward and clear overview article considering all the usual sub-topics: epidemiology, causation, consumption change patterns by cohort and age, health interactions and debilitation related to alcohol abuse, and diagnostic and treatment issues. Five issues are discussed in the summary section: defining and diagnosing alcoholism, issues related to cohort and categorization of late- versus early-onset drinkers, need for additional treatment outcome studies, educational needs of service providers, and lastly, the need for causation research and longitudinal studies of alcoholism.

007   Beresford, T. P., Blow, F. C., & Brower, K. J. (1990). Alcoholism in the elderly. Comprehensive Therapy, 16(9), 38-43.
        Coming from the University of Michigan Alcohol Research Center, the authors of this article aim to translate for the therapist, "factors that hinder the recognition of this illness" and suggest "ways for clinicians to improve their ability to diagnose alcoholism among the elderly," and discuss what the ingredients for successful treatment are for the elderly. The authors systematically take up each issue and clearly explain what the accurate information should be. Practical insights are made throughout the discussion. An example of this is within the discussion of late-onset drinking the authors caution the clinician-reader not to try to deal with major causative stressors, e.g., the grief related to loss of a spouse, "until sobriety has been achieved and well established for some time." Another example of the immediate utility of information in this article is in a discussion of withdrawal syndrome in an elderly patient. The actual medications and medication levels are recommended with precision and detail. One final example of the usefulness of this paper is in a discussion of treatment effectiveness, in which the authors emphasize to the clinician, "The one overriding principle in the treatment of alcoholism should be the provision of hope in the clinical solution;" they go on to say that providing this hope and enhancing self-esteem is particularly salient to the elderly because having grown up in the Prohibition Era and having viewed alcohol dependence as a moral issue only, self-esteem can be restored when the elderly person can view alcoholism as "an illness that will improve."

008   Beresford, T. P., Blow, F. C., Brower, K. J., Adams, K. M., & Hall, R. C. W. (1988). Alcoholism and aging in the general hospital. Psychosomatics, 29(1), 61-72.
        In this article authors discuss the problem of late-life alcoholism focusing primarily on diagnosis and treatment. In the introduction they note that alcoholism is a serious problem in the current generation of elders, and will be an even greater problem as baby boomers grow old in future years. They also point out that health professionals often underdiagnose alcohol abuse in older patients. They note many reasons for lack of detection of older alcoholics and

underdiagnosis of late-life alcohol abuse.

Current screening instruments used to identify alcoholics may not be reliable or valid for those 60 and older. Graham's research on methodological problems is reviewed. The following sources of error are noted: impaired short-term memory affecting quantity-frequency assessment; isolation, living alone, no longer driving affecting responses to items in social and legal problems; age-related increased incidence of health problems affecting responses to questions on health problems; and social or cultural values that intensify shame and promote denial, affecting questions on self-recognition of problems.

Authors present a disguised case history to discuss four factors important to consider in making a diagnosis of alcohol abuse: tolerance, withdrawal, loss of control, and social decline. The importance of a geropsychological assessment is also discussed.

The final section focuses on treatment. The goal of treatment is to replace alcohol with people who do not drink. Clinicians must offer hope for recovery. Authors suggest that clinicians point out the need for total abstinence from alcohol.

009   Bienenfeld, D. (1987). Alcoholism in the elderly. American Family Physician, 36(2), 163-169.

Alcohol abuse and alcohol dependence are defined as separate illnesses by the author. Prevalence figures are presented. Early-onset alcoholics, who began drinking heavily before age 40, are compared to late-onset alcoholics, who began drinking after age 60. Late-onset alcoholics are more likely than early-onset alcoholics to be separated or divorced, have organic mental disorder, and suffer from serious health problems. Compared to early-onset alcoholics, late-onset alcoholics are less likely to have spent time in jail or to have a family history of alcoholism. The author also compares alcoholic and non-alcoholic elders. Compared to non-alcoholic elders, alcoholic elders are more likely to live alone, have marital problems, have health problems, and have organic mental disorder. Their risk of suicide is also higher.

Diagnosis and treatment are discussed. Several signs of late-life alcoholism are highlighted. These include: self-neglect, falls and injuries, confusion, malnutrition, hypothermia, and other signs. The author suggests obtaining an alcohol use history. Treatment involves: accurate identification, detoxification, and counseling and rehabilitation.

010   Bloom, P. (1983). Alcoholism after sixty. American Family Physician, 28(2), 111-113.

The article presents data on prevalence of alcohol use and

abuse in older and younger adults. Problems in prevalence data are noted. Medical problems such as malnourishment and drug-alcohol interactions are discussed. Signs of late-life alcoholism are presented. These include: bruises and broken bones, frequent use of the emergency room, and refusal to answer the door. Two types of alcoholics are described: early-onset drinkers, who began drinking early in life; and late-onset drinkers, who began drinking for the first time in later years. Alcoholism is described as a coping mechanism and as a response to helplessness characteristics of late-life. Treatment should include AA involvement, home health care, and involvement with the physician, as well as various other social service providers and agencies.

011   Brody, J. A. (1982). Aging and alcohol abuse. Journal of the American Geriatrics Society, 30(2), 123-126.

Four factors which contribute to alcoholism in the elderly are identified and discussed. These are: retirement; loss of loved ones; poor health and discomfort; and loneliness. The author reviews survey data and treatment studies. Based on survey data available, 1 to 5% of those 65 and older have a serious alcohol problem. Data from treatment populations suggests that 10 to 15% of those 65 and older have a serious problem. The author feels these estimates are too low and that future cohorts of elders, who will not have experienced Prohibition, will be more likely to abuse alcohol than the present cohort of older adults.

Clinical studies identify two types of alcohol abusers: long-term abusers who survive into old age; and those in whom the onset of alcoholism occurs late in life. The author notes that many older alcoholics live in federally funded housing projects and present major problems for housing managers. Elderly alcoholics are easier to treat than are younger alcoholics. The author pleads for better methods of detection of alcoholism in this group.

In the discussion section the author calls for more and better research. In particular, he notes the need for more research about late-onset alcoholism; case control studies to identify people at high risk; and case-finding studies in hospitalized settings and carefully documented treatment trials.

012   Closser, M. H., & Blow, F. C. (1993). Special populations. Women, ethnic minorities, and the elderly. Psychiatric Clinics of North America, 16(1), 199-209.

This article presents an overview of substance abuse prevalence and problems with identification; and also examines the impact of alcoholism and treatment programs tailored to specific subgroups of the population. Among subgroups, the authors look at the elderly alcoholic and specially designed treatment programs to see if they show greater treatment outcomes than standard ones. They also review other studies to see whether the elderly prefer treatment programs with their own cohorts over a mixed-age group.

Closser and Blow note that there is emerging evidence which states that alcoholism among the elderly is a significant and growing health problem. Figures from the National Institute of Mental Health's Epidemiological Catchment Area report that: of the general population, 14% of older men and 1.5% of older women are alcoholics. Elderly alcoholism is underreported, primarily due to inappropriate screening measures that are used for younger adults, undersampling of the elderly, lack of education by health professionals and a reluctance to want to acknowledge alcoholism in older adults. Alcohol figures for elderly patients being seen in health care settings is substantially higher, and have been reported to be between 15% and 58%. However, research suggests that older alcoholics are more likely to seek inpatient care for diagnoses other than alcoholism. The article then discusses the three general patterns of elderly drinking: early-onset, late-onset and intermittent alcoholism. The reasons why older people are at high risk for alcohol-drug interactions is followed by a discussion of the problems with identifying elderly substance abusers. Alcohol and drug abuse mimic both mood and anxiety disorders, so proper diagnosis is very important to establish in this age group.

Evidence suggests that older adults respond as well as younger adults to traditional alcoholism treatment programs. One study concluded that treatment of older adults was more successful when conducted among their own cohorts. Specialized programs on aging or grief, more medically complex cases, required increased lengths of stay and use of more intensive health care levels may be reasons for elder-specific treatment. The authors conclude that "treatment for alcoholism is important for economic as well as humane reasons because underrecognition may result in the ineffective use of health care resources without treatment for the underlying cause" (p. 209).

013   Dufour, M. C., Archer, L., & Gordis, E. (1992). Alcohol and the elderly. Clinics in Geriatric Medicine, 8(1), 127-141.

This article considers the effects of alcohol on older adults. The authors point out that age-related changes in lean body mass and adipose tissue result in decreases in the volume of total body water. As a result, an alcohol dose identical to that administered to a younger individual produces a higher blood alcohol concentration (BAC) in an older individual. Although the effects of alcohol consumption on nutrition are minimal in adequately nourished, non-alcoholic elders, at higher levels of consumption alcohol inhibits the absorption of thiamine, riboflavin, niacin, and folic acid and promotes the loss of magnesium, calcium and zinc. On the positive side, authors review studies that conclude that drinking alcohol enhances social interactions, reduces feelings of stress and tension, and increases feelings of euphoria and self-confidence.

Alcohol produces negative changes in the central nervous system (CNS), which in combination with age-related changes, result in numerous sleep problems. Alcohol exacerbates sleep dysregulation and sleep apnea. One study reviewed reported that alcohol worsened all of the following breathing disturbances in sleep: severe obstructive sleep apnea, mild sleep apnea, and snoring. Alcohol also induced hypoxia in all subjects. With respect to appetite and digestion, however, alcohol has positive effects. Small amounts of alcohol stimulate appetite and improve bowel regularity in older adults.

Findings on the effects of alcohol on the heart are controversial. However, heavy drinking has been noted as a factor in heart disease. In the last part of the article authors discuss various dangers of recommending moderate alcohol consumption including: exacerbating an existing alcohol problem; drug-alcohol interactions; and exacerbation of existing dementia or cognitive impairment.

014   Dunne, F. J. (1989). Alcohol and the elderly. British Medical Journal, 6689(298), 1660-1661.

This brief article identifies factors increasing the risk of alcoholism such as retirement, bereavement, and loneliness; discusses medical problems exacerbated by alcoholism such as cirrhosis of the liver, Parkinsonism, depression, and cerebellar degeneration; and identifies warning signs to watch for such as poor hygiene, hypothermia, and drug-alcohol interactions. Authors also discuss diagnosis and treatment. They recommend obtaining a history of alcohol use and determining blood alcohol concentrations.

Detoxification, education, and rehabilitation are all effective parts of treatment.

015   Egbert, A. M. (1993). The older alcoholic: Recognizing the subtle clinical clues. Geriatrics, 48(7), 63-69.

Dr. Egbert presents a social and clinical overview of the problems in recognizing and treating alcoholism in older adults. Ten percent of the older community are abusers, although the rate of alcoholism is even higher in institutionalized patients: 18-20% in hospitals, 28% in psychiatric hospitals and 40% in nursing homes. The diagnosis is frequently missed due to atypical physiologic changes, non-specific symptoms that may mimic "geriatric syndrome" of self-neglect, bruising, poor diet, depression and falls, and social isolation which prevents hidden drinking from being exposed. Clinical clues to active alcoholism in the older patient are listed as: 1) therapy not working for a normally treatable illness; 2) the patient reports poor sleeping patterns; 3) diarrhea, urinary incontinence and weight loss; 4) trauma; 5) anxiety coupled with use of anxiolytics, sedatives, or hypnotics; and 6) unexplained behavior following surgery such as agitation, anxiety, confusion and/or seizures.

The author discusses the adverse physical and cognitive effects of alcoholism in the older adult, as well as the concept of late-onset alcoholism. Further segments deal with screening tests' reliability, detoxification and therapy issues. Dr. Egbert notes that older alcoholics have the same recovery rate as their younger counterparts; however, untreated alcoholism in older adults is more likely to be fatal.

016   Giordano, J. A., & Beckham, K. (1985). Alcohol use and abuse in
         old age: An examination of type II alcoholism. Journal of
         Gerontological Social Work, 9(1), 65-83.

This article gives an overview of the support and non-support for late-onset alcoholism. There is a review of bereavement, retirement, health problems, and loneliness as causative factors which lead to alcoholism. The authors find considerable disagreement and a lack of research evidence to support crises leading to excessive drinking in the elderly. Instead, they posit some theoretical alternatives which they find more useful than the Type II explanation. They discuss issues related to personality, contingency theory, social motivational theory, and learning theory. In the summary section they discuss family crisis-related situational variables and propose family life education as a system of intervention and prevention. They also make the point that Type II alcoholism may not even be alcoholism, but situational drinking which may also explain why Type II "alcoholics" have such successful treatment outcomes. A final suggestion is that there should be more concentration on issues such as gender and drinking because women make up a large portion of those who increase drinking behavior in late-life.

017   Glantz, M. D., & Backenheimer, M. S. (1988). Substance abuse
         among elderly women. Clinical Gerontologist, 8(1), 3-26.

This review article gives the usual overview of alcohol abuse, over-the-counter medication use, prescription psychoactive drug use, and abuse; and includes a very thorough discussion of the high rate of prescriptions for mental health problems written by the non-psychiatrically trained physician. In terms of women, this overview points out that some of the problems in the near future will be that since younger generations of women are high users of alcohol and other drugs, in the future when the women are older, they should have greater problems. The current cohort of elderly women are high users of prescription and over-the-counter medications, and this makes them vulnerable to abuse and problems of misuse. Finally, elderly women are heavier users than men of psychoactive drugs and tend to use these drugs for longer periods of time, thus enhancing the probability of experiencing drug-related problems. The last dramatic point made in this article is that elderly women may be at greater risk for "physician-perpetrated" drug abuse than any other age/gender group. Despite the interesting review included in this article, it is still quite clear that there is much more research needed in the area of elderly women and substance abuse.

018   Gomberg, E. L. (1982). Alcohol use and alcohol problems among the elderly. In Alcohol and health monographs No.4 Special population issue (pp. 263-290). Rockville, MD: U.S. Department of Health and Human Services Public Health Service Alcohol, Drug Abuse, and Mental Health Administration National Institute on Alcohol Abuse and Alcoholism.

In this comprehensive overview of existing literature and accepted knowledge about alcoholism and aging, Gomberg discusses social drinking patterns of older people. The article provides information about and reviews studies on the incidence and prevalence of problem drinking in the elderly; and discusses the psychosocial variables, antecedent conditions, and symptoms associated with problem drinking in late life. In addition, Gomberg reviews what is known and what is needed in terms of outreach and treatment, discusses prevention, and lists research priorities. Many tables are included to organize data and to present findings from literature reviewed.

Based on her review of literature, Gomberg notes that there is a decrease in the percentage of drinkers among people 60 and older and a decline in the amount of alcohol consumed after the age of 50. She explains this drop may be related to economics, physiology, unique historical aspects (Prohibition), or increased medical problems related to age.

Prevalence studies indicate that older alcoholics occupy a disproportionate number of hospital beds in the U.S. and represent a large percentage of patients in psychiatric facilities.

Differences in patterns of alcohol abuse are identified for the young-old and old-old, males and females, and different ethnic groups. The young-old, males, and caucasians are more likely to abuse alcohol than are the old-old, women, or minorities.

Gomberg identifies and discusses three types of older alcoholics: early-onset alcoholics, who began drinking early in life; reactive problem drinkers, who began drinking late in life as a response to some late-life loss or stress; and intermittents, who have intermittent histories of alcohol abuse. Stresses that may trigger late-onset alcoholism, according to Gomberg, include depression, bereavement, retirement, marital stress, and physical health problems. Gomberg suggests that older alcoholics, compared to their younger counterparts, report more binge drinking, more problems with spouse and relatives and more health problems. They also have more problems with police.

Gomberg briefly discusses outreach and treatment. She recommends education for police, physicians, and other caregivers and professionals and for children and relatives about alcoholism in the elderly. This would increase case finding. She recommends social therapies, including AA and other self-help organizations and family therapy. She suggests that prevention efforts be aimed at self-help organizations and pre-retirement training programs to target the reactive problem drinker. Several research needs are identified including the need for research on societal attitudes toward older persons' drinking. The effects of alcohol on the biology of older persons, differences among subgroups of older problem drinkers (e.g., gender, ethnicity, age of onset), and the effectiveness of different outreach and case finding methods are also discussed.

019   Gulino, C., & Kadin, M. (1986). Aging and reactive alcoholism. Geriatric Nursing, 7(3), 148-151.

Many older alcoholics remain unidentified and untreated. Authors note the distinction between early-onset and late-onset alcoholism. They focus their attention on the late-onset alcoholic, who drinks for the first time late in life, as a way to cope with the overwhelming problems of aging. Loneliness and social isolation are identified as major causes of alcoholism in the elderly. Anxiety and depression are common among alcoholic elders. Late-onset alcoholics, unlike early-onset drinkers, display few social and emotional problems early in life.

Diagnosis and treatment are discussed in the last part of the article. The Short Michigan Alcoholism Screening Test (SMAST) is recommended as a good diagnostic tool. Clues to look for such as falls are also identified. In discussing treatment, authors caution against using Disulfiram (Antabuse) and recommend social and emotional support. Education is a cornerstone of treatment. Approaching alcoholism from a medical standpoint may be useful with older alcoholics. A case is presented to demonstrate clues to alcoholism and effective treatment techniques.

020   Gupta, K. L. (1993). Alcoholism in the elderly: Uncovering a hidden problem. Postgraduate Medicine, 93(2), 203-206.

The article begins by citing the statistic that 2-10% of the elderly population suffers from alcoholism; in the U.S. about 3 million people 60 and over are alcoholics. The author discusses age-related changes such as decline in lean body mass, loss of neurons in the brain, and reduced efficiency of liver enzymes, which increase the negative effects of alcohol in the elderly. A detailed chart of negative physiological effects on the endocrine, musculoskeletal, cardiovascular, gastrointestinal, hematological, and central nervous systems is included. In one chapter the problem of underdetection of late-life alcoholism is examined. Older alcoholics are less likely to be identified by police, employers, or family members. The remainder of the article focuses on diagnosis and clinical features of the disease. The importance of taking a detailed patient history, including personal drinking history, is emphasized. The following clinical features are identified: confusion, depression, sleep disturbance, falls, burns, recurrent lung infections, self-neglect, high mean corpuscular volume, abnormal results on liver function studies, and loss of weight.

021   Gurnack, A. M., & Thomas, J. L. (1989). Behavioral factors related to elderly alcohol abuse: Research and policy issues. The International Journal of the Addictions, 24(7), 641-654.

This article is primarily an overview of selected research studies done between 1965 and 1987. The introduction cites five major reasons for increased concern about late-life alcohol abuse. The research section is laid out in two different ways for the reader: in chronological chart form and as a discussion. The chart summarizes studies performed with information pertaining to the authors, year, geographical area, focus of study, major findings and limitations. As a discussion, the authors describe various consistent research findings such as "the elderly show a decreased tolerance to alcohol as a result of the aging body's slowed metabolism," note descriptive studies that deal with specific populations of older problem drinkers, and include research that compares older problem drinkers who differ in drinking histories. The authors also note that little research has been written on late-life-onset alcohol abusers and suggest that the reason might be because this group is most responsive to treatment. Two other research sections cite possible causes of and treatments for alcohol abuse among older adults. The article concludes with four research issues that need further investigation, and suggest that the future challenge will be matching appropriate services to specific elderly subgroups.

022   Haldeman, K., & Gafner, G.   (1990).   Are elderly alcoholics
        discriminated against?   Journal of Psychosocial Nursing,
        28(5), 7-11.
        Authors contend that because of ageism, lack of education, and
other factors, older alcoholics are not recognized or treated.   As a
result, many become worse or even die or kill others.   Case examples
are provided.
        Haldeman and Gafner argue for early intervention with older
alcoholics.   Client resistance to treatment is a major barrier.   Lack of
information about alcoholism and aging and general underutilization of
behavioral and social services by older adults, as well as stigma
associated with alcoholism in this population, also hinder treatment
efforts.   There is also a notable lack of elder-specific alcohol treatment
facilities.
        Older alcoholics can be helped.   It is important to develop a
supportive, trusting relationship with the older alcoholic.   Emphasizing
the medical model and the disease concept may be useful.   One alcohol
treatment facility designed specifically for the elderly, the Day
Treatment Center, is recommended and is described in detail.

023   Hartford, J. T., & Samorajski, T. (1982).   Alcoholism in the geriatric
        population.   Journal of the American Geriatrics Society, 30(1),
        18-24.
        This overview article examines the many negative effects of
alcohol on older adults.   They point out that due to age-related changes
in lean body mass and adipose tissue, which result in decreased body
water levels, there is an age-related increase in blood ethanol levels
when ethanol dosage is based on body surface.   With aging, the rate of
blood flow through the liver decreases, which could produce changes
in metabolism of alcohol.   Declining liver function, associated with
aging, is likely to produce an interaction between ethanol and a wide
variety of prescribed drugs.   Alcohol also causes various sleep
disturbances in older adults.   Ethanol may reduce rapid eye movement
(REM) sleep and Stages 3 and 4 of Non-rapid Eye Movement (NREM)
sleep.   The older alcohol abuser's sexual drive may also be impaired.
Men who have a long history of alcoholism may have testicular atrophy
and experience chronic impotence.
        Authors discuss several other negative effects of alcohol on
health and longevity including: damage to the central nervous system
(CNS); pancreatitis; cirrhosis of the liver; nutritional and vitamin
deficiencies; and Wernicke's disease.   Authors review literature which
links alcoholism to organic brain syndrome (OBS) in older adults.
        In the last section of this article, authors discuss alcohol-drug
interactions, focus specifically on chloral hydrate, barbiturates, tricyclic
antidepressants, benzodiazepines, and neuroleptic drugs.

024   Haugland, S. (1989). Alcoholism and other drug dependencies.
        Primary Care, 16(2), 411-429.
        The author has written a straight forward overview of
alcoholism and other drug dependencies (AODD) of the elderly to assist
the professional who treats elderly patients. Haugland begins by
delving into the major differences between the elderly and the younger
chemically dependent. Next, Haugland defines terms and definitions,
followed by historical and theoretical considerations. The author points
out that many changes in the elderly due to alcoholism mimic normal
aging. The differences between early- and late-onset elderly alcoholics
are discussed, as are common clinical symptoms of possible alcohol
abuse. Clarification is made between addiction and dependency
followed by information on prescription drug dependency and
detoxification from prescription drugs. The article continues with a
discussion of eight practices, principles and guidelines to successful
interventions. Criteria for inpatient or outpatient treatment is clearly
outlined for the reader, as well as alcoholism/chemical dependency
staging and treatment recommendations. Haugland's closing remarks
remind us of the value and satisfaction of helping those who have
problems with alcoholism and drug dependencies.

025   Johnson, L. K. (1989). How to diagnose and treat chemical
        dependency in the elderly. Journal of Gerontological Nursing,
        15(12), 22-26.
        This article focuses on diagnosis and treatment of chemical
dependency in older people. Signs and symptoms are identified. Some
psychological symptoms highlighted are: memory deficits, confusion,
and anger. Physical symptoms listed include: heart problems, fatigue,
sexual dysfunction, and bruises. Social factors of retirement, isolation,
and loss of friends and family members are discussed. The Michigan
Alcoholism Screening Test (MAST) is described as a good diagnostic
tool. Barriers to treatment of late-life alcoholism are noted. These
include: labeling the elderly as a poor risk of recovery; ageism; and
reluctance to use limited financial resources to treat older people when
funds could be used for younger alcoholics. The prognosis for the
older alcoholics is excellent. Specific treatment recommendations are
made. For example, the detoxification process is different and over-
medication should be avoided. Group treatment is recommended.
Inpatient and outpatient programs should be available.

026   King, C. J., Van Hasselt, V. B., Segal, D. L., & Hersen, M. (1994).
        Diagnosis and assessment of substance abuse in older adults:
        Current strategies and issues. Addictive Behaviors, 19(1), 41-
        55.

In this article authors review evaluation and intervention methods for younger alcoholics, looking at the appropriateness of these strategies for older substance abusers, and offer suggestions for future work in this area.

The authors review relevant literature on the extent of the problem of alcohol abuse and drug misuse in older people. They discuss the inappropriateness of DSM-III-R criteria for diagnosis in older adults, pointing out that the DSM-III-R was standardized primarily on younger age groups. Specifically, criteria concerning social and occupational dysfunction may not be appropriate for older adults. They also point out that the quantity of alcohol or other substances necessary to produce impairment is substantially less for older adults. Diagnosis of alcohol and substance abuse in older adults is also complicated by the myth that young addicts either die or "outgrow" their addiction. In addition, many symptoms of late-life alcoholism may be erroneously accepted as "normal" aspects of aging rather than as consequences of alcoholism in older members.

In the next section authors examine correlates and risk factors associated with substance abuse in older adults focusing on physical/biological changes with age; cognitive factors; social influences; and psychiatric or co-morbid pathology. Relevant literature is discussed under each topic. The last part of the article deals with assessment; and the following instruments are examined: The Michigan Alcoholism Screening Test (MAST); the Brief Michigan Alcoholism Screening Test (BMAST); CAGE; and the Minnesota Multiphasic Personality Inventory (MMPI). The authors conclude that the appropriateness of these measures for older adults is uncertain. They suggest that existing assessment instruments must be specifically validated with older clinical populations; elder-specific alcohol and substance abuse measures must be constructed and appropriately validated; and discriminant analytic studies are needed to identify correlates and risk factors that are particularly salient to elderly substance abuse.

027   Lamy, P. M. (1984, July/August). Alcohol misuse and abuse among the elderly. Geriatrics and Gerontology Issue on Drug Intelligence and Clinical Pharmacy, 18, 649-651.

Literature is reviewed which reports on the extent of the use of alcohol among older people. Problems of underreporting and underdiagnosing of older alcoholics are discussed. The conclusion is that alcohol consumption among the elderly is on the rise. Adverse consequences of alcohol abuse and alcoholism among the elderly are identified. These include medical problems, psychological problems, and social problems. Alcohol-drug interactions are another serious problem noted. A profile of the older alcohol abuser is presented. The older drinker most often seeks relief from social and psychological problems or drinks to be accepted.

028   Liberto, J. G., Oslin, D. W., & Ruskin, P. E. (1992). Alcoholism in older persons: A review of the literature. Hospital and Community Psychiatry, 43(10), 975-984.

This article presents a comprehensive review of the literature on elderly alcoholism. Literature in the following areas is reviewed: epidemiology, psychiatric co-morbidity, medical aspects, and treatment. Under epidemiology authors discuss limitations of current studies, emphasizing problems of definition of alcoholism and problems of validity of current instruments, as well as prevalence data obtained from cross-sectional and longitudinal studies. Findings from community based studies are compared with findings from studies of hospitalized patients. Findings from various prevalence studies are presented in tabled form. Based on their review, the authors summarize results of cross-sectional community-based studies as follows: elderly men drink larger amounts of alcohol and drink more often than elderly women; no definitive relationship exists between ethnic origin and alcohol abuse in later years; lower income elderly persons consume less alcohol than higher-income populations; and hospitalized and outpatient populations have higher prevalence rates of alcoholism than community-based samples. The most consistent findings from longitudinal studies are summarized: abstainers tend to remain abstinent, and alcohol consumption by light drinkers tends to remain stable with age; the alcohol consumption of heavy drinkers decreases over time; and men drink more often and in greater quantities than women.

Summarizing findings from studies of age of onset which were reviewed, authors conclude that about one-third to one-half of elderly alcohol abusers experience the onset of problem drinking late in life. Late-onset drinkers are more psychologically stable than early-onset drinkers; and late-onset drinkers stay in treatment longer than early-onset drinkers.

Based on review of literature on psychiatric co-morbidity, it is clear that many older alcoholics suffer from alcoholism and either anxiety or depression. Many older alcoholics warrant dual diagnosis. Alcohol dementia and cognitive changes seen in alcoholics may be due to nutritional deficiencies. Review of literature on medical aspects reveals that older adults are more likely to suffer greater medical morbidity than are their younger counterparts. Older alcoholics have an increased risk of major illness, poorer physical functional status, impaired ability to perform activities of daily living, and higher total and cardiovascular mortality rates.

Studies on treatment are contradictory with some concluding that age-specific treatment is more effective than traditional treatment, and others citing good results from traditional treatment in mixed-age groups.

029   Marcus, M. T. (1993). Alcohol and other drug abuse in elders. Journal of ET Nursing, 20(3), 106-110.

This article written for ET nurses examines the problem of alcohol and drug abuse in older people. Several barriers that prevent the nurse from identifying and dealing with drug abuse in elders are identified. These include: lack of understanding about the aging process and stereotypes about aging; lack of comprehensive research on the effects of alcohol and other drugs in the aging individual; inappropriate assessment measures; and lack of education about alcoholism and drug abuse in elders. Denial can also be a barrier.

Marcus discusses age-related risk factors which contribute to the vulnerability of elders to alcoholism and drug abuse. These include: biologic sensitivity and increased susceptibility to toxic effects of drugs and alcohol; decreased total body water and lean body mass and increased body fat, which result in changes in distribution and increased body concentrations of drugs; changes in the liver and kidneys, which result in slowed metabolism of drugs and alcohol; retirement, widowhood, relocation, and other socio-cultural and developmental events; changes in health status; decrease in short-term memory, increased anxiety, and depression.

Warning signs of alcoholism are identified. These include: falls, poor nutrition, confusion, mood swings, sleep disturbances, depression, denial, and negative self-concept. Two brief cases are presented to help illustrate clues and warning signs. Finally, the author offers suggestions for dealing with the problem. These include: AA, outpatient treatment, inpatient treatment, detoxification programs, long-term residential programs, and pharmacologic therapy.

030   Maypole, D. E. (1989). Alcoholism and the elderly: Review of theories, treatment and prevention. Activities, Adaptation and Aging, 13(4), 43-54.

This review article is divided into five major sections offering a discussion of theories of causation, treatment issues, and prevention issues and ends with a section entitled conclusions in which the author offers suggestions for what needs to be done in the immediate future to deal with elderly alcoholism. In the epidemiology section, the usual incidence rate of 2-10% prevalence is given and the issue of early- versus late-onset is discussed. In the theories section, beginning with a brief discussion of the inadequacy of "loss theory" as lacking empirical support when used to explain drinking for late-onset elderly alcoholics, Maypole then gives an overview of a number of social and psychological theories which apply to an individual's use of alcohol. The theories include Freud's work, learning theory, genetic-constitutional theory, and sociological theories such as "social pathology" theory, "social disorganization" theory, "deviant behavior" theories and "labelling" theories.

Under the heading of treatment issues, Maypole gives a historical perspective of the development of treatment programs. The author begins with recognition of alcoholism as a disease by one American physician in the late 18th century and the prevalence of the "moral perspective," through the development of AA followed by an era of expanded resources from the Great Society, which fostered many new social programs to the current day burgeoning of employee assistance programs. The author then gives a brief description of treatment programs developed specifically for the elderly during the 1980's. In the last two sections of this review article, the author discusses the need for primary prevention programs for the elderly and offers in the conclusion section the need for more education of the public and the practitioner; the need for more funding for program development; primary prevention; and the recognition of the need for whole family treatment focus in any treatment intervention. He ends with an admonition to faculty in the "ivory tower" to become more involved in their communities and to incorporate into their research programs research in this area.

031   Milhorn, H. T., & Gardner, L. C.   (1990).   When to suspect alcoholism: How to help when you do. Senior Patient, 2(7), 41-46.

In this article the authors identify negative physiological effects of geriatric alcoholism. They include increased risk of cardiovascular problems and adverse effects on pulmonary function, nutritional deficiency, problematic drug/alcohol interactions, and increased risk of premature dementia.   The last part of the article focuses on the importance of accurately diagnosing alcoholism in older people. The authors point out that older people, who have a drinking problem are more likely than younger drinkers to remain hidden because of their isolation, denial of family members, the myth that older alcoholics are skid row bums, and the fact that symptoms of alcoholism mimic those of dementia and other age-related medical conditions.

To accurately diagnose alcoholism in older patients, the physician should look for clues such as falls, incontinence, self-neglect, and stomach problems. Laboratory tests such as serum gamma-glutamyltransferase should be performed to assist in diagnosis, and screening tests such as the CAGE and the Michigan Alcoholism Screening Test can also be used to aid in diagnosis.

Treatment of late-life alcoholism is also discussed. The importance of confronting denial is recognized. The importance of reassurance that things can change and kind acceptance of the elderly are important to successful treatment. Inpatient treatment, outpatient treatment, AA and other support therapies are recommended. Detoxification takes longer in older adults, and drug dosages must be lower for them than for younger people. Nutrition therapy is essential. Individual counseling is effective. The authors recommend small groups with limited noise, no rough language, and no smoking. The aftercare phase of treatment involves close follow-up by a personal physician, as well as increased attention to personal health and living arrangements. AA meetings should be regularly attended.

032   Miller, N. S., Belkin, B. M., & Gold, M. S. (1991). Alcohol and drug dependence among the elderly: Epidemiology, diagnosis, and treatment. Comprehensive Psychiatry, 32(2), 153-165.

This article presents an overview of epidemiology, diagnosis, and treatment of drug abuse in the elderly. Prevalence studies reviewed indicate that individuals 65 and older in the community have the lowest rates of alcoholism of all age groups. Older adults very rarely use illegal drugs, although alcoholic elders are much more likely to use such substances than are elders in general. Many older adults abuse prescription and over-the-counter drugs. Analgesics and hypnotics and sedatives are the most abused drugs. The prevalence of alcoholism and drug abuse among older adults in medical populations and psychiatric populations is very high.

One section of the paper focuses on diagnosis. In this section the DSM-III-R criteria for dependence syndrome are defined. Denial is highlighted as a serious problem which can interfere with proper diagnosis. Signs and symptoms of alcohol dependence such as depression and insomnia are identified.

In the section on epidemiology, the reader is informed that alcoholism is an inherited disorder. Treatment considerations are addressed in the last section. Advice is offered on how to treat acute withdrawal in the elderly. Particular drugs are recommended and appropriate dosages are suggested. The need to treat coexisting psychiatric diseases is emphasized. The AA model is outlined as an appropriate treatment model.

033   Morse, R. M. (1988). Substance abuse among the elderly. Bulletin of the Menninger Clinic, 52(3), 259-268.

Older adults abuse alcohol, prescription drugs, and over-the-counter drugs. Due to increased biological sensitivity, which accompanies aging, older adults are more negatively affected by drug taking than are younger people. Stresses such as retirement, death, health problems, and family conflicts place older adults at increased risk for substance abuse. The most often abused drugs are analgesics and tranquilizers. Many older adults mix these drugs with alcohol. Treatment is briefly discussed. Three phases of treatment are: detoxification, maintaining abstinence, and rehabilitation.

034   Olsen-Noll, C. G., & Bosworth, M. F. (1989). Alcohol abuse in the elderly. American Family Physician, 39(4), 173-179.

Three types of elderly drinkers are described: survivors, who began drinking early in life; intermittents, who are occasional binge drinkers; and reactors, who start drinking late in life in response to the stresses of aging. They identify the following as particularly vulnerable: widowed elders, those with criminal records, and those living in disadvantaged areas.

Several physiological consequences of alcoholism in older adults are noted. In late-life the efficiency of liver enzymes is decreased. Central nervous system sensitivity to alcohol increases in late-life. These and other age-related changes increase the adverse health effects of alcohol in the aged. Cardiovascular problems, reduced pulmonary function, gastritis, diarrhea, and a variety of other health problems associated with alcoholism are discussed. Drug-alcohol interactions pose a major problem in late life.

Diagnosis and treatment of alcoholism are given attention in the last part of the article. The importance of medical history and a good physical exam are emphasized. Signs to look for such as falls, changes in sleep patterns, burns, and confusion are noted. Authors suggest that treatment should focus on day-to-day problems such as adjustment to relocation and other transitions. Better community and family education and improved coordination of physicians, social agencies, and geriatric mental health personnel and agencies is recommended. Specific treatment modalities discussed include: AA, counseling, gentle persistence to break down learned helplessness, day hospital care, and home visits.

035   Pascarelli, E. F. (1979). An update on drug dependence in the elderly. Journal of Drug Issues, 9(1), 47-54.

In this overview article the author discusses the present status (1979) of drug abuse patterns in older adults. The use of opiates is discussed, and the author notes that the number of older residents in methadone treatment is steadily growing. The author rightly points out, however, that overall larger numbers of older adults are dependent upon depressants, such as barbiturate and non-barbiturate sedatives and hypnotics and alcohol than on opiates. The threat to various body organ systems posed by the use of such substances and the serious, sometimes life-threatening, dangers of mixing alcohol with other drugs are the focus of most of the paper. Each category of drug use is examined separately, and the dangers of mixing drugs are examined in a separate section. The article concludes with a recommendation to include education on techniques of treatment and diagnosis of drug dependence in hospitals, medical schools, and geriatric services.

036   Pattee, J. J. (1982). Uncovering the elderly "hidden" alcoholic. Geriatrics, 37(2), 145-146.
The physician is identified as the key figure in a position to recognize and help the older alcoholic. Three very brief cases are presented. Early- and late-onset alcoholics are defined. Signs to look for to identify alcoholism such as evidence of falls, confusion, and deepening depression are highlighted. Medical problems associated with alcoholism are also mentioned, such as gastritis, hypertension, and insomnia.

037   Ruben, D. H. (1986). The elderly alcoholic: Some current dimensions. Advances in Alcohol & Substance Abuse, 5(4), 59-70.
The author presents an overview of major factors related to alcohol abuse in late-life. Ageism, bereavement, marriage/family problems, retirement, money problems, and negative attitudes of professionals toward the elderly are all discussed. The last part of the article focuses on treatment of late-life alcoholism. Some approaches discussed are: behavioral counseling and outreach projects to senior centers, nursing homes, and other environments. Additionally, educational programs and group and supportive therapies are also mentioned.

038   Schuckit, M. A. (1982). A clinical review of alcohol, alcoholism, and the elderly patient. Journal of Clinical Psychiatry, 43(10), 396-399.
A discussion of alcohol-related problems is presented. Hypertension, cardiomyopathy, and other cardiovascular problems associated with alcoholism are discussed. The increased risk of cognitive impairment and organic brain syndrome (OBS) are also highlighted. Characteristics of older alcoholics are identified. White widowed males are at particularly high risk. Diagnosis of alcoholism is discussed. Factors to look for include: separation or divorce related to alcohol abuse, physical evidence that alcohol has harmed health, job

loss due to alcohol abuse, multiple arrests related to alcohol use.

The last part of the article focuses on treatment of alcoholism. The first step is identification and confrontation. Next, withdrawal must be treated. Vitamin therapy and antidepressants are often necessary. The next stage involves rehabilitation and education about alcohol and its consequences. The patient is helped to reorganize life without alcohol. Family involvement is important in treatment. This group has more medical needs and medical treatment is important.

039   Schuckit, M. A., & Pastor, P. A. (1978). The elderly as a unique population: Alcoholism. Alcoholism: Clinical and Experimental Research, 2(1), 31-38.

In this overview article the state of the present literature is discussed and shortcomings of existing literature are presented. A series of hypotheses are offered for future testing. Based on review of existing literature, the authors conclude that older alcoholics show a lower rate of social problems but a higher rate of physical problems than younger alcoholics. Older alcoholics drink daily but drink less alcohol per occasion than younger alcoholics. The socially isolated older adult is at particular risk.

Three research areas were identified: the definition of alcoholism and the formulation of useful diagnostic criteria; the manner in which an individual becomes recognized as a "case;" and the etiology of alcoholism.

040   Sellers, E. M., Frecker, R. C., & Romach, M. K. (1983). Drug metabolism in the elderly: Confounding of age, smoking, and ethanol effects. Drug Metabolism Reviews, 14(2), 225-250.

In this lengthy overview article the authors describe in detail the effects of age, smoking, and drinking on drug metabolism. They put forth the following generalizations about age and drug metabolism. The body mass decreases and adipose tissue mass increases relative to total body weight in the older person, affecting drug distribution. The extent of protein bonding of some drugs may be reduced in old age due to the age-related decline in plasma albumin. Liver size and total cardiac output decrease in the elderly, which affects total drug clearance. Glomerular filtration rate declines with age affecting drug clearance for those drugs cleared by renal excretion.

One section of the article discusses the connection between cigarette smoking and drinking. The level of consumption of either drug (nicotine or alcohol) increases as a function of the level of consumption of the other. Acute and chronic ethanol ingestion alters the pharmacodynamics and disposition of drugs; however, these effects have rarely been examined with respect to age. Many effects of ethanol consumption on drug metabolism are discussed. Some of these include the following: ingestion of ethanol inhibits the mixed-function oxidase enzymes; the clearance of acetaminophen, various benzodiazepines, and phenytoin decreases; and plasma half-life of amitriptyline, chlordiazepoxide, diazepam, meprobamate, and pentobarbitone is increased.

041   Solomon, K., Manepalli, J., Ireland, G. A., & Mahon, G. M. (1993). Alcoholism and prescription drug abuse in the elderly: St. Louis University grand rounds, Journal of the American Geriatrics Society, 41(1), 57-69.

This grand rounds presents a comprehensive overview of geriatric addiction. Six cases of alcoholism and prescription drug abuse in the elderly are presented first. Then the pharmacokinetics of alcohol, barbiturates, benzodiazepines, and narcotic analgesics are discussed. Physicians who conducted the grand rounds at St. Louis University also discuss the clinical diagnosis of addictions in the elderly. They emphasize that addictions in the elderly are not usually secondary to other medical psychiatric disorders. They co-exist with these other disorders as co-primary. They note that, compared to younger patients, elderly patients are more likely to have a dual psychiatric diagnosis.

In one section doctors discuss the factors necessary to the development of an addiction, including: a biological vulnerability to become an addict; the addictive potential of the drug; long enough time of exposure to a drug for addiction to develop; psychological stress, depression, loneliness; anxiety; the burden of caregiving; and loss of a spouse or other social losses. Older adults who are addicted complain of the following: anxiety, depressed mood, appetite disturbances, panic attacks, sleep problems, and hallucinations. A table is included which presents these psychiatric consequences of addictions.

The authors also discuss the hallmark symptoms of addiction: denial and rationalization. The stages in the addiction process are also highlighted. The first stage of learning is when the individual experiences euphoria and episodes of binging, attempts to control drug use, and experiences occasional shame. The second stage of seeking is when the consequences of drug use become apparent, and there are alternating periods of use and abstinence. In the third stage, dependency, unreasonable behaviors begin. The next stage is harmful dependency. The last stage is addiction.

The next section of this article focuses on assessment and treatment. DSM-III-R criteria are outlined. The CAGE and the MAST screening tools are reviewed. Medical consequences and presenting symptoms to look for are described. The authors discuss withdrawal symptoms, emphasizing anxiety as the key symptom. Delirium tremens (DTs) are described. Medical consequences of alcoholism to look for, which are discussed in the text and also summarized in a table, are: alcoholic liver disease, pancreatitis, GI track diseases, protein-calorie malnutrition, central and peripheral nervous system diseases, anemias, and electrolyte and other metabolic disturbances. The authors also recommend checking for addiction if falls, sensual dysfunction, or incontinence are problems.

The treatment plan used in the Geriatric Alcoholism and Substance Abuse Program at St. Louis University is briefly described. The program is based on the 12-Step model developed by Alcoholics Anonymous(AA). The first step in treatment is abstinence and medical detoxification and treatment of mild withdrawal syndromes. The next stage of treatment is the stage of admission, in which denial and rationalization are confronted and the principles of the 12-Step program are presented. The next stage is the stage of compliance, in which the patient is introduced to the Big Book and other AA literature. The next stage is the stage of acceptance in which the patient admits he of she is an addict and tries to reverse some of the problems caused by the addiction. Surrender is the final stage. In this stage the patient moves out of the hospital or treatment facility, and finds a sponsor and participates in outpatient therapy. Cognitive therapy, group therapy, family therapy, and attendance at AA meetings are all valuable forms of outpatient therapy. The family is included in every phase of treatment.

042   Stall, R. (1987). Research issues concerning alcohol consumption among aging populations. Drug and Alcohol Dependence, 19(3), 195-213.

This overview concentrates on a review of the literature in order to examine reasons for change and stability in alcohol consumption in the elderly. The author proposes seven hypotheses to be further examined through empirical research. The paper includes a historical overview with methodological concerns accompanying each study and survey review. Examples of the hypotheses which might explain the lower rate of alcohol consumption in the elderly are: the mortality hypothesis, in which the heavy drinkers die at an earlier age and are no longer represented in the elderly group; the morbidity hypothesis, in which the elderly experience more disease and must lower alcohol consumption due to fear of aggravating their conditions from drug interactions; the biological aging hypothesis, in which the aging body itself limits the amount of alcohol that can be comfortably/safely consumed; the cohort hypothesis, in which differences are explained by historical events experienced by the current elderly generation and not indicative of remission; the measurement hypothesis, in which the differences are explained by the lack of appropriate measures available to test the elderly, that is, the current measuring instruments were normed for younger populations and therefore do not apply to the elderly; and finally the social learning or "socialization to old age" models are discussed as possible explanations. This is a very thorough article which offers a good starting point for a chapter on methodological concerns and interpretation of current data in this area.

043   Sumberg, D. (1985). Social work with elderly alcoholics: Some practical considerations. Special Issue: Gerontological social work practice in the community. Gerontological Social Work Practice in the Community, 8(3-4), 169-180.

This article is directed toward social workers interested in helping elderly alcoholics stop drinking. After presenting a brief introduction about our negative attitudes toward older adults and alcoholics, the author identifies three major types of older alcoholics: the chronic alcohol abuser, who has been drinking heavily for many years; the reactive drinker, who drinks in response to loss of spouse, job, or loved ones and develops the disease of alcoholism; and the binge drinker, who maintains abstinence or social drinking for long periods of time in between short bursts of out of control drinking. Four issues facing the concerned social worker are highlighted. First, the false notion that alcohol is one of life's few remaining pleasures for the old. Alcoholism is no longer a pleasure; it produces profound negative changes in physical, mental, emotional, and social life. Second, the social worker must deal with the notion that alcoholics are hopeless cases. Older alcoholics can be helped. Third is the issue of denial. The elderly drinker who finds many "reasons" to drink is suffering from denial. Finally, the issue of loss is important. The absence of alcohol represents a major loss for older adults, who have already experienced many significant losses.

The author presents seven steps in the treatment of alcoholism in older adults. They are: 1) identifying the alcoholic; 2) encouraging recognition by the older client; 3) dealing with denial; 4) meeting concrete needs; 5) monitoring recovery; 6) support services (AA, family groups, community groups); and 7) dealing with the loss of alcohol.

044   Szwabo, P. A. (1993). Substance abuse in older women. Clinics in Geriatrics Medicine, 9(1), 197-208.

In this article Szwabo reviews the problem of alcohol abuse and abuse of other drugs in two separate sections. She notes that roughly 10-15% of women over age 65 suffer from physical, psychiatric, or functional impairment related to alcohol. She points out that alcoholism is more often recognized in older men than in older women. The DSM-III-R criteria for alcohol abuse are discussed. The article focuses on medical and psychiatric problems associated with alcohol abuse, including liver disease, gastritis, pancreatitis, falls, AIDS, depression, organic delusional disorder, anxiety, and other conditions. The CAGE questionnaire, Michigan Alcoholism Screening Test (MAST), and other assessment tools are described. Treatment issues are also considered. The author notes that few treatment services are available for older women who abuse alcohol.

045   Thibault, J. M., & Maly, R. C. (1993). Recognition and treatment of substance abuse in the elderly. Primary Care, 20(1), 155-165.

Thibault and Maly have written a straight forward overview on the problems of recognizing and treating substance abuse in the elderly. The authors cite 4.1% to 8.3% of those elderly 65 years and older as alcoholic or drug dependent. Since primary physicians are usually the first to treat the health problems of the chemically dependent, they are also in the unique position to screen and treat older abusers. Problems of identification of alcohol and prescription drug abuse are discussed, followed by symptoms that should be screened for substance abuse. A profile of the older alcohol abuser is described as most commonly a man, between the ages of 60 and 74, non-white, separated or divorced, living with another person, and without a high school diploma. Because the older abuser does not exhibit behavior like the antisocial younger abuser, the problem may be overlooked.

Use of screening instruments like the Michigan Alcoholism Screening Test (MAST) and the CAGE questionnaire are most useful in those patients already exhibiting signs of alcoholism. Treatment for prescription drug dependency may require hospitalization followed by education of the patient, family and health professionals. Many of the interventions helpful to alcoholics may also be employed for the drug-dependent patient. However, there are few treatment programs developed specifically for the elderly. Components of therapy include detoxification, as an inpatient and outpatient, education and personal character challenges. Intervention by confrontation, a technique used with younger alcoholics, may be used with carefully selected elderly patients. Abstinence, however, is the core component of treatment.

046   Thienhaus, O. J., & Hartford, J. T. (1984). Alcoholism in the elderly. Psychiatric Medicine, 2(1), 27-41.

This is an overview written from the medical perspective and includes the usual discussion of diagnosis, biological factors, psychosocial factors, sensory changes, illness, cognitive changes, and therapeutic considerations. The unique aspect of this article is the inclusion of a good discussion of sleep problems associated with alcohol consumption and abuse and a thorough overview of sexual function and dysfunction which accompanies alcohol intake. All of the aforementioned topics are discussed in the context of how they interact with normal age changes.

047   Ticehurst, S. (1990). Alcohol and the elderly. Australian and New
        Zealand Journal of Psychiatry, 24(2), 252-260.
        This article is a comprehensive overview of late-life alcoholism. Several bodies of existing literature from various countries are reviewed. Highlights from prevalence studies are also presented in tabled form. The author highlights physiological changes related to aging which increase the negative effects of alcohol abuse. Some of the changes noted are decreased body water and volume of distribution; changed absorption, metabolism, and excretion; and lower lean body mass. He suggests that the widely used "total consumption" criteria may need to be adjusted downward to remain valid measures of dangerous intake levels in the elderly. The article contains a detailed and critical discussion of current literature on prevalence. The author points out, using relevant literature, that elderly alcoholics constitute a significant minority in general hospitals, psychiatric facilities, and nursing homes.

        One section of the article describes the clinical presentation of late-life alcoholism. Clinicians are cautioned to look for evidence of falls, self-neglect, malnutrition, and aggression that precipitates family quarrels. It is pointed out that alcoholics often present with depression, anxiety disorders or other psychiatric problems. One-third of all older offenders in forensic settings are alcoholics. Late-onset alcoholism is defined in detail. Treatment considerations are highlighted in the last section. Home visits and careful assessment of drinking behavior are recommended. After detoxification is accomplished, the author suggests treatment of underlying social stressors, family casework, treatment of depression, and social support therapy. The basic recommendation is that treatment should revolve around established treatment regimens, adapted to the unique medical, psychological, and social aspects of aging. An eclectic approach based on flexibility and use of a variety of treatment approaches and settings is called for with older alcoholics.

048   Tobias, C. R., Lippmann, S., Pary, R., Oropilla, T., & Embry, C. K.
        (1989). Alcoholism in the elderly: How to spot and treat a

problem the patient wants to hide. Postgraduate Medicine, 86(4), 67-79.

Early-onset and late-onset alcoholics were compared and contrasted. Early-onset alcoholics are under 60 when they begin drinking, and are likely to have a family history of drinking, criminal arrests, and an unstable personality. They have a poor response to treatment. Late-onset alcoholics, by contrast, begin drinking at 60 or older and do not have an unstable personality, and are less likely to have a family history of alcoholism or criminal arrests. Their response to treatment is favorable. To diagnose alcoholism, a careful review of medical records is important to reveal alcohol-related illnesses such as recurrent stomach problems or diseases of the liver or pancreas.

The Short Michigan Alcoholism Screening Test (SMAST) can also be an aid in diagnosing alcoholism. Lab tests (i.e., liver function tests and fasting blood glucose) provide valuable information for diagnosing alcoholism. Various medical conditions related to alcoholism such as dementia, pancreatitis, anemia, cirrhosis, and gastritis are identified. Psychological problems related to alcoholism were identified as depression and organic mental disorders. Family disruption, job problems, and legal difficulties were cited as some of the sociological problems related to alcoholism.

Treatment was also discussed. Treatment includes detoxification and rehabilitative intervention. Various forms of rehabilitation were recommended, including: AA, family therapy, group therapy, religious counseling, and community services such as senior citizens' groups.

049   Widner, S., & Zeichner, A. (1991). Alcohol abuse in the elderly: Review of epidemiology, research and treatment. Clinical Gerontologist, 11(1), 3-17.

This review article tries to go beyond just a simple review of the area of elderly alcohol abuse and provide some insight into methodological problems which are encountered when doing research in this area. The sections of this article are: discussion of prevalence data; screening instruments and procedures for identification of the elderly alcoholic; a discussion of late-versus early-onset elderly alcoholics; a discussion of the physiological and psychological impact of drinking; a review of treatment types and effectiveness; and lastly a look at future research. In each of these sections important generalizability issues are included. Some of these are the fact that prevalence data vary because there is no standard use of an age which defines "elderly" (some studies use 50, 55, 60, etc.); not all studies use the standard DSM-based definition of alcoholism; many of the studies are cross-sectional and therefore cohort differences may lead to underreporting of problems; screening instruments may not be age-sensitive; medical diagnoses rarely reflect alcohol abuse as a cause and alcohol-related problems are ascribed to physical changes accompanying normal aging. Another issue discussed in this review is the "maturing out" phenomenon. In the last section under future research the authors clearly state the need for "well-controlled longitudinal studies" and the need to answer questions about why treatment services are underutilized by the elderly, what role psychotropic medication has in treating the elderly, and the effectiveness of established treatment interventions for use with the elderly alcoholic.

050   Zimering, S., & Domeischel, J. R. (1982). Is alcoholism a problem of the elderly? Journal of Drug Education, 12(2), 103-111.

The authors present figures on the extent of the problem of alcoholism in older adults nationally and in the State of New York. They emphasize the future forecast, examining the expected increases in the elderly population in the future. Characteristics of elderly alcoholics are discussed. Aging males are identified as a group at particularly high risk. The distinction is made between early-onset and late-onset alcoholism. Case examples are presented.

The importance of accurate identification and treatment of the elderly alcoholic is stressed. Education is identified as a key need for physicians and other caregivers, older adults, and family members of older adults. Authors emphasize the role federal, state, and local government can play. They outline one approach to treatment which has been used successfully. Team treatment involves many professionals and many different therapies. Recreation programs are recommended as one important component of treatment.

Books and Book Chapters

051   Abrams, R. C., & Alexopoulos, G. (1991). Geriatric addictions. In R. J. Frances & S. I. Miller (Eds.), Clinical textbook of addictive disorders (pp. 347-365). NY: Guilford.

This chapter focuses on alcoholism, prescription drug abuse and misuse in the elderly, and over-the-counter and illegal drug abuse in the elderly. The first part of the chapter examines geriatric alcoholism -- its epidemiology, clinical features, negative consequences, and treatment. The authors point out that 2-10% of older people are alcoholics. They challenge the findings of community studies that report a decline in alcohol use with age on several bases: differential mortality of alcoholics and non-alcoholics; greater likelihood that older alcoholics are institutionalized; and cohort differences, which may be responsible for the findings. Late-onset and early-onset elderly drinkers are distinguished as two different groups clinically. Age-related physiological changes such as decreased activity of the hepatic enzymes, reduction of lean body mass and increased sensitivity of the central nervous system increase the negative effects of alcohol in older people. Authors also point out that alcohol-drug interactions are more likely to occur in older people. Other negative consequences of geriatric alcoholism are cognitive impairment, cardiomyopathy, sleep disturbance, impotence, and depression. With respect to treatment, the authors stress the need to accurately detect alcoholism in elders and the need for education and rehabilitation.

The next sections focus on abuse of medications (prescription and OTC drugs) and illegal drug abuse in older adults. The authors note that older people are the heaviest users of prescription and OTC drugs. Twenty-five percent of older persons use psychoactive drugs.

Analgesics and anxiolytics/sedatives/hypnotics are the drugs most abused by older adults living independently. Benzodiazepines are also frequently abused by elders. Many older adults abuse OTC drugs. Eighty percent of elderly patients taking an OTC drug daily also use alcohol. The authors include a helpful table listing commonly used OTC drugs such as aspirin and their common adverse interactions. The authors point out that illegal drug use is quite rare in elderly populations, perhaps because of a "maturing out" or "burning out" process. Treatment of illegal drug use generally requires hospitalization and rehabilitation.

052   Akers, R. L., & La Greca, A. J. (1988). Alcohol, contact with the legal system, and illegal behavior among the elderly. In B. McCarthy & R. Langworthy (Eds.), Older offenders: Perspectives in criminology and criminal justice (pp. 51-61). New York: Praeger.

Akers and La Greca conducted a study to determine if there was a relationship between alcohol and criminal or deviant behavior in older adults. Most elderly who come into contact with the legal system do so for alcohol-related offenses such as DWI and public drunkenness. DWI's account for 52% of all arrests in the elderly, compared with 29% of other persons ages 15-59.

Using self-reports, the authors interviewed over 1,400 adults ages 60 or older. Four types of communities were selected: two were retirement communities and two were age-integrated communities. The authors were measuring "offensive" behavior, which included committing assault, shoplifting, public intoxication, intoxicated while driving and illegal gambling. The results were as expected. That is, the elderly very infrequently commit any of these acts. Only about 6% of the elderly in one community reported committing one of the five offenses. Gambling was the most reported offense, followed by DWI's. Assaults and public drunkenness tied for third. Elderly men were shown to be more likely to have some kind of contact with the legal system in the past year than were elderly women. The authors concluded that there is a relationship between elderly drinking and crime, albeit a small percentage. The problem drinker is more likely to commit deviant behavior and to get into trouble with the law than the abstainer.

053   Akers, R. L., & La Greca, A. (1991). Alcohol use among the elderly: Social learning, community context, and life events. In D. Pittmen & H. White (Eds.), Society, culture, and drinking patterns reexamined (pp. 242-262). New Brunswick, NJ: Rutgers Center of Alcohol Studies.

This chapter can best be characterized by an opening statement of the two sociologist authors in which they express the hope to relate problem drinking of the elderly to "social psychological and social structural variables." The authors report the results of 1,410 in-home interviews with elderly in four communities: two retirement, and two age-integrated. The dependent variable measurements were: frequency of drinking in the past 12 months, frequency of drinking in the past month, quantity/frequency combined, frequency of alcohol-related problems during the past year, and drinking patterns after age 60. Seven sociodemographic variables were also examined: age, race, sex, marital status, education, income, and occupational prestige. Akers and La Greca report the results within three theoretical contexts: social learning theory, community context, and a life-event stress framework. The results reported were that the social learning model accounted for 59% of the variance in drinking behavior.

Using a LISREL model with measures of community context, the authors found that "the structural variable of community contest is mediated through the micro-level process of social learning." Because of the many and complex analyses performed, we recommend the reader look at this article in detail. The findings and discussion of the life event stressors' effects are interesting. The authors found that the greater the social support and coping skills, the less likely the subjects were to drink, but that life-event had "essentially no effect" on drinking behavior.

054   Anthony, J. C. (1984). Alcohol abuse and dependence as a risk factor across the adult male age span. In G. Maddox, L. N. Robins, & N. Rosenberg (Eds.), Nature and extent of alcohol problems among the elderly (Vol. 14, pp. 245-274). Rockville: USDHHS.

This article is part of the proceedings of a National Institute on Alcohol Abuse and Alcoholism (NIAAA), National Institute on Aging (NIA) National Institute for Mental Health (NIMH) sponsored state of the art workshop which took place in 1983 at the Alcohol Research Center at Washington University. The major focus of this paper is to examine prospective data from the Baltimore Epidemiological Catchment Area (ECA) program. This study reports a 1-year follow-up of the initial sample of 982 males surveyed on alcohol use and abuse. One of the most intriguing findings was: "On the surface, this study's findings were contrary: age was not generally a prognostic factor that helped to predict the follow-up state of cases" (p. 269). The authors do a very thorough job of discussing this finding as it is affected by numerous methodological constraints. The article is complex and offers a great deal of information.

055   Atkinson, R. M. (1984). Substance use and abuse in late life. In R.
             M. Atkinson (Ed.), Alcohol and drug abuse in old age (pp. 2-
             21). Washington, DC: American Psychiatric Press, Inc.

        Atkinson provides a short and easy-to-read overview of
prevalence, etiology and treatment of geriatric alcoholism and drug
abuse, including comments on both prescription and illicit drug use.
The issue of apparent age-related declines in alcohol and drug use is
thoroughly addressed along with a brief reference to lifetime patterns
of usage. Six types of risk factors are discussed: genetic
predisposition; age-related increases in biologic sensitivity to alcohol
and drugs; psychosocial stressors; chronic illness; over-prescribing; and
family and cohort influences. The commonly held belief that late-life
stress increases consumption is called into question and Atkinson urges
more systematic study in this area. Following comments on several
outcome studies of outpatient treatment in elders, the chapter closes
with a look at future trends in geriatric substance abuse. Several
helpful tables are included throughout the chapter.

056   Baker, S. L. (1985). Substance abuse disorders in aging veterans. In
             E. Gottheil, K. A. Druley, T. E. Skoloda, & H. M. Waxman
             (Eds.), The combined problems of alcoholism, drug addiction,
             and aging (pp. 303-311). Springfield, IL: Charles C.
             Thomas.

        In this overview chapter Baker focuses on the problem of
alcoholism and substance abuse in aging veterans. He notes that 30%
of VA domiciliary residents suffer from alcoholism. He also points out
that a substantial increase is projected in veterans 65 years of age and
older during the next 10 years. He discusses the fact that many older
alcoholics are not diagnosed as alcoholic, and gives attention to the
serious problems of alcohol-drug interactions in older alcoholics. The
author mentions that the VA's audio-visual center in St. Louis is
developing a training packet and tape for specialized medical education
of physicians for improved recognition and clinical management of
alcoholism and alcohol-related secondary diseases and other
complications of alcoholism.

        Treatment issues are also considered with a focus on
reintegration into the family, age-appropriate AA groups, leisure
activities, and the need for warm, caring people who help the alcoholic.
Geriatric Research, Education and Clinical Centers called "GRECCS"
were funded in 1975 and established in eight VA centers to provide a
needed focus on aging veterans. In the future funding will be provided
to establish a VA alcoholism research program, which will include
special concerns for the aging veteran.

057   Barnes, G. M. (1982). Patterns of alcohol use and abuse among older
       persons in a household population. In W. G. Wood & M. F.
       Elias (Eds.), <u>Alcoholism and aging advances in research</u> (pp.
       3-15). Boca Raton, FL: CRC Press.

       In this chapter Barnes presents findings from a household
survey of drinking patterns in Erie and Niagara Counties in Western
New York State. The focus in on patterns of drinking among older
persons, as compared with drinking among younger and middle aged
groups. A stratified random sample of adults 18 years and older living
in households in the two counties was selected. The final sample size
was 1,041. Questions on drinking followed Jessor's slightly modified
version of the methodology used in Cahalan's national survey of
American drinking practices. Questions of quality, frequency, and
variability of drinking were used to derive the Absolute Alcohol (AA)
Index, an average daily consumption estimate.

       Results indicate that the rate of drinking is lower among people
in the older age groups than among those in younger comparison
groups. Compared to males, elderly females have significantly lower
rates of heavier drinking. There are many fewer alcohol-related
problems such as driving after drinking too much, among those 60 and
older than among those in younger age groups. Not being married and
being retired, two commonly cited stresses of late life, did not
significantly affect drinking patterns in the older age group. There
were no significant differences in the percent of heavy drinkers in the
married group as compared with the widowed group, or in the retired
group as compared to those still working. There was also no
significant relationship between the degree of satisfaction with life and
drinking. Neither participation in social activities nor health status
were related to drinking.

058   Barr, H. L. (1985). What happens as the alcoholic and the drug
       addict get older? In E. Gottheil, K. A. Druley, T. E.
       Skoloda, & H. M. Waxman (Eds.), <u>The combined problems
       of alcoholism, drug addiction, and aging</u> (pp. 193-200).
       Springfield, IL: Charles C. Thomas.

       This chapter focuses on drug and alcohol abusers who received
treatment at Eagleville, and what happens as they get older. Two
studies were discussed: (1) a study of mortality among ex-residents
and (2) a long-term follow-up study of residents who were interviewed
seven years after their first treatment episode. Substance use or abuse
was ascertained for each subject at the time of his or her two-year
follow-up or in the case of those who died within the first two year, up
to the time of death. During the eight years of observation, 708
persons died. The death rate for alcoholics was 25.9 per 1,000 years

at risk; and for drug addicts it was 8.8 per 1,000 years at risk. Also, violent deaths, i.e., deaths due to accidents, suicide, and homicide, were excessive in both groups. The general conclusion from data analyses was stated as follows: "As they get older, they either recover or they don't. If they don't stop being substance abusers, they are very likely to die prematurely so that they do not get much older" (p. 193). Very brief cases of older alcoholics are presented in the chapter.

059   Bell, R. A., Lin, E., Ice, J., & Bell, R. J. (1979). Drinking patterns and suicidal ideation and behavior in a general population. In M. Galanter (Ed.), Currents in alcoholism, Volume 5: Biomedical issues and clinical effects of alcoholism (Vol.2, pp. 317-332). New York: Grune & Stratton.

A random sample of 2029 individuals 18 and older drawn from a three-county area in the Southeastern United States, was administered an interview which included a depression scale, questions on frequency of alcohol use, and questions about suicidal ideation and behavior. In addition, basic demographic and other data were gathered. Characteristics of respondents are discussed in detail.

Analysis of data on depression, alcohol consumption, and suicidal ideation and behavior revealed some statistically significant relationships. The authors found a significant relationship between suicidal ideation and behavior. As the frequency of suicidal ideation increases, the percentage of attempters significantly increases. The presence of suicidal ideation was associated with high depression scores in both high and low drinking categories, indicating that depression, rather than drinking, is related to suicidal ideation and behavior.

060   Berkman, L. F. (1985). Stress, social networks and aging. In E. Gottheil, K. A. Druley, T. E. Skoloda, & H. M. Waxman (Eds.), The combined problems of alcoholism, drug addiction, and aging (pp. 14-35). Springfield, IL: Charles C. Thomas.

This chapter explores stress, social networks and aging. In the first section the author notes that compared to younger individuals, older people are less likely to maintain extensive social contacts. Older widowed males have a particularly difficult time maintaining social contacts. The author reviews existing literature on social support and stress. Loss of a spouse is linked to higher levels of morbidity and mortality. The author discusses literature which supports the "buffer hypothesis," which posits that social ties and social support buffer negative effects of stress.

In the last section of the chapter the author briefly reviews empirical findings from a study in Alameda County. The study conducted by the California State Department of Health in 1965 consisted of sending questionnaires to a sample of adults in the county requesting information on social contacts with family, friends, church and other social groups, smoking and drinking practice, obesity, and physical activity, and collecting mortality data for 1965-1974. Analyses of data revealed that, with the exception of men 70 years and over, people lacking social and community ties are about three times more likely to maintain high risk practices than their counterparts with the most social contacts. Specifically, "the more isolated one becomes, the more likely he or she is to smoke, drink heavily, be physically inactive, obese or underweight, and sleep more or less than seven or eight hours per night." They also found that people who consume 46 or more drinks per month are found to have an elevated mortality risk. These findings were true across all age groups.

061   Bienenfeld, D. (1990). Substance abuse. In D. Bienenfeld (Ed.), Verwoerdt's clinical geropsychiatry (3rd. ed., pp. 164-177). Baltimore, MD: Williams & Wilkins.

In this brief overview chapter, Bienenfeld presents data and information on epidemiology, recognition and diagnosis, consequences and complications, and treatment of alcoholism. He also presents data and information on illicit drug use and abuse and misuse of prescription and over-the-counter drugs. Bienenfeld notes that about 10% of those 65 and older have some form of drinking problem; however, research shows drinking decreases with age. There are two types of older alcoholics: early-onset alcoholics, who began drinking before age 40; and late-onset alcoholics, who began drinking after age 40. Both types drink less than younger alcoholics, but drink more frequently and have higher blood alcohol concentrations with the same amount of alcohol. Clinical presentation of late life alcoholism is covered, and a table of symptoms is included. Some of the consequences and complications of alcoholism discussed are: marital problems, health problems, and suicide. Alcohol-drug interactions are also noted.

Treatment of late life alcoholism includes detoxification, group work and individual therapy. Alcoholics Anonymous is one of the most effective elements of treatment. About one-third of all AA members in North America are over age 50. The last part of the chapter focuses on abuse and misuse of prescription and over-the-counter drugs. A table of adverse effects of over-the-counter medications is included.

062   Bland, J. (1985). Services for the elderly with alcohol-related problems: A systems approach. In E. Gottheil, K. A. Druley, T. E. Skoloda, & H. M. Waxman (Eds.), The

combined problems of alcoholism, drug addiction, and aging (pp. 272-277). Springfield, IL: Charles C. Thomas.

This chapter presents a brief description of procedures used by the Maryland State Alcoholism Control Administration in Baltimore, Maryland between 1975-1979 designed to respond to the needs of elderly alcoholics and problem drinkers. An investigation revealed lack of knowledge about alcoholism in older adults and negative attitudes toward the elderly in alcoholism treatment personnel. With the help of representatives from various agencies, several goals were formulated including: (1) to raise consciousness about alcoholism in the elderly; (2) to provide workshops and seminars to enhance the knowledge base about alcoholism and aging; and (3) to train a cadre of trainers within the alcoholism provider network and the geriatric provider network. Goals one and two were pursued. Records indicated that since 1979 there was an increase in the number of patients 60 or over who were admitted for treatment.

063   Blazer, D., George, L., Woodbury, M., Manton, K., & Jordan, K. (1984). The elderly alcoholic: A profile. In G. Maddox, L. Robins, & N. Rosenberg (Eds.), Nature and extent of alcohol problems among the elderly (Vol. 14, pp. 275-297). Rockville: NIAAA.

This chapter is part of the proceedings of a National Institute on Alcohol Abuse and Alcoholism (NIAAA), National Institute on Aging (NIA), National Institute for Mental Health (NIMH) sponsored state-of-the-art workshop which took place in 1983 at the Alcohol Research Center at Washington University. The major focus of this paper is to report analyses of data from almost 4,000 respondents 18 years or older, with 1,500 persons 60+ as part of the North Carolina Epidemiological Catchment Area (ECA) project. Several findings were reported. One such finding was that the elderly had heavy levels of alcohol intake less often, but were more likely to ascribe to the answer that they needed a drink before breakfast. The elderly are more likely to have spoken to a doctor about their drinking, admit that they wanted to stop drinking and could not, and used more drugs than their younger counterparts. The elderly were also more likely to report more physical symptoms and to report more fighting while drinking (51% versus 19%). Data are also reported on race and urban versus rural status. Methodological considerations are detailed throughout the discussion.

064   Blazer, D. G., & Pennybacker, M. R. (1984). Epidemiology of alcoholism in the elderly. In J. T. Hartford & T. Samorajski (Eds.), Alcoholism in the elderly: Social and biomedical issues (Vol. 25, pp. 25-32). New York: Raven Press.

Published in 1984, this chapter presents an overview of the area of alcoholism and aging which decries the lack of needed epidemiological data that allows researchers to begin to understand the depth of the problem. The chapter is divided into six sections: definition of a case, in which the typical criteria used to define a case of alcoholism is critiqued considering the differences in social problems of younger versus older alcoholics; case finding, in which the problems of misdiagnosis and nondiagnosis due to age are discussed; clinical relevance, in which the findings of ten community surveys/research projects are discussed showing major differences in prevalence rates, etc.; etiologic factors, in which late-onset versus early-onset causative factors are discussed; treatment, in which the good prognosis for elderly alcoholics is pointed out with added discussion of the need for more and better age-specific treatment programs; and the last section, need for research, discusses the then unique opportunity for gathering large data samples represented by the National Institute for Mental Health sponsored Epidemiologic Catchment Area (ECA) program, and the need for further development of long-term longitudinal studies of elderly alcoholism.

065   Bosmann, H. B. (1984). Pharmacology of alcoholism and aging. In
        J. T. Hartford & T. Samorajski (Eds.), Alcoholism in the
        elderly: Social and biomedical issues (Vol. 25, pp. 161-174).
        New York: Raven Press.

        In the first part of the chapter Bosmann states that "the tremendous toxicity and abuse potential of alcohol make it the most dangerous 'drug' taken by the elderly." He briefly highlights degenerative effects of ethanol on the heart muscle, stomach, pancreas, and liver, and on sexual functioning in the elderly. Bosmann notes that because older adults have less total body water, less extracellular fluid, and higher body fat, the same ingested dose of ethanol will result in a higher blood level in an elderly adult than in a young adult. Secondary effects of ethanol metabolism include: hypoglycemia, hyperlipidemia, fatty liver, and severe liver damage.

        Ethanol has profound negative effects on the brain. The author reviews literature which confirms behavioral changes and changes in performance on various neuropsychological tests. Endocrine function is impaired following ethanol ingestion. Current empirical studies are briefly reviewed. The combination of aging and sustained use of ethanol can be fatal. Organ function is greatly reduced and organ damage is more serious in older people.

        Addiction and tolerance are discussed in the next part of the chapter. The author points out that chronic maintenance of high concentrations of blood ethanol can produce a state of physical dependence and psychological craving. Addiction is similar to that seen with other sedative/hypnotics. Ethanol is a classic example of drug tolerance, because not only tolerance to ethanol occurs, but also cross-tolerance to several classes of drugs occurs, particularly other sedative-hypnotics, benzodiazepines, and to general anesthetics.

When ethanol intake is reduced or eliminated, withdrawal occurs. Tremors, nausea, anxiety, and sweating occur. In severe ethanol withdrawal, a period of hallucination follows and grand or petit mal seizures are common. As the syndrome progresses to tremulous delirium, cardiovascular shutdown and death may occur.

Ethanol combined with certain other drugs has severe adverse effects. The combination of Valium and ethanol can be fatal. Some drugs that adversely interact with ethanol are: benzodiayepines, anesthetics, morphine, tranquilizers, antidepressants, antihypertensives, anti-convulsants, and antibiotics. Antabuse (disulfiram) is a drug which violently interacts with ethanol and is used to intervene in alcoholism.

066   Brody, J. A. (1985). Alcohol and aging — The extent of the problem from limited data. In E. Gottheil, K. A. Druley, T. E. Skoloda, & H. M. Waxman (Eds.), The combined problems of alcoholism, drug addiction, and aging (pp. 5-13). Springfield, IL: Charles C. Thomas.

This chapter begins by noting that "careful studies of the degree and extent of the problems of aging and alcohol abuse do not exist" (p. 5). The chapter presents basic demographic information on the aging population in the United States including: number and percentage of elders in the population; life expectancy figures; and information on socio-economic status and living arrangements.

The last section of the chapter reviews existing studies, which confirm that many older adults abuse alcohol. Four conditions which increase the risk of alcohol abuse in older adults are noted: retirement, deaths among relatives and friends, poor health, and loneliness. Early- and late-onset alcoholics are described. Treatment issues are briefly discussed, and the author notes that elderly alcoholics are easier to treat than young alcoholics. The author concludes by calling for prevention and education strategies to help prevent alcoholism in older adults.

067   Bulsewicz, M. J., Cannon, W. C., & Dustman, R. E. (1982). Alcoholism and aging: Similarities and differences in neuropsychological performances. In W.G. Wood & M.F. Elias (Eds.), Alcoholism and aging advances in research (pp. 47-60). Boca Raton, FL: CRC Press.

This chapter reports on two studies of the similarities and differences in neuropsychological performance between chronic alcoholics and aging individuals. The first study conducted at the Salt Lake City VA Medical Center administered nine neuropsychological tests to 60 males (20 young normals who did not have a history of heavy drinking; 20 young alcoholics selected from inpatient and outpatient alcoholism rehabilitation centers; and 20 elderly normals with no history of heavy drinking).

One-way analyses of variance were performed on the scores from each test. An Impairment Index Score was calculated for each subject from his/her scores on tests selected from the Halstead-Reitan Battery. Impairment Index scores provide a global indication of neuropsychological functioning. Results of statistical analyses revealed that in comparison to the young normals, the young alcoholic group and the elderly normals demonstrated neuropsychological deficits. In general, the alcoholic and elderly groups performed at equivalent levels on those tests which required higher level processing of information (like short-term memory and learning). They were most different on tests which required fundamental sensory-motor functions such as reaction time and the perceptual functions of vision and audition. The researchers then divided the young alcoholic group into two subgroups: those that had experienced severe neurological symptoms including delirium tremors and seizures during withdrawal from alcohol, and those who had not experienced severe neurological symptoms during withdrawal. Analyses were then performed again on all measures. Based on these analyses, it was evident that the poor performance of the total sample of young alcoholics on neuropsychological tests was overwhelmingly due to the performances of the subgroup which had experienced severe neurological symptoms during withdrawal. Results also showed that nonverbal short-term memory is extremely vulnerable to any degree of chronic alcohol use.

The second study reported on evoked potentials recorded from 120 males ranging in age from 21 to 90 years. Visually Evoked Responses (VERs) were recorded from frontal (F3), central (C3, C4), and occipital (O1, O2) areas. Peak to peak amplitudes of three consecutive wave components in each VER were measured. For each recording site the three component amplitudes were summed to provide one measure of late wave amplitude. Separate analyses of variance (ANOVA) were computed to evaluate age, area, and intensity effects for amplitudes of VERs from frontal and central sites and from the occiput. Results indicate that with brighter flashes, frontal and central VERs of the older subjects were significantly larger than those of younger subjects. Results from both studies cast doubt on the premature aging hypothesis, which posits a relationship between alcoholism and early aging.

068   Cermak, L. S. (1985). The effects of alcohol on the aging brain. In
        E. Gottheil, K. A. Druley, T. E. Skolada, & H. M. Waxman
        (Eds.), The combined problems of alcoholism, drug addiction
        and aging (pp. 77-87). Springfield, IL: Charles C. Thomas.
        This chapter reviews two experiments designed to differentiate
the "premature aging" theory from the "continuum" theory of ethanol's
effects on the aging brain. According to the authors, the theory of
premature aging assumes that alcohol consumption accelerates a
general, widespread deterioration of the central nervous system, while
the continuum theory assumes a specific deterioration of midline-
diencephalic structures as seen in Wernicke-Korsakoff's syndrome.
The authors therefore hypothesize that if the continuum theory holds
true chronic alcoholics' performance on neuropsychological tests should
approximate patterns of performance seen in Korsakoff's patients. The
two experiments were given to two separate age groups of chronic
alcoholics and normal controls. All four groups comprised adult males
with 20 subjects in each of the "older" groups (45-60 years) and 10
subjects in each of the "younger" groups (20-35 years). The first
experiment involved a series of non-cued versus cued verbal recall
tasks; the second experiment required the same subjects to engage in
repetition, phonemic, and semantic tasks after listening to word lists of
varying lengths.
        Group effects under different task conditions were determined
using analysis of variance (ANOVA). Results of the first experiment
yielded main effects for age and alcohol use, but no interaction effects.
Alcoholics of all ages appeared to perform below their controls. In
addition, pattern of performance appeared to be essentially the same for
all groups across task conditions. The second experiment yielded no
age or diagnostic group effects; again, the same pattern of performance
held across all groups. The authors conclude that a continuum theory
of ethanol's effects on the aging brain could not be substantiated,
although mild support was obtained for the premature aging theory.
Examination of specific patterns of deficits versus overall decline is
highlighted as an exemplary experimental procedure for future research
in this area.

069   Cohen, D. (1985). The relationship between serum immunoglobulins
        and neuropsychological functioning in older alcoholics. In E.
        Gottheil, K. A. Druley, T. E. Skolada, & H. M. Waxman
        (Eds.), The combined problems of alcoholism, drug addiction
        and aging (pp. 88-93). Springfield, IL: Charles C. Thomas.
        Cohen describes a pilot study that investigates serum
immunoglobulin levels and psychological test performance in chronic
alcoholic males aged 45-60 years. Based on previous reports of

correlations between serum immunoglobulin levels and cognitive performance in both healthy and demented older adults, the author hypothesizes that a relationship will exist between these two indices in patients with chronic alcoholism. The study was conducted in the Alcohol Treatment Unit of a Veterans Administration Medical Center. Thirty-four patients with a primary diagnosis of alcohol addiction were tested on admission to the unit; 28 of these patients were tested again three weeks later. Serum IgG, IgA and IgM were assayed by single radial immunodiffusion. Cognitive measures included the Hooper Test of Visual Organization as well as four performance subtests of the Wechsler Adult Intelligence Scale. Spearman R calculations for individual immunoglobulins x cognitive tests revealed four significant correlations. However, no consistent relationship was found across any one test or type of immunoglobulin. In addition, paired t-tests revealed no significant differences on pre- and post-admission measures. The author recommends continued study of immune system response to ethanol induced changes in the brain.

070   Counte, M. A., Salloway, J. C., & Christman, L. (1982). Age and sex related drinking patterns in alcoholics. In W. G. Wood & M. F. Elias (Eds.), Alcoholism and aging advances in research (pp. 17-27). Boca Raton, FL: CRC Press.

This chapter reports on a study conducted on an inpatient alcoholism treatment unit. Participants included 534 patients ranging in age from 15 to 78, who were admitted to the treatment program over a three-year period. Approximately 36 to 48 hours after admittance, each subject completed a lengthy questionnaire that included: background and sociodemographic information, treatment history, psychological and social incidents surrounding their drinking, experience of drinking symptoms, multiple drug use, and factors that prompted their seeking present help.

Respondents were grouped by five age groups: adolescence (15-20); early adulthood (21-34); middle age (35-49); late adulthood (50-64); and elderly (65 and older). Data were submitted to factor analyses and four factors emerged: alcoholic symptomatology, social isolation, onset of heavy drinking, and gregarious drinking. Each factor was converted into a factor-based scale. Each subject was assigned a total score on each scale. Analyses were performed by age and sex for each scale. Results of analyses revealed that although age was a significant predictor for two factors (alcoholic symptomatology and onset of heavy drinking), it was not as significant a predictor as sex. Men and women of all ages differ significantly in terms of their drinking patterns.

071   Crook, T., & Cohen, G.   (1984).   Future directions for alcohol
         research in the elderly.   In J. T. Hartford & T. Samorajski
         (Eds.), Alcoholism in the elderly: Social and biomedical
         issues (Vol. 25, pp. 277-282). New York: Raven Press.
         This chapter addresses the following questions: How serious
is the problem posed by alcoholism in the elderly? and How should
future research questions be directed? To answer the first question
Crook and Cohen note that existing epidemiological data confirm that
older people drink less than younger people and alcohol consumption
decreases with age.   However, due to age-related changes in
concentrations of water and fat, older adults who consume the same
amount of alcohol as younger adults demonstrate a much higher local
organ concentration of alcohol per unit dose. Alcohol is a particularly
toxic drug to older people, and older brains may be more sensitive to
the deleterious effects of alcohol. Memory loss, confusion, accidents,
falls, and many medical illnesses and mental health problems are
exacerbated or precipitated by alcohol use.
         Authors call for more, better designed epidemiological studies
of the prevalence of alcohol use by the elderly.   More studies are
needed to identify the principal demographic and psychosocial factors
related to alcohol usage. Additional studies should focus on similarities
and differences in early-onset and late-onset alcoholism. Other studies
need to be conducted which focus on life course of alcohol use and
abuse. More studies need to be conducted to determine the effects of
alcohol on sleep, appetite, sexual function, and other aspects of normal
daily function.   There need to be better quality studies on the
physiological effects of alcoholism and alcohol abuse. Greater attention
needs to be devoted to the relationship between alcoholism and other
mental disorders. Finally, Crook and Cohen recommend more research
on differential effectiveness of various treatment modalities.

072   Di Clemente, C. C., & Gordon, J. R. (1984). Aging, alcoholism,
         and addictive behavior change: Diagnostic treatment models.
         In J. T. Hartford & T. Samorajski (Eds.), Alcoholism in the
         elderly: Social and biomedical issues (Vol. 25, pp. 263-275).
         NY: Raven Press.
         This chapter presents a discussion and critique of important
issues in developing treatment models. The authors emphasize that
behavior change in alcohol consumption is the critical dimension in
alcoholism treatment.   The decision to enter treatment and follow
through on intervention techniques is relevant to treatment. Decision-
making deserves more attention in research. The authors point out that
there are many types of elderly alcoholics and patterns of drinking over
the life course.   Several studies are cited which demonstrate that

treatment is effective for older alcoholics.

In the last part of the chapter the authors present their own model of behavior change, emphasizing that change is continuous and progresses in stages. They identify seven stages of addictive behavior change, immotive, precontemplation, contemplation, decision-making, active change, maintenance, and relapse. This framework raises important questions such as: What are the most effective ways of helping immotive elderly alcoholics to begin to think of changing their alcohol consumption? What are the most tempting relapse situations for the elderly? What kinds of coping skills does the aged alcoholic need to maintain sobriety?

The treatment model presented delineates four levels of a person's functioning in connection with the alcohol problem. They are symptomatic, interpersonal, system and intrapersonal. The levels of problem involvement can help clinicians develop effective interventions to move individuals through the stages of addictive behavior change and to monitor change at each level.

073   Douglass, R. L. (1984). Aging and alcohol problems: Opportunities for socio-epidemiological research. In M. Galanter (Ed.), Recent developments in alcoholism, (Vol. 2, pp. 251-266). New York: Plenum Press.

This chapter reviews the current (1984) state of knowledge regarding published research in the area of aging and alcoholism and proposes areas in which research is badly needed. The author points out two major shortcomings of existing literature. First, it is primarily descriptive and few good empirical studies exist. Second, most studies have been done on clinical populations (medical wards, psychiatric facilities, or nursing homes) and thus suffer from a bias of selection. Prevalence studies reveal that about 25 to 45% of older male patients in these populations and 10% of older females are alcoholics. Douglass points out that we have no national studies of elderly drinking, alcohol problems, or alcoholism. He describes three types of elderly alcoholics and suggests that we need better studies of the similarities and differences between these types. The three types are those who have been alcoholic for a large portion of their lives (early-onset); those who have had repeated cycles of problems with alcoholic and problem-free periods; and those who became problem drinkers or alcoholics late in life (late-onset). Douglass also points out that there are numerous problems in measurement and conceptual variability in existing literature.

The chapter concludes with research suggestions from the 1981 White House Conference on Aging. The major suggestions are: (1) it is critical to determine as exactly as possible the nature and extent of problems associated with alcohol use among the elderly; (2) elderly must be defined; (3) it is important to determine who is at risk among the aged; (4) a focus should be on specific concentrations of the elderly population subgroups; (5) differences by gender, age of onset, and other characteristics should be identified; and (6) barriers to treatment and the most effective modes of treatment should be identified.

074   Druley, K. A., & Pashko, S. (1985). Development and evaluation of a treatment program for older veteran alcoholics. In E. Gottheil, K. A. Druley, T. E. Skoloda, & H. M. Waxman (Eds.), The combined problems of alcoholism, drug addiction, and aging (pp. 336-344). Springfield, IL: Charles C. Thomas.

This chapter describes the Chronic Alcohol Rehabilitation Program for older chronic alcoholics initiated at the Coatesville VA Medical Center in 1975. A therapeutic community was developed in which residents were responsible for their own behavior. Self-government, community meetings, and counseling were part of the program. The program was well attended and resulted in decreased drinking.

Two follow-up studies of residents were conducted, both of which found that there was a significant reduction in drinking and days intoxicated and veterans felt better mentally and physically several months after discharge from the program. The authors concluded that this program freed up staff-intensive psychiatric beds by developing a cost-efficient/effective nurse-coordinated therapeutic community.

075   Dunham, R. G. (1982). Aging and changing patterns of alcohol use. In D. M. Peterson & F. J. Whittington (Eds.), Drugs, alcohol and aging (pp. 33-41). Dubuque, Iowa: Kendall/Hunt.

Data for the study reported on in this chapter were drawn from interviews with 310 persons 60 year of age and older, who were living in government-funded, low income housing in Miami, Florida. Only 100 respondents in the sample reported drinking some alcohol during their lifetimes. Many of the samples were Latin and female, two groups that are less likely to drink in late life.

A self-reported retrospective measure of life drinking patterns was constructed, focusing on key events in drinking history such as the ages one drank the most or least. Six life patterns of drinking were identified: life-long abstainers, rise and fall pattern, rise and sustained pattern, light throughout life pattern, light with a late rise pattern, late starters, and highly variable. Females and Latins were most likely to be abstainers. Two-thirds of the sample were abstainers. Late starters usually began drinking in their 50's, with 54 being the mean age.

Males were twice as likely as females to be late starters. Fifty-five percent of the late starters reported having some alcohol-related illnesses. Females are most likely to not drink or to drink and then abstain. Males are more often found in the heavy, continuous drinking groups. Blacks are most often found in the highly variable group.

076   Dustman, R. E. (1984). Alcoholism and aging: Electrophysiological parallels. In J. T. Hartford & T. Samorajski (Eds.), Alcoholism in the elderly: Social and biomedical issues (Vol. 25, pp. 201-225). New York: Raven Press.

This chapter summarizes studies of brain wave activity in abstinent alcoholics and healthy older adults versus young adult control subjects. Sections are devoted to the electroencephalogram (EEG), sleep patterns, and cortical evoked potentials (EPs), with the latter section including brief discussions of sensory cortical EPs, brainstem auditory EPs, pattern reversal EPs, and late positive or P300 components. Comments are also offered on stimulus intensity and EP amplitude. The author concludes that electrophysiological studies, overall, neither support nor refute the premature aging theory. Although wave activity during sleep of abstinent alcoholics and healthy older adults suggests some commonality of brain dysfunction for the two groups, resting EEG recordings during wakefulness demonstrate few similarities and appear to be relatively insensitive to changes associated with chronic alcohol use or normal aging. Interpretation of EP studies is hampered by use of a wide variety of experimental procedures. Dustman does make particular note of the finding that both alcoholics and healthy older subjects tend to augment visually evoked responses (increase amplitude) to stimuli of increasing intensity, and that perhaps this is related to reduced inhibitory function in both groups. A number of illustrations and graphs accompany the text.

077   Elliott, N., & Smith, D. G. (1985). The elderly alcoholic: Nursing considerations. In E. Gottheil, K. A. Druley, T. E. Skoloda, & H. M. Waxman (Eds.), The combined problems of alcoholism, drug addiction, and aging (pp. 326-329). Springfield, IL: Charles C. Thomas.

In this chapter the focus is on treatment and rehabilitation of older alcoholics. The following key points should be addressed by nurses such that the care and treatment of older alcoholics may be improved: (1) a positive attitude that sees older alcoholics as treatable and worthy of respect and help is essential; (2) careful history taking and accurate assessment and diagnosis of alcoholism is needed; (3) detoxification must be done carefully, recognizing that it will take longer for the process in older alcoholics and precautions must be taken to prevent injury and wandering off; (4) therapeutic communities work well; family contact is essential; follow-up and an ongoing process of education are critical to recovery.

078   Etemad, B. (1980). Alcoholism and aging. In J. H. Masserman (Ed.), Current psychiatric therapies (pp. 111-114). New York: Grune & Stratton.

This chapter is written by a medical doctor who briefly reviews several models of treatment for older alcoholics. Models discussed include moral, medical, and psychiatric models. The medical approach emphasizes medical complications related to alcoholism such as nutritional deficiencies, metabolic disorders, diseases of the central nervous system, and withdrawal symptoms. Drug therapy is the major backbone of the medical approach. Specific drug doses are suggested for detoxification. The psychiatric model emphasizes group therapy, improved coping skills, behavioral therapy, and relaxation.

079   Finney, J. W., & Moos, R. H. (1984). Life stressors and problem drinking among older adults. In M. Galanter (Ed.), Recent developments in alcoholism (Vol. 2, pp. 267-288). New York: Plenum Press.

In this chapter Finney and Moos critically examine the empirical evidence relating life stressors to the onset of problem drinking in older age and to the continuation of drinking problems in later years. A comprehensive conceptual framework to guide future research is presented. In the first section of the chapter the authors review data from prevalence studies gathered in household surveys and clinical studies. They conclude that the prevalence of alcohol problems and alcoholism is much higher in clinical populations than among older adults living in the community. They also argue that sampling inadequacies and measurement problems have produced underestimates of the prevalence of alcohol abuse in the elderly. They predict higher rates of alcoholism in future cohorts of elders, particularly among females.

Two types of older alcoholics are defined: late-onset drinkers, who began to drink excessively late in life; and early-onset problem drinkers, or elderly persons whose abuse of alcohol in younger years has continued into old age. Some early-onset alcoholics have shown a pattern of intermittent problem drinking. Stress has been implicated in triggering new episodes of alcohol abuse among intermittents or in perpetuation of excessive drinking among early-onset alcoholics. Stress is also cited as a major factor which precipitates late-onset alcoholism. Empirical studies linking stress with alcoholism are reviewed. The authors conclude that: "In general, studies of the association between widowed or retired status do not seem to support the stress hypothesis. Results of studies in the other two categories--age of onset of problem drinking and the responsiveness of older problem drinkers to treatment--tend to support the stress theories" (p. 278).

In the last part of the chapter a conceptual framework to guide future research is presented. The model emphasizes that the link between stressful life circumstances and problem drinking is affected by sociodemographic factors (e.g., sex, ethnicity) and personal characteristics (e.g., depression, self-concept, beliefs about alcohol use). Life stress should be better defined. Authors distinguish three types of stress: long-term strains; stressful life events; and daily hassles. Mediators of stress must also be considered. Social resources and appraisal/coping responses are the two mediators described.

080   Forni, P. J. (1978). Alcohol and the elderly. In R. C. Kayne (Ed.), Drugs and the elderly (pp. 75-83). San Francisco, CA: The Ethel Percy Andrus Gerontology Center.

Two types of alcoholics are identified: those who began drinking early in life (early-onset); and those who began drinking late in life (late-onset). Alcohol-drug interactions are noted as a serious problem for older adults who abuse alcohol. The clinical effects associated with ingesting various quantities of alcohol, ranging from 30 to 500 milligrams, are specified.

The National Council on Alcoholism (NCA) criteria for diagnosing alcoholism are presented and discussed. Altered blood sugar metabolism, liver disease, gastrointestinal complications, nutritional deficiencies, and other medical problems associated with alcoholism are also discussed.

081   Freund, G. (1984). Neurobiological relationships between aging and alcohol abuse. In M. Galanter (Ed.), Recent developments in alcoholism (Vol. 2, pp. 203-221). New York: Plenum Press.

This chapter provides an overview of what is currently (1984) known about the neurobiological effects of alcohol abuse and the potential neurobiological interactions between aging and alcohol abuse. Evidence from a variety of different types of studies are reviewed. These include: studies on animals, autopsy studies, CT and blood flow, microscopic pathology, studies using the electroencephalogram (EEG), evoked potentials, and studies of neurochemical change.

The CNS toxicity of alcohol has been confirmed in animal studies. In addition, autopsy studies more often reveal grossly atrophic brains in older populations with increasing alcohol-use severity. Based on CT studies it is clear that both aging and alcohol abuse induce atrophy of the cerebral cortex, of central structures around the third ventricle, and of parts of the cerebellum, independent of trauma, liver disease, or thiamine deficiency. Rapid Eye Movement (REM) sleep is decreased in both aging adults and alcoholics. The decrease in REM sleep is correlated with impairment on intelligence and memory tests. Results from evoked potential studies show that sensory evoked potentials for visual, auditory, and somatosensory modalities are decreased in amplitude and delayed in latency with both aging and alcohol abuse. Neurochemical changes are also associated with aging and alcohol abuse. Both aging and alcohol abuse result in loss or impairment of synaptic function. In turn, changes in behavior accompany changes in synaptic function. The chapter concludes that "both normal aging and alcohol abuse are associated with behavioral, morphological, electrophysiological, and neurochemical changes in humans and animals" (p. 218). The last part of the chapter calls for specific research to allow us to delineate possible interactions between aging and alcohol abuse.

082   Gambert, S. R., Newton, M., & Duthie, E. H. (1984). Medical issues in alcoholism in the elderly. In J. T. Hartford & T. Samorajski (Eds.), Alcoholism in the elderly: Social and biomedical issues (Vol. 25, pp. 175-191). New York: Raven Press.

This chapter discusses common medical issues that need to be considered in caring for the older adult who either drank to excess in the past or is presently abusing alcohol. Several physiological problems related to acute alcohol intoxication are discussed. Alcohol has a deleterious effect on cardiac muscle leading to increased cardiac rate and output and increased systolic blood pressure. Acute pancreatitis, stomach problems, and hypoglycemia often result from ingestion of alcohol. There is a greater prevalence of gout and cirrhosis in heavy drinkers. Alcohol affects the central nervous system, and may lead to depression of central nervous system respiratory centers with eventual coma.

Alcohol also induces metabolic abnormalities. Alcoholic liver disease is common The hydroxylation of vitamin D_3 to its more active 25-hydroxated form by the liver may be compromised, leading to osteomalacia. Decreased concentration of plasma testosterone and decreased testosterone production result from alcohol ingestion, which results in decreased sexual function in males.

A section is included on alcohol and the cardiovascular system, and alcohol and its effects on nutrition and body components. Some of the cardiovascular problems discussed are cardiomyophathy, cardiac fibrosis, and microvascular infarcts and swelling. Gastrointestinal problems addressed include glossitis and stomatitis, esophageal disorders, erosive gastritis, peptic ulcer disease, and pancreatitis.

Alcohol ingestion chronically affects nutrition and may cause malnutrition. Protein malnutrition is manifested by muscle wasting, hypoproteinemia, and edema. Lactase-deficiency syndromes can be precipitated by alcohol ingestion. Alcohol ingestion aggravates diarrhea and external losses of all nutrients. Iron-deficiency anemia is common in alcoholics. These and other alcohol-related medical problems are discussed in some detail.

083   Garver, D. L. (1984). Age effects on alcohol metabolism. In J. T. Hartford & T. Samorajski (Eds.), Alcoholism in the elderly: Social and biomedical issues (Vol. 25, pp. 153-159). New York: Raven Press.

In this chapter, Garver reviews evidence on blood ethanol levels and rates of elimination of ethanol in older persons, and age-related changes in ethanol distribution in the body. Literature reveals that a relative decrease in total body water/body weight accompanies aging. Since ethanol distributes only to the body water compartments, the consequence of such a decrease in body water is greater concentration of ethanol in the blood of the elderly as compared with younger adults following comparable intake of ethanol. With respect to metabolism, there is no evidence that the activity of the enzyme alcohol dehydrogenase (the liver enzyme that metabolizes ethanol) changes as a function of age. The elimination time of ethanol is not related to age. Gout and fatty liver are conditions which are secondary effects of the metabolism of ethanol.

Ethanol has been shown to result in urinary obstruction and a decline in sexual function. Ethanol also interacts with a number of sedative-hypnotic drugs in a manner that lowers the threshold at which effects of intoxication occur. Sometimes combining ethanol and sedatives produces supra-additive effects.

084   Glynn, R. J., Bouchard, G. R., LoCastro, J. S., & Hermos, J. A. (1984). Changes in alcohol consumption among men in the normative aging study. In G. Maddox, L. Robins, & N. Rosenberg (Eds.), Nature and extent of alcohol problems among the elderly (Vol. 14, pp. 101-116). Rockville: USDHHS.

This article is part of the proceedings of a National Institute on Alcohol Abuse and Alcoholism, National Institute on Aging, National Institute for Mental Health sponsored state-of-the-art workshop which took place in 1983 at the Alcohol Research Center at Washington University. Data from the Normative Aging Study begun in 1963 at the

Boston VA yield some informative data as it applied to alcohol consumption. A 15-page survey was returned by 1,897 of the 2,025 men canvassed in 1973, and a follow-up survey in 1982 yielded a return of 1,570. One of the most interesting findings was supportive of the caution one must have in interpreting the findings of cross-sectional research in this area. Attrition due to death was more likely to occur in the nondrinker and the "two or more drinks a day" groups from the first sample. Also, nonrespondents to the 1982 study tended to be from the extreme drinking groups and were more likely to be from the youngest or oldest age groups. The other findings were that the drinking patterns were stable over time, and that men in their forties and fifties at the first sampling were particularly consistent in their drinking habits.

085   Gomberg, E. L. (1985). Life events and drinking behavior in later years. In E. Gottheil, K. A. Druley, T. E. Skoloda, & H. M. Waxman (Eds.), The combined problems of alcoholism, drug addiction, and aging (pp. 51-73). Springfield, IL: Charles C. Thomas.

Gomberg addresses two questions in this chapter: (1) is there such an issue as early- versus late-onset alcoholism, and (2) what in the aging process supports or causes substance abuse? To answer the first question, Gomberg reviews studies conducted by Zimberg, Bogue, Bahr, and others, which confirm that some older alcoholics begin abusing alcohol after age 45 (late-onset). These studies agree that about one-third of all older alcoholics are late-onset. Gomberg briefly discusses definition problems pointing out that late-onset could mean after age 40 or after age 60. She proposes a new term, "recent onset" for those drinkers who began abusing alcohol within the last 10 years. She points out that many older adults begin abusing alcohol as a response to recent loss or stressful life experiences.

The answer to the second question, according to Gomberg, requires a mini-course in gerontology so that those interested in alcohol abuse and aging know what the aging process entails. She focuses on three areas: stress and life events such as retirement and widowhood, coping mechanisms, and social supports and social networks. She explores the arguments for and against the linkage of negative life events with alcohol abuse and the buffer effect of social support.

086   Gomberg, E. L. (1993). Drugs, alcohol, and aging. In L. T. Kozlowski, H. M. Annis, H. D. Cappell, F. B. Glaser, M. S. Goodstadt, Y. Israel, H. Kalant, E. M. Sellers, & E. R. Vingilis (Eds.), Research advances in alcohol and drug problems (Vol. 10, pp. 171-213). New York: Plenum Press.

This lengthy overview chapter reviews existing literature in the following areas: demographics of the elderly; psychosocial issues for the elderly; medication use; tobacco; alcohol use by older adults; biological effects of alcohol; problem drinking and alcoholism; and treatment and rehabilitation of older alcoholics.

In the chapter Gomberg discusses the role of loss (i.e., retirement, widowhood) in contributing to alcohol problems among the elderly. She also notes the important role of social networks and social resources as protecting against alcoholism in older adults. The chapter also includes a brief discussion about depression and dementia in late life.

With respect to drinking, Gomberg reviews research that indicates that older adults drink frequently but lesser quantities than younger people. She also discusses early- versus late-onset alcoholism and reviews prevalence data in late-life drinking. Gomberg discusses negative effects of alcohol on various body systems and the problem of alcohol-drug interactions.

The last part of the chapter focuses on treatment and rehabilitation. Gomberg addresses the following types of questions: how do older alcoholics come to the attention of caretakers? and are there special problems in diagnosis, management, and treatment of older alcoholics?

087   Green, N. M., & Bridgham, J. D. (1991). The older adult alcoholic client. In R. F. Young & E. A. Olson (Eds.), Health, illness, and disability in later life (pp. 61-72). Newbury Park: Sage.

This chapter presents an overview of the older adult alcoholic and examines the causes of alcohol abuse, as well as the special problems that occur with diagnosis and treatment. In discussing the older alcoholic, the authors point out statistical differences in various studies dealing with elderly alcoholics. Several reasons are cited for differences, including denial of addiction among older adults, hospitals that treat an organ rather then the person, and how one defines "alcoholism." Under causes of alcohol abuse, Green and Bridgham found that their clients were typically proportioned between early- and late-onset with one-third the latter and two-thirds the former. They mention boredom, stress, age-related problems, depression and lost ability to choose where and when and how much to drink as major factors that lead to alcoholism. Misdiagnoses occur frequently because many symptoms of alcoholism are stereotypical symptoms of aging. Professionals are reluctant to treat older alcoholics because "the cost of being treated becomes greater than the benefit to be accrued" (Maletta, 1982). Abstinence is advocated by the authors who believe that older adults can make productive use of leisure time without alcohol.

088   Hall, E. P. (1983). Substance abuse in the aging. In G. Bennett, C. Vourakis, & D. S. Woolf (Eds.), Substance abuse: Pharmacologic, developmental, and clinical perspectives (pp. 192-205). New York: John Wiley.

In this chapter the author discusses the developmental tasks of aging, coping patterns in aging, the epidemiology of substance abuse, factors influencing drug abuse, and prevention. Three developmental tasks and one psychosocial crisis of aging are highlighted: redirection of energy to new roles, acceptance of one's life, developing a point of view about death, and the crisis of integrity versus despair. Several age-related losses and stresses are discussed including retirement, illness, loss of spouse and relocation. Substance abuse is one method of coping with these losses.

The last two sections of the chapter focus on epidemiology of substance abuse (alcoholism, abuse of over-the-counter, and/or prescription drugs) and factors contributing to substance abuse. After reviewing major prevalence studies, Hall distinguishes early- from late-onset alcoholics: early-onset including those who began drinking in their 30's and 40's, and late-onset including those who began drinking in their late 40's or 50's. Factors related to late-life alcoholism include marital and family problems, social isolationism, and severe antisocial problems.

089   Hartford, J. T., & Thienhaus, O. J. (1984). Psychiatric aspects of alcoholism in geriatric patients. In J. T. Hartford & T. Samorajski (Eds.), Alcoholism in the elderly: Social and biomedical issues (Vol. 25, pp. 253-262). New York: Raven Press.

In this chapter the descriptive symptomatology of alcoholism according to the Diagnostic and Statistical Manual of Mental Disorders (DSM-III) is reviewed. The mechanisms by which alcoholism interfaces with other types of psychiatric pathology and its causative, concurrent and reactive nature in relationship to major mental disorders are discussed. The chapter presents various treatment modalities and examines their clinical applicability to elderly patients.

The DSM-III makes the diagnosis of alcohol dependence contingent on the presence of two symptom clusters: (a) a pattern of pathological alcohol use or alcohol-related impairment in social or occupational functioning; and (b) signs of either tolerance or withdrawal. The author defines two types of alcoholism: primary or early-onset alcoholism, which is present from an early age and continues in late life; and secondary, or late-onset alcoholism, which develops in the context of a pre-existing problem such as depression or life stress. Personality disorders that seem to be especially predisposed to substance abuse are borderline, passive-aggressive, and to a lesser degree, compulsive and dependent personality disorders. Stressors which precipitate reactive alcoholism are bereavement, moves, retirement, and the leaving of children.

Alcoholism is often found to exist with and compound other mental disorders, primarily affective disorders and schizophrenia. Alcoholism also accelerates and mimics the dementing process, can produce confusion and memory loss, and also precipitates suicide.

There is no predictable cure for alcoholism. There are, however, many different approaches and therapeutic techniques to treat the problem. The clinical management of the older alcoholic combines pharmacological approaches with psychosocial therapies. A thorough physical and appropriate laboratory tests should be conducted, and medical illnesses should be treated. Treatment includes the use of Antabuse, proper nutrition, and multivitamin therapy, education and counseling, and group and individual psychotherapies (e.g., Alcoholics Anonymous is recommended as a particularly good therapy for older alcoholics).

090   Helzer, J. E., Carey, K. E., & Miller, R. H. (1984). Predictors and correlates of recovery in older versus younger alcoholics. In G. Maddox, L. Robins, & N. Rosenberg (Eds.), Nature and extent of alcohol problems among the elderly (Vol. 14, pp. 83-99). Rockville: USDHHS.

This article is part of the proceedings of a National Institute on Alcohol Abuse and Alcoholism, National Institute on Aging, National Institute for Mental Health sponsored state-of-the-art workshop which took place in 1983 at the Alcohol Research Center at Washington University. The intent of this research was to more closely examine recovery differences in older versus younger alcoholics. Interviews were conducted five to eight years after inpatient treatment. Though there seemed a slight trend toward more elders sustaining recovery, the findings were complicated by a much higher mortality rate in the older group. Despite the lack of clear differences between the older and younger alcoholics, this article is a good starting point for reviewing comparisons of recovery between different age groups.

091   Hermos, J. A., LoCastro, J. S., Bouchard, G. R., & Glynn, R. J. (1983). Influence of cardiovascular disease on alcohol consumption among men in the normative aging study. In G. Maddox, L. Robins, & N. Rosenberg (Eds.), Nature and extent of alcohol problems among the elderly (Vol. 14, pp. 117-132). Rockville: USDHHS.

This article is part of the proceedings of a National Institute on

Alcohol Abuse and Alcoholism, National Institute on Aging, National Institute for Mental Health sponsored state-of-the-art workshop which took place in 1983 at the Alcohol Research Center at Washington University. Data were taken from the Normative Agency Study which was begun at the Boston VA in 1963. A 15-page survey was returned by 1,897 of the 2,025 men canvassed in 1973 and a follow-up survey in 1982 yielded a return of 1,570. This report examines the question of whether recently diagnosed hypertension or heart disease would influence alcohol consumption over time. The findings were ambiguous, and the authors acknowledged that "the participants with hypertension reduced their drinking significantly between 1973 and 1982, but we were unable to detect the factors predicting that reduction, other than the initial higher consumption levels" (p. 128). As in other articles dealing with this data, the methodological constraints of this survey study are discussed.

092   Hochhauser, M. (1982). Learned helplessness and substance abuse in the elderly. In D. M. Peterson & F. J. Whittington (Eds.), Drugs, alcohol and aging (pp. 17-24). Dubuque, Iowa: Kendall/Hunt.

This chapter presents an analysis of psycho-social factors related to problems of substance abuse among the elderly. Substance abuse is conceptualized in a learned helplessness framework. The loss of control (and subsequent feelings of helplessness) that may occur as a response to a life crisis such as widowhood may produce increased mental and physical distress in the elderly. This increased stress may lead to the increased use of alcohol, nicotine, or food as a way to alleviate stress by providing an experience over which the older adult has some control. Two types of stressful events are discussed: external events such as death of a spouse, and internal events such as health changes. Individual biological and psychosocial differences affect the way an older person responds to stressful events. Two outcomes are discussed: learned mastery and successful coping, and learned helplessness which results in substance abuse or suicide. Alcoholism is described as both a form of slow suicide and a precipitant of suicidal behavior. The conclusion of the chapter is that "the extent to which the elderly believe that they can predict and/or control environmental events will similarly have important effects on their levels of substance use, misuse, and abuse, and possibly their life- and death" (p. 22).

093   Hoffman, A., & Heinemann, M. E. (1986). Alcohol problems in elderly persons. In N. J. Estes & M. E. Heinemann (Eds.),

Alcoholism development, consequences, and interventions (pp. 257-272). St. Louis: Mosby.

This is a comprehensive overview of alcoholism and the elderly. The authors include information on etiology, physiological (covering the CNS, the GI system, the cardiac system, electrolyte balance, the hematopoietic system, pulmonary disease, cancer and endocrine function) and psychological consequences of the disease, diagnostic issues and instrumentation, and finally treatment approaches and management of the disease. Also discussed in this paper is the stress-reaction hypothesis, as well as treatment goals, which can help the professional assist the older patient to achieve and maintain sobriety (p.269).

094   Holzer, C. E., Robins, L. N., Myers, J. K., Weissman, M. M., Tischler, G. L., Leaf, P. J., Anthony, A., & Bednarski, P. B. (1983). Antecedents and correlates of alcohol abuse and dependence in the elderly. In G. Maddox, L. Robins, & N. Rosenberg (Eds.), Nature and extent of alcohol problems among the elderly (Vol. 14, pp. 217-244). Rockville: USDHHS.

This article is part of the proceedings of a National Institute on Alcohol Abuse and Alcoholism, National Institute on Aging, National Institute for Mental Health sponsored state-of-the-art workshop which took place in 1983 at the Alcohol Research Center at Washington University. The major focus of this paper is to examine in-depth data from the NIMH Epidemiological Catchment Area (ECA) program, which was a multi-site community survey providing diagnostic assessment of many psychiatric disorders. Some of the findings are that married respondents have low rates of abuse, with the separated/ divorced groups having the highest. The rate of alcoholism is greater for those who have not finished high school than among those with more education. Also, there is a trend which shows increased alcoholism among individuals from the poorest households. Although the elderly have much lower rates of alcohol abuse and dependence than younger individuals, they do appear to have the same sociodemographic correlates of abuse. Included in this article is a section on cohort effects and data interpretation.

095   Horton, A. M., Jr., & Fogelman, C. J. (1991). Behavioral treatment of aged alcoholics and drug addicts. In P. A. Wisocki (Ed.), Handbook of clinical behavior therapy with the elderly client (pp. 299-315). New York: Plenum Press.

This chapter begins with a brief review of definition changes for substance abuse and dependence in the last decade according to the

Diagnostic and Statistical Manual of Mental Disorders. It discusses major criteria for the diagnosis of psychoactive substance dependence, lists the nine substances associated with abuse and dependence, and points out how aging affects different substance use disorders in different ways. The authors devote most of their attention to the assessment and behavioral treatment of elderly alcoholics primarily because of the lack of information about elderly drug use and treatment research.

Topics on aging alcoholics include the epidemiology, subtypes, stresses associated with aging, and treatment of the elderly alcoholic. The authors discuss methods of assessment, including the Minnesota Multiphasic Personality Inventory and the Comprehensive Drinker Profile, measuring neuropsychological and psychopathological effects, treatment studies, and guidelines for treatment of the aging alcoholic. In addition, problems in identifying appropriate patients and treatment settings were raised. Next, the authors briefly touch upon both the use of legal and illegal drugs among the elderly, and suggest that the model used for elderly alcoholics has some merit for the elderly drug addict. The authors conclude that at this point, suggestions for behavioral treatment rests more on clinical lore than on empirical practice, and hence, there is an urgent need for expanded research efforts on aging alcoholics and drug addicts.

096   Hyman, M. M. (1985). Aging and alcoholism: A 15-year follow-up study. In E. Gottheil, K. A. Druley, T. E. Skoloda, & H. M. Waxman (Eds.), The combined problems of alcoholism, drug addiction, and aging (pp. 215-227). Springfield, IL: Charles C. Thomas.

This chapter reports on a 15-year follow-up of a cohort of alcoholics, all of whom were age 60+ at follow-up and had experienced serious alcohol-related problems before middle age. The study group consisted of White male residents of Middlesex County, New Jersey aged 30-54, who had made one or more visits to the Alcoholism Treatment Center (a county-run outpatient clinic at Roosevelt Hospital in Metuchen, NJ) and whose cases were closed for the first time in 1958. The number in the cohort was 54 (age 30-39, N=21; age 40-44, N=17; age 45-54, N=16). Fourteen to 16 years later, 48 of the 54 (89%) were dead. At follow-up (three years after intake) 30 people were alive and 25 were interviewed. Interview topics included: family relations, leisure and organizational activities, employment and income, health and hospitalizations, contact with AA, trouble with the law, traffic accidents, and citations, and drinking practices and changes in drinking patterns.

Of the 20 mentally alert locatables at follow-up, on whom

adequate information was available, five had been total abstainers during the previous three years and two were abstainers with occasional "slips." Seven were frequent drinkers. Five were frequent, but moderated drinkers with great reductions in alcohol consumption. One frequent drinker had less severe alcohol problems at follow-up than at intake, but could not be confidently classified as a non-problem drinker.

Twelve of the cases (five total abstainers, two near-abstainers, and five moderated drinkers) were classified as having favorable outcomes, 15 as having irreversible (six mentally deteriorated, nine alcohol-implicated deaths) and eight having unfavorable but reversible outcomes (mentally alert but with continuing problem drinking). These groups are compared on various dimensions. Compared to other groups, the "irreversibles" were older, less educated, and lower in occupational level, were more often without work, living in poverty and not with wives, and more frequently had digestive and neurological impairments or symptoms. They also received lower scores on scales of early achievement and social resources. As compared to frequent drinkers, abstainers were older, less educated, and in lower occupational groups and had had more stays in psychiatric and rehabilitation facilities and had had more contact with AA, more often used social intervention services provided by the clinic and had been in more trouble with the law. The researcher concludes that experiences with the law and stays in psychiatric and rehabilitation facilities make it more difficulty to deny one's alcoholism and help to contribute to favorable outcomes.

097   Kofoed, L. L., Tolson, R. L., Atkinson, R. M., Turner, J. A., & Toth, R. F. (1984). Elderly groups in an alcoholism clinic. In R. M. Atkinson (Ed.), Alcohol and drug abuse in old age (pp. 36-47). Washington, DC: American Psychiatric Press, Inc.

In this chapter one particular alcohol treatment program for older adults is described. "The Class of 45" is a specialized, elderly-oriented outpatient component of a comprehensive Alcohol and Drug Dependence Treatment Section (ADDTS) of the Psychiatry Service at the Portland, Oregon VA Medical Center. The group is open to any veteran accepted for outpatient alcoholism treatment who was on active military duty in 1945 or earlier. Groups meet weekly for 1 1/2 hours. At least monthly all groups meet together for informal dinners. The mean age of participants is 61 and almost all are men.

Observations of the group indicate that older adults respond in treatment at least as well as younger patients, but the tempo is slower. Humor is abundant in meetings. Self-disclosure is slow and cautious. Members rapidly develop a strong attachment to one another. Group members commonly reminisce about "the good old days."

"The Class of 45" group showed an 81% rate of attendance at scheduled meetings and treatment activities and an average length of stay of more than 10 months. For the outpatient program as a whole attendance rate is only 58% and average length of stay is 5.8 months.

Two cases are presented. A strong argument is made for elderly-specific treatment. The type of group described could be effectively implemented in a variety of settings such as senior centers, churches, and alcoholism treatment programs.

098   Kunz, G. D., Stammers, T. W., Pashko, S., & Druley, K. A. (1985). Factors that differentiate treatment placement among older chronic alcoholics. In E. Gottheil, K. A. Druley, T. E. Skoloda, & H. M. Waxman (Eds.), The combined problems of alcoholism, drug addiction, and aging (pp. 345-353). Springfield, IL: Charles C. Thomas.

The question addressed in this chapter was "can historical, psychosocial, or medical markers be identified which differentiate those alcoholic veterans of age 55 or older who are deemed capable of functioning satisfactorily in a fast-track rehabilitation program from those whom it is felt would be more appropriately placed in a slow-track rehabilitation program?" (pp. 345-346). To answer this question, researchers present statistics compiled on 200 older veterans who graduated from a fast-track and a slow-track rehabilitation program at the Coatesville VA Medical Center. The slow-track program is very basic in structure and makes more scaled-down demands on participants than does the fast-track program. The fast-track program is more complex, intensive, and insight-oriented. Graduates of the fast-track program showed significant improvement on factors of employment, alcohol consumption, criminal activity, and psychological functioning. Graduates of the slow-track program showed significant improvement on factors of employment, alcohol consumption, criminal activity, and psychological functioning, while graduates of the slow-track program showed significant improvement on the medical factor, psychological functioning, and alcohol consumption.

A sample of 25 graduates from the slow-track and 21 graduates from the fast-track programs for whom there were complete sets of routine testing available were compared. From these samples it was possible to collect additional demographic, historical, and medical information on 11 graduates from slow-track and 13 graduates from fast-track program. Results indicated that on admission, veterans who are referred to a slow-track program display a significantly higher level of global psychopathology (MMPI F Scale, Beck Depression Scale) than those who are referred to the fast-track program.

Candidates for the fast-track program had a higher level of education and a prior history of vocational status at a higher level than did those referred to the slow-track program. They also had more intact interpersonal support systems.

099   Lawson, A. W. (1989). Substance abuse problems of the elderly: Considerations for treatment and prevention. In G. W. Lawson & A. W. Lawson (Eds.), Alcohol and substance abuse in special populations (pp. 95-113). Rockville, MD: Aspen.

In this comprehensive overview, the author discusses drug misuse and abuse, as well as alcoholism among the elderly. Abuse of prescription and over-the-counter drugs is considered. Alcohol-drug interactions are recognized as a serious problem in this age group. Factors are identified which increase the risk of substance abuse. Physical factors identified include: changes in drug tolerance and absorption resulting from physical changes accompanying aging; loss of spouse, friends, job, social activities, and available sexual partners, which result in stress, depression, and isolation; and other psychological factors such as loneliness, boredom, negative changes in self-concept, and lowered self-esteem; and sociological factors such as retirement, loss of income, and changing status.

Drug misuse is usually not intentional and does not involve use of illegal substances. Drug misuse can result from the physician's lack of knowledge, errors in physician judgment, lack of supervision by physician, and excessive use of over-the-counter drugs. The major form of misuse is underuse. Unlike misuse, abuse is intentional and may involve the use of illegal drugs. The drugs most commonly abused are analgesics, sedatives, and narcotics. The most common form of abuse is overuse. Abuse of over-the-counter drugs can cause serious problems. Even caffeine and nicotine contribute to serious problems in older adults.

Two types of older alcoholics are identified: early-onset, who begin to have drinking problems early in life and continue to drink in old age; and late-onset alcoholics, who begin experiencing problems related to drinking later in life, usually as a reaction to some late life stress or problem. Empirical studies of late life alcoholism are discussed.

Treatment of substance abuse in the elderly is discussed in the last section. Therapies identified as helpful include: socialization therapy, group therapy, case work, and cognitive therapy. It is suggested that in many cases antidepressant medications may be helpful. The importance of treating older adults in places they already frequent is mentioned. Treatment in senior centers is appropriate. Home visits are also recommended. Other older adults can be helpful in therapy. Treatment goals must be realistic and implemented in small increments. Marriage and family therapy can be effective.

Prevention of substance abuse in the elderly is an important goal. Education and counseling can be effective. It is important to reduce psychological and environmental stress and increase the social contacts older people have.

100   Maletta, G. J. (1982). Alcoholism and the aged. In E. M. Pattison & E. Kaufman (Eds.), Encyclopedic handbook of alcoholism (pp. 779-791). New York: Gardner Press.

The hidden nature of alcohol abuse in the older population is discussed. For a variety of reasons older adults are less likely to be recognized as alcoholics than are younger people. First, they are less likely to work and be identified at work. Also, they drive less often and are less often picked up in traffic accidents. They may not live with family members who can recognize their problem. Older alcoholics less often seek treatment. Their problem often remains undiagnosed. Many studies in the literature report fewer problems with alcohol and decreased drinking in older people. The author suggests that, due to problems of underreporting and methodological problems in many of the studies, these conclusions may be unwarranted. A more accurate statement is that we currently do not know the extent of the problem of alcohol abuse in late life.

The author suggests that alcohol problems of the elderly may be grouped into several categories: (1) symptoms developed as a result of drinking; (2) psychological dependence; (3) problems with relatives, friends or neighbors related to alcohol; (4) problems with employment, finances, or other socioeconomic indicators as a result of alcohol use; and (5) problems with law enforcement officers, secondary to alcohol use.

Literature is reviewed on the characteristics of older alcoholics and causes of late-life alcoholism. Based on literature reviewed, the author notes that males, Caucasians, and those with a lower level of education are more likely to abuse alcohol than are females, non-caucasians, and the more highly educated. Older alcoholics in treatment are more likely than younger alcoholics to be voluntary admissions and have a better prognosis. Some of the causes of alcoholism identified were: feelings of uselessness, feelings of dependency, poverty, reactions to alienation, and feelings of low social status.

Two types of older alcoholics are discussed: those who begin drinking early in life and continue (early-onset); and those who begin drinking for the first time in late, usually as a reaction to the problems and stresses associated with growing old (late-onset). The importance of a comprehensive treatment plan that takes into account the unique psychosocial features of the older alcoholic and his/her family members is noted.

101   Marco, L. A., & Randels, P. M. (1985). Medical and psychiatric management of the older alcoholic veteran. In E. Gottheil, K. A. Druley, T. E. Skolada, & H. M. Waxman (Eds.), The combined problems of alcoholism, drug addiction and aging (pp. 312-325). Springfield, IL: Charles C. Thomas.

Despite the focus suggested by its title, this chapter actually provides a general overview of the topic of aging and alcoholism. Alcoholism as a public health problem is first discussed, followed by a brief examination of mechanisms of ethanol metabolism, criteria for accurate diagnosis, risk factors, and inheritability. The older alcoholic is described as unique in terms of medical and psychiatric management, particularly because of the physiologic changes that accompany aging. Although treatment approaches are summarized in two paragraphs, the authors make several specific recommendations regarding detoxification: outpatient detoxification is advised only when patients have adequate family supervision and support; use of antihistamines, anticholinergic agents, and highly sedating neuroleptics should be avoided in older patients.

102   Mayfield, D. G. (1974). Alcohol problems in the aging patient. In W. E. Fann & G. L. Maddox (Eds.), Drug issues in geropsychiatry (pp. 35-40). Baltimore, MD: The Williams and Wilkins Company.

In this chapter the author discusses national studies of drinking behavior, which reveal lower levels of drinking among older adults, compared to younger individuals. Complete abstinence is also common among people 60 years and older. The reduction in drinking may be explained by a reduction in energy level, diminution in vigor and appetite, constriction in social activities associated with drinking, or by financial constraints imposed by age. This generation of older adults was raised in a historical time period when abstinence was much more common and abuse of alcohol was viewed in a much more negative light than is true today.

The author also points out that many alcoholics never reach old age because of an early death from liver disease, homicide, suicide, accidents, cardiovascular disease, and various forms of cancer.

Two types of alcoholics are discussed: "delayed problem drinkers," or individuals who were heavy drinkers prior to age 50 and became problem drinkers between ages 50 and 60; and "decompensated social drinkers," or individuals who were moderate drinkers and over several years developed excessive drinking in their 60's. Elderly alcoholics from either group are likely to be underdetected, underdiagnosed, and undertreated.

Treatment of late-life alcoholism is the focus for the last half of the chapter. Drug treatment is defined as the cornerstone of management and is discussed in detail. The use of chlordiazepoxide is recommended. General guidelines for administering the drug are provided. Multi-vitamin therapy for management of withdrawal syndromes is also recommended.

103   Meyers, A. R. (1985). The epidemiology of late-life problem drinking: What a survey says. In E. Gottheil, K. A. Druley, T. E. Skoloda, & H. M. Waxman (Eds.), The combined problems of alcoholism, drug addiction, and aging (pp. 228-239). Springfield, IL: Charles C. Thomas.

This chapter reports results of a study of a sample of adults in the Boston, Massachusetts, Standard Metropolitan Statistical Area (SMSA). The study design is not discussed in the chapter. The reader is referred to earlier published studies, which describe the study in detail.

Results of the study are summarized. The older problem drinkers in their sample were more likely to be "young-old" (i.e., 70-years-old or younger), native born, and male. Compared to non-problem drinkers, problem drinkers were significantly more dissatisfied with their relationships with spouse, family members, and friends. Many problem drinkers reported that they drank to "escape" or for hedonistic reasons. All of the older problem drinkers reported that they had experienced drinking problems earlier in their life. Results also indicated that many older problem drinkers had experience with treatment programs, but with mixed success.

104   Miller, M. J. (1991). Drug use and misuse among the elderly. In R. F. Young & E. A. Olson (Eds.), Health, illness and disability in later life: Practice issues and interventions (pp. 45-51). Newbury Park: Sage Publications.

This chapter is a lay-oriented overview of the problems of medication use and abuse by the elderly. The author focuses on prescription drug expenditures among the elderly, as well as their use of over-the-counter drugs. As the greatest consumers of medications in our country, the elderly are at great risk for medication use problems. The author discusses factors that can contribute to drug misuse by older adults, which include intentional and unintentional medication misuse, adverse drug reactions, lack of appreciation of the effects of aging, and inaccurate medical diagnosis. Miller concludes the article by citing eight suggestions for better patient-provider prescription practices (Vestal, 1984), and notes that as the number of geriatric patients increases in the decades to come, skilled management for elderly medication problems will be essential.

105   Mishara, B. L. (1985). What we know, don't know and need to know about older alcoholics and how to help them: Models of prevention and treatment. In E. Gottheil, K. A. Druley, T. E. Skoloda, & H. M. Waxman (Eds.), The combined problems of alcoholism, drug addiction and aging (pp. 243-261). Springfield, IL: Charles C. Thomas.

This chapter begins with a discussion of factors related to the development of alcoholism in the later years. The major causal factor is loss--loss of spouse, job, health, or home. The author argues for the need for a "balanced view" about alcoholism and aging, citing data which indicates that individuals who drink moderately live longer than those who abstain from drinking alcohol.

The major discussion in the chapter focuses on prevention of alcoholism in late life. Mishara argues strongly for primary, secondary, and tertiary prevention of alcoholism among the elderly. As he notes, "primary prevention is aimed at inhibiting the development of alcohol problems before they begin" (p. 247). "Secondary prevention efforts focus upon new problem drinkers" (p. 247). "Tertiary prevention is aimed at the chronic alcoholic" (p. 251).

Primary prevention efforts need to be aimed at older individuals who are not alcoholics or alcohol abusers, but who are at risk of developing problems with alcohol. Research efforts should focus on identifying who is most at risk for alcoholism in late life and what interventions are most effective in preventing alcoholism. Support for the stress theory would suggest that the recently widowed and recently retired should be targeted. Programs should be developed to help older people prepare for the stresses and challenges of aging, and in particular for the stresses of widowhood and retirement. Mishara calls for more programs for the recently bereaved and for more pre-retirement programs to help those who are going to retire. Wellness programs, which emphasize positive mental, physical, and emotional health, and provide education about the values of good nutrition, physical exercise, and social involvement are another primary prevention strategy. Self-help groups and age-based support groups would aid the transition to late-life.

Another prevention strategy might be to involve older people in activities that nurture self-worth and increase feelings of self-esteem. Part-time work, community activities, and volunteer opportunities in health care and other settings are all valuable. Mishara also suggests improving housing quality for elders, new career programs in later life, and aid to families with dependent older people as preventive measures which could help reduce the incidence of alcoholism in old age. Primary prevention is the most cost effective form of prevention.

Secondary prevention efforts target new problem drinkers, who have not yet become alcoholics or who have recently become alcoholics. Late-onset alcoholics, or reactive program drinkers, are prime targets for secondary prevention efforts. These older adults need to be identified early and referred for treatment where the goal is lasting cure. The major barrier to successful secondary prevention efforts is what Mishara calls the "tardive referral syndrome," or refusing to seek help until it is almost too late. Denial on the part of older alcoholics and their family members and caregivers is a major reason treatment is not sought earlier. Another reason intervention does not occur earlier is that older adults and their caregivers, as well as physicians and other service providers, fail to recognize the warning signs of alcoholism in older alcoholics. Education and early case identification and active outreach are essential elements of secondary prevention.

106   Mishara, B. L., & Kastenbaum, M. R. (1980). Alcohol and old age. NY: Grune & Stratton, Inc.

This book brings together existing knowledge about alcohol and age. Chapters address epidemiology, physiological effects, types of older alcoholics, methods of treatment and review of existing data. Chapter One presents a historical overview of alcohol and age. Alcohol was used by Babylonians, Egyptians, Romans, Greeks and others for religious, ceremonial and/or medicinal purposes. References to the positive uses of alcohol are made in the Bible. The authors suggest that the widespread abuse of alcohol is a recent phenomenon. Chapter Two discusses various physiological effects of alcohol including: depressant effects on the central nervous system, effects on sleep pattern, effects on nutrition, and cardiovascular effects. Chapter Three reviews prevalence studies of alcohol consumption in old age. Epidemiological studies are reviewed. These studies reveal that the elderly drink less than younger people.

Chapter Four focuses on problem drinking. Studies are reviewed on problem drinking in the elderly who are in institutions and treatment programs. In these settings there are several older problem drinkers. Early-onset and late-onset drinkers are compared. Early-onset drinkers have a long standing history of alcohol abuse, whereas late-onset drinkers began drinking late in life. Several factors contributing to problem drinking in late life are highlighted, including the nature of the family system, health difficulties, and depression. A large body of empirical literature is reviewed in this chapter. Treatment is the focus in Chapter Five. Outcome studies are reviewed, and the conclusion is that treatment is as successful for the old as for the young. Two treatment models exist: the medical model and the socio-cultural model. Literature is reviewed on drug treatment, outpatient psychotherapy, Alcoholics Anonymous, and inpatient treatment.

Chapter Six discusses alcohol and health. Alcoholic elders show a higher level of CNS impairment, lower levels of psychosocial functioning, and higher mortality than do non-alcoholic elders. Moderate use of alcohol, however, like other drugs if used in proper dosages, may have beneficial effects on the health of older adults. It is an appetite stimulant, relaxes people, and aids in digestion. Chapter Seven continues the discussion of the positive effects of alcohol for older people as a stimulant to socializing and social activity and a way to encourage group cohesion, particularly among nursing home residents. Chapter Seven includes detailed tables presenting the results of a number of empirical studies conducted in nursing homes and other institutions.

The last chapter presents results of the authors' own research on elderly living in the community. Based on their research they found that using wine in moderate to low doses heightened zest, raised morale, increased energy level, and improved cognitive and psychosocial functioning.

107   Mittelman, A. P. (1985). Re-entry house and other dispositional alternatives for the aging alcoholic. In E. Gottheil, K. A. Druley, T. E. Skoloda, & H. M. Waxman (Eds.), The combined problems of alcoholism, drug addiction, and aging (pp. 330-335). Springfield, IL: Charles C. Thomas.

In this chapter Re-Entry House is discussed as a treatment facility for older veterans. Re-Entry House is a 64-bed unit, staffed by two social workers, a psychologist, nurses, and other personnel from various services. The facility serves about 300 veterans a year. Approximately 70 to 80% are substance abusers. Many are elderly. The Re-Entry House Program is a 90-day program of structured treatment and discharge planning designed to provide support and counseling. The veteran is encouraged to engage in productive activities that will reinforce a sense of achievement and self-worth. This is accomplished utilizing rehabilitative medical services, social work services, vocational counseling, nursing services, and individual and group therapy.

Options for dispositional planning for the aging alcoholic include: residential care homes, nursing homes, halfway houses, and

VA state domiciliaries. One alternative often recommended is the Residential Care Home and a Day Treatment Program. The most utilized option is domiciliary placement.

108   Parsons, O. A., & Leber, W. R. (1982). Premature aging, alcoholism, and recovery. In W. G. Wood & M. F. Elias (Eds.), Alcoholism and aging advances in research (pp. 79-92). Boca Raton, FL: CRC Press.

In this chapter Parsons and Leber present results of their own empirical studies over the last decades, and briefly review other empirical studies which test the premature aging hypothesis. This hypothesis suggests that alcoholism hastens and accentuates the aging process. In summarizing their work for the last decade the researchers conclude that they have found consistent evidence for age by alcoholism interaction in performance on a variety of intelligence, problem-solving, and other neuropsychological tests in male alcoholics but only sporadic effects for duration of alcoholism effects. Based on a review of existing empirical research and results of their own study with 35 recovered female alcoholics and a matched control group, the researchers found that on some tests recovered alcoholics did better than alcoholics, but they were still significantly lower than controls. Parsons and Leber call for more studies of recovery of function in alcoholics. They conclude that while the premature aging hypothesis is not entirely supported in empirical research, older alcoholics do perform more poorly relative to peer nonalcoholics than do younger alcoholics; however "the questions as to whether alcoholism results in cumulative changes in the brain or whether the aging brain is differentially sensitive to alcoholism or whether both effects are present remains to be answered" (p.91).

109   Petersen, D. M., & Whittington, F. J. (1987). Drug use among the elderly: A review. In C. D. Chambers, J. A. Inciardi, D. M. Petersen, H. A. Siegal, & O. Z. White (Eds.), Chemical dependencies: Patterns costs, and consequences (pp. 127-151). Athens, OH: University Press.

This chapter presents a review and summation of the relevant literature and available research evidence on drug use and misuse among the elderly (including alcohol). Several studies on the nature and extent of alcohol use and public intoxication among different age groups are reviewed. Based on studies reviewed, the conclusion is that drinking decreases with age. A summary of findings from all studies is presented in table form, so methodology and findings from each can be easily compared. The literature on types of older alcoholics is reviewed. The literature on the use of alcohol as a social stimulant for the elderly is reviewed.

Drug use and misuse are considered in the second part of the chapter. Literature is reviewed on the use and misuse of legal drugs, as well as with the abuse of illegal drugs. Misuse of legal drugs is a much more serious problem than is abuse of illegal drugs. Abuse of illegal drugs is growing, however. The authors conclude by stressing the need for more research in order to increase our basic knowledge about the population of older alcoholics and addicts and the best ways to treat them.

110   Pinsker, H. (1985). Outpatient treatment of older alcoholics. In E. Gottheil, K. A. Druley, T. E. Skoloda, & H. M. Waxman (Eds.), The combined problems of alcoholism, drug addiction, and aging (pp. 278-283). Springfield, IL: Charles C. Thomas.

This chapter describes the Beth Israel Medical Center Alcoholism Treatment Program's Outpatient Clinic. A club was organized called the 55+ Club. The focus was on activity and socialization. Refreshments were served at meetings and sometimes trips were taken. The club was not successful. Members avoided discussion of problems of aging and never spoke of their feelings.

111   Rathbone-McCuan, E. (1982). Health and social intervention issues with the older alcoholic and alcohol abuser. In W. G. Wood & M. F. Elias (Eds.), Alcoholism and aging advances in research (pp. 29-43). Boca Raton, FL: CRC Press.

The focus of this chapter is the assessment and treatment of older alcoholics and alcohol abusers. The author suggests that older alcoholics are easier to treat than their younger counterparts; socialization-oriented treatment may be the most important component for older adults; and counseling, education, and self-help are effective with older alcoholics. She suggests that ageist practitioners are erroneous in their thinking that older alcoholics can not be effectively treated. The first step in treatment is assessment. In addition to determining quality and frequency of alcohol consumption, assessment of the following should also be made: physical illness, sexual functioning, and mental illness.

In the second part of the chapter treatment is discussed. The emphasis is on immediate and long-term outcomes of the intervention. The author concludes with recommendations for future research and training in the areas of: (1) case identification techniques; (2) interviewing skills; (3) community education skills; and (4) environmental modifications techniques.

112   Rathbone-McCuan, E. (1988). Group intervention for alcohol-related problems among the elderly and their families. In B. W. MacLennan, S. Saul & M. B. Weiner (Eds.), Group psychotherapies for the elderly (pp. 139-148). Madison, CT: International Universities Press.

The author introduces us to group therapy for older alcoholic adults by first discussing the bilateral theory of aging and alcoholism, known as early- and late-onset, and then talking about nine myths concerning alcoholism among the elderly. She writes that the debates continue as to the nature and treatment of alcoholism, and cites the efforts of the governor of Michigan (1977) to appoint a Citizen Task Force on Seniors and Substance Abuse whose work then leads to a series of co-sponsored formal demonstration projects. These projects were successful because they "attempted to introduce cooperation among aging and alcoholic source administrators" and the combination of the two groups are what the authors feels is the key to an effective elderly alcoholic program. Besides the two agencies working together, Rathbone-McCuan notes that a comprehensive adult care program combines systematically organized inpatient and outpatient services. AA groups are another source that older alcoholics benefit from.

The author maintains that there are any number of positive group interventions for the older alcoholic, although no one treatment has been widely accepted. She suggests three sets of goals according to Glassman and Wright (1983): therapy-in-the-group, therapy-with-the-group, and membership-in-the-group whose use should match "the interactional capabilities" of the elderly members in order to be most effective. The article then stresses the importance of group intervention to be reality-directed and emphasizes the studies of Dunlop, Skorney and Hamilton (1982), particularly for using family-directed intervention in elderly alcoholism treatment. Closing remarks again focus on the need for administrators from both gerontology and alcohol-related agencies to work closer together in order to better deal with elderly alcoholics.

113   Rathbone-McCuan, E., & Hashimi, J. (1982). Isolated elders: Health and social intervention (pp. 211-236). Rockville, MD: Aspen Systems.

In this overview chapter on elder alcohol abuse, a brief review of literature on geriatric alcoholism is provided. Prevalence figures are presented and methodological problems of epidemiological studies conducted are discussed. The concept of isolation is defined and several isolating factors which promote increased drinking in elders are highlighted. These factors include retirement, loss of social relationships and accompanying loneliness, and the increased awareness of death. Stress, depression, and the labeling process are discussed in relation to elder alcohol abuse and mental health. Two case studies are presented to illustrate the relationship of various factors contributing to elder alcoholism. Depression is discussed in some detail, and eleven major signs and symptoms of depression are listed.

The second half of the chapter focuses on assessment and treatment. The role of the physician in assessment is discussed. The need to assess functional status of older adults is emphasized. The authors offer suggestions on how to establish an effective outreach program to find vulnerable elders. They discuss multiple treatment modalities including Alcoholics Anonymous and other support groups, socialization therapy, aversion therapy, family therapy, and education. Health components to include in an effective alcoholism program are regular health status screening, physical and occupational rehabilitation, linkages to nursing homes, nutrition and pharmacy input. Social components in an effective program are involvement in AA and other self help groups, intensive case management, community involvement, and leisure/interest counseling.

114   Robins, L. N. (1983). Introduction to the ECA project as a source of epidemiological data on alcohol problems. In G. Maddox, L. Robins, & N. Rosenberg (Eds.), Nature and extent of alcohol problems among the elderly (Vol. 14, pp. 201-216). Rockville: USDHHS.

This article is part of the proceedings of a National Institute on Alcohol Abuse and Alcoholism (NIAAA), National Institute on Aging (NIA), National Institute for Mental Health (NIMH) sponsored state-of-the-art workshop which took place in 1983 at the Alcohol Research Center at Washington University. The major focus of this paper is to explain the utility of the NIMH Epidemiological Catchment Area (ECA) program, which was a multi-site community survey providing diagnostic assessment of many psychiatric disorders. One intriguing finding was that alcohol abuse or dependence was the most common diagnosis for men at every site; for women it was the fifth most common diagnosis. Also the elderly had the lowest rate ranging from 4-8% "at some time in their lives." Another component of this paper is the inclusion of a history of surveys and results in this area, with an added discussion of methodological problems throughout.

115   Ruben, D. H. (1992). The elderly and alcohol and medication abuse. In C. E. Stout, J. L. Levitt, & D. H. Ruben (Eds.), Handbook for assessing and treating addictive disorders (pp. 215-235). Westport, CT: Greenwood Press.

This chapter overviews etiology and treatment of elderly

alcoholism and medication (drug) abuse. In the introductory sections, Ruben looks at the addictive properties of alcohol, drinking as a moral issue, and lack of knowledge and myths about alcohol and alcoholism in older people.

In the next section common problems and patterns of prescription drugs are discussed including overuse, underuse, improper prescribing practices, lack of medication monitoring, and 10 common myths about generic and brand name drugs.

The common causes of alcohol and drug abuse are the focus of the next section. Bereavement, family relations, retirement, relocation, and physician mistakes are highlighted.

The last part of the chapter deals with prevention. Primary and secondary prevention are defined and discussed. Some of Ruben's suggestions for primary prevention include: training workshops focusing on elderly clients; workshops for health care professionals on issues related to alcoholism, drug abuse, and aging; programs and literature aimed at seniors; clearly spelled out geriatric dosages on medicine labels; local or national pharmacy hot lines for questions on drugs and drug information; and providing meaningful roles and activities for older people. Recommendations for secondary prevention include behavioral pharmacology and behavioral psychotherapy.

116   Ryan, C., & Butters, N. (1984). Alcohol consumption and premature aging: A critical review. In M. Galanter (Ed.), Recent developments in alcoholism (Vol. 2, pp. 223-250). New York: Plenum Press.

This chapter reviews a decade of empirical research to examine the premature-aging hypothesis, which posits that alcohol abuse causes a premature aging of the brain. Various studies are reviewed. These include: geropsychological, computerized-tomography, and evoked potential studies. The authors point out serious methodological flaws in many early studies, which claimed to support the premature-aging hypothesis. They present evidence from more sophisticated recent studies which do not support the hypothesis. Based upon their extensive review and critique of existing empirical evidence, Ryan and Butters conclude that alcohol abuse does not cause premature aging. However, excessive consumption of alcohol will produce changes within the brain that mimic those changes in the brain associated with aging and seen in non-alcoholic elderly persons.

117   Sherouse, D. L. (1983). Professional's handbooks on geriatric alcoholism. Springfield, IL: Charles C. Thomas.

This handbook covers major areas of treatment, assessment, and recovery in geriatric alcoholism. In the first chapter, Sherouse offers a demographic overview of aging and discusses age-related issues. She focuses in detail on age-related changes in the skin, musculoskeletal system, digestive system, endocrine system, and reproductive system. Chapter two discusses myths and facts about alcohol. An alcohol equivalency chart, chart of blood alcohol concentration levels (BALs), a chart indicating the stages of the disease, and other reference aids are included. The disease concept is presented in chapter three. Chapter four deals with assessment. A self-report questionnaire published in Florida is presented. Diagnostic tips such as the following are offered: ask direct, open-ended questions; accept the person as he/she is; and be aware of denial.

In the next chapter, the author addresses the negative effects of alcohol on each body system and suggests how to manage withdrawal with appropriate drugs. She provides a detailed table of products containing alcohol such as cough syrups, anti-diarrheal agents, and laxatives. A cumulative loss questionnaire is provided to assess loss. Depression is another factor discussed. Symptoms of depression are outlined. Chapter Seven highlights the serious problem of polydrug use, mixing drugs and/or alcohol and drugs. The final chapters all address treatment, emphasizing individual and group psychotherapy; AA and other support self-help groups; family therapy; and nutrition and exercise.

118   Smart, R. G., & Liban, C. B. (1982). Predictors of problem drinking among elderly, middle-aged and youthful drinkers. In D. M. Peterson & F. J. Whittington (Eds.), Drugs, alcohol and aging (pp. 43-53). Dubuque, Iowa: Kendall/Hunt.

For this study a household survey of the adult population aged 18 years and over was conducted in Durham, Ontario. Interviews were conducted with 1,103 individuals in 1,480 households. The questionnaire included 133 items on demographics, drinking patterns, alcohol-related problems, and other areas. Respondents were asked whether or not they had experienced 14 drinking symptoms indicative of alcohol abuse or alcoholism. A dependency symptom score was calculated for each respondent. Three groups were compared: Young (18-25); Middle-aged (26-39); and Old (60+).

Dummy variable multiple regression analyses were conducted separately for each age group to: (1) predict the probability of dependency and problem symptoms from background variables; (2) identify the most important variables; and (3) identify the unique contribution of each variable to the prediction. Some of the results are: (1) the probability of experiencing at least one alcohol dependency symptom in the prior year was negatively related to age; those least likely to experience such a symptom were 60 years of age and older;

(2) the most important variable in predicting the probability of dependency symptoms for the young and the middle-aged was volume of consumption, but for the old (60+) was frequency of consumption; (3) the probability of experiencing one or more alcohol problem symptoms in the prior year decreased with age; and (4) for those 60 and older the most important predictor of alcohol problem symptoms was birthplace. The elderly problem drinker was most likely to be male, from outside Canada, in the lower income and socioeconomic groups, and drinking several times a week, but not in particularly large quantities.

119   Stirling, J. M., Largen, J. W., Jr., Shaw, T., Mortel, K. F., &
       Rogers, R. (1984). Interactions of normal aging, senile
       dementia, multi-infarct dementia, and alcoholism in the
       elderly. In J. T. Hartford & T. Samorajski (Eds.),
       Alcoholism in the elderly: Social and biomedical issues (Vol.
       25, pp. 227-251). New York: Raven Press.

       The authors summarize studies of both age- and alcohol-related declines in brain morphology and histology, neurotransmitter function, neuro-psychological function, and regional cerebral blood flow (rCBF). Brief discussions of patterns of impairments seen in various types of dementia (DAT, multi-infarct, and Wernicke-Korsakoff's) are also included. Some emphasis is placed on rCBF. CBF declines in normal aging because of neuronal cell death accompanied by reduced metabolic demand, and because of rigidity of cerebral vessels due to atherosclerosis. Studies reviewed suggest that normal reductions in rCBF with advancing age are more pronounced in chronic alcoholics. In one study of normal aged volunteers and Korsakoff's patients, resting rCBF was found to correlate negatively with daily alcohol consumption. Although the lowest mean rCBF values were found for the Korsakoff's patients, the authors note that even mild consumption of alcohol in normal subjects was associated with slight rCBF declines. The effect was exacerbated in subjects with risk factors for atherosclerosis. The chapter concludes by calling for more research to clarify the interactions between effects of aging and the direct and indirect effects of chronic alcohol use.

120   Straus, R. (1984). Alcohol problems among the elderly: The need for
       a biobehavioral perspective. In G. Maddox, L. Robins, & N.
       Rosenberg (Eds.), Nature and extent of alcohol problems
       among the elderly (Vol. 14, pp. 9-28). Rockville: USDHHS.

       This article is part of the proceedings of a National Institute on Alcohol Abuse and Alcoholism (NIAAA), National Institute on Aging (NIA), National Institute for Mental Health (NIMH) sponsored state-of-the-art workshop which took place in 1983 at the Alcohol Research Center at Washington University. This article provides a historical overview of alcoholism and aging research during the preceding 40 years. Some of the topics reviewed are the changes in alcohol consumption, changes in causes of intoxication, and changing liabilities of alcohol misuse. The article ends with a suggested classification for alcohol problems and a look at some questions which need to be answered about alcohol and aging; the author includes nine major research areas where intriguing questions exist. It is interesting to note that nearly one decade later many, if not most, of these questions still go unanswered.

121   Weiss, K. M. (1984). The evolutionary basis of alcoholism: A question of the neocortex. In J. T. Hartford & T. Samorajski (Eds.), Alcoholism in the elderly: Social and biomedical issues (Vol. 25, pp. 5-23). New York: Raven Press.

Weiss reviews existing literature on why people drink from the biological and evolutionary perspectives. More specifically, the following questions are addressed: (1) are there genes whose expression is related to the trait; (2) are these genes manifest in the individuals who carry them, and can we specify which individuals carry them; and (3) are the genes expressed in the normal natural history of the animals bearing them?

After briefly reviewing animal studies, which demonstrate that most animals avoid drinking alcohol and prefer to drink water, and studies of twins and adoptees, which show genetic variation in alcoholism, the author suggests that a great deal of this previous work is wholly irrelevant to the problem of evolutionary explanation.

In the final part of the chapter the author emphasizes that human beings are the only animals who choose to drink alcohol and to compromise their alertness and possibly place themselves in a dangerous position. Weiss suggests that humans are the only animals who use symbols, a result of the brain's evolution. In the world of symbols, alcohol can produce courage, relieve anxiety, and enhance social functioning. Weiss concludes that drinking is a cultural and social phenomenon. He argues for the general irrelevance of genes related to animal alcohol use and to human physiological response to alcohol.

122   Westermeyer, J. (1984). Cross-cultural aspects of alcoholism in the elderly. In M. Galanter (Ed.), Recent developments in alcoholism (Vol. 2, pp. 289-299). New York: Plenum Press.

This chapter explores available data on alcoholism among the elderly across cultures. Cross-cultural studies provide an opportunity to determine universal aspects of alcoholism in the aging, and to identify aspects of alcoholism that can be modified or exacerbated by social and cultural influences. Existing knowledge on three areas is reviewed: aging and culture, alcoholism and culture, and aging and alcoholism.

Studies on aging and culture reveal that traditional societies with few elderly people assign high status to the old. By contrast, in modern industrialized societies aging and the old are seen in negative terms and held in low esteem. Cultural norms about alcohol use and abuse also vary from one culture to another. For example, in many Asian societies opium smoking is condoned for elders and condemned for youth. Some cultures approve alcohol use only in a social context such as at rituals or ceremonies. Literature on aging and alcoholism suggests that alcohol has negative physiological effects and that these effects are exaggerated in the old. These effects should not vary by culture.

The chapter concludes that the cultural universals are: (1) elderly people encounter alcohol-related problems at lower doses than do younger people; (2) falls, burns, alcoholic dementias, and exacerbations of medical conditions are frequent manifestations of alcoholism in the elderly; and (3) elderly alcoholics are more often found in cities than in rural areas. Certain other factors vary by culture. These include: social status and role of the elderly, ability of family or other social groups to alter or disrupt drinking patterns, and integration or isolation of the widowed, among others.

123   Whittington, F. J. (1984). Addicts and alcoholics. In E. Palmore (Ed.), Handbook on the aged in the United States (pp. 279-294). Westport, CT: Greenwood Press.

This chapter summarizes existing knowledge on older drug addicts and alcoholics. Addicts abuse illegal substances or legal substances illegally obtained. The size of the addict population is growing. Most attention in the chapter is devoted to alcoholics. Epidemiological studies are reviewed and prevalence figures are presented. Characteristics of older alcoholics are identified. More older alcoholics are male and widowed. Treatment literature is reviewed in the last section. Summarizing this literature, there seems to be agreement that various social therapies and family involvement are effective.

124   Wilkinson, D. A., & Carlen, P. L. (1982). Morphological abnormalities in the brain of alcoholics: Relationship to age, psychological test scores and patient type. In W.G. Wood &

M.F. Elias (Eds.), <u>Alcoholism and aging advances in research</u> (pp. 61-77). Boca Raton, FL: CRC Press.

This chapter concerns the relationship between age, brain morphology, and psychological test performance in chronic alcoholics. An evaluation was made of the premature aging hypothesis, which posits that alcoholism results in premature aging of the brain, and accounts for fundamental neuropsychological changes in alcoholics.

Study subjects were 93 chronic alcoholics (10 women and 83 men) who had been admitted to the hospital for treatment of their alcohol consumption, or associated medical problems. Subjects were required to have a reported mean ethanol intake in excess of 80 g/day for at least 10 years. A comparison group of 154 subjects (90 men and 64 women) were patients of the neuroradiology clinic of a local general hospital. All subjects received CT scans on the EMI head scanner (Model 1000/S) with a 160 x 160 matrix. Tomographic slices were 8 mm thick. For each subject the following scores were computed: the width of the lateral ventricles at the anterior horns (V1); the width of the lateral ventricles measured at the level of the caudate nucleus (V2); the width of the waist of the lateral ventricles (V3); and the traverse width of the eight largest visible sulci. All subjects were assessed psychometrically using the Wechsler Adult Intelligence Scale (WAIS), the Wechsler Memory Scale (WMS), and tests from the Halstead-Reitan Neuropsychological Test Battery (HRB).

Scores of alcoholics and controls were compared using analysis of covariance with age as a covariate. T-test comparisons between experimentals (chronic alcoholics) and controls revealed marked morphological changes in the brain among alcoholics. Correlational analyses confirmed that neuropsychological tests scores from the HRB were significantly correlated with morphological scores computed derived from the CT scan. Two groups of alcoholics were identified: Wernicke/Amnesic Group (WA) and Other Alcoholics (OA); and the two groups were compared on all measures. Analyses revealed that the two alcoholic groups differed in respect to the age-relatedness of their morphological scores. Morphological scores for the WA group were not related significantly to age as they were in the OA group. This finding suggests that the premature aging hypothesis may be appropriate for the OA group, but not for the WA group. Further analyses revealed significant correlations of test performance on neurological tests with both age and brain morphology for both the WA group and the OA group. In the OA group when age is eliminated the correlations of performance with morphology are eliminated. The converse (morphology controlled) does not hold. In the WA group statistical control of age or morphology does not affect degree of correlation. The authors conclude that alcoholics (OA) show a pattern of impairment consistent with the hypothesis of premature aging.

125   Wood, W. G. (1985). Mechanisms underlying age-related differences
         in response to ethanol. In E. Gottheil, K. A. Druley, T. E.
         Skolada, & H. M. Waxman (Eds.), The combined problems
         of alcoholism, drug addiction and aging (pp.94-109).
         Springfield, IL: Charles C. Thomas.
         Wood examines three possible mechanisms of age-related
increases in alcohol sensitivity by summarizing animal studies in this
area. The chapter opens with a brief review of the increased effects of
both acute and chronic ethanol administration on aged mice and rats,
including more severe signs of intoxication and withdrawal, and
declines in locomotor performance and acetylcholinesterase (Chat)
activity. The remainder of the chapter is devoted to a discussion of
each of the three mechanisms: age-related changes in metabolism of
ethanol, body composition and brain sensitivity. Some brief evidence
is provided for the conclusion that rate of liver metabolism and
clearance of ethanol are decreased in aged animals, while rate of
elimination is similar across age groups. Two studies in favor of the
body water hypothesis are highlighted. According to this theory, age-
related increase in ethanol sensitivity is due to decreases in percentage
of body water to body weight in aged animals. Wood goes on to note,
however, that correction of dose administration for differences in
percentage of body water does not alleviate observed differences in
behavior. For example, aged mice lose the righting response at lower
brain and blood alcohol levels than younger mice. The chapter
concludes with complex and inconclusive evidence for age differences
in brain sensitivity to ethanol. A study by the author and his colleagues
suggests less alteration of synaptic membrane fluidity upon in vitro
ethanol exposure in aged animals as opposed to younger animals. This
appears to conflict with the observation of greater in vivo sensitivity
of aged animals.   Other studies indicate greater ethanol-induced
inhibition of $Na+K+$ ATPase activity in synaptic plasma membranes
in aged versus young animals.

126   Wood, W. G. (1987). Alcoholism. In G. L. Maddox (Ed.) The
         encyclopedia of aging (pp. 25-27). New York: Springer.
         The author comments on the increased attention devoted to
aging and alcoholism in recent years, and cites evidence both for and
against the view that alcoholism is a significant health problem in the
elderly. A brief but detailed review of animal studies of the differential
effects of alcohol on young versus aged organisms is provided. In
particular, Wood refers to several studies that demonstrate greater
ethanol-induced membrane fluidity and cellular tolerance (mediated

through depolarized release of gamma-aminobutyric acid, or GABA) in young animals as opposed to aged animals. It is suggested that older adults may be more susceptible to alcohol-induced pathology, whether as a result of social drinking or from chronic alcohol abuse.

127   Zimberg, S. (1984). Diagnosis and management of the elderly alcoholic. In R. M. Atkinson (Ed.), <u>Alcohol and drug abuse in old age</u> (pp. 24-31). Washington, DC: American Psychiatric Press, Inc.

Zimberg presents his own Scale of Alcohol Abuse Severity and cautions that older problem drinkers typically exhibit more subtle manifestations of alcoholism than their younger counterparts. Based on experience treating patients in both outpatient and inpatient settings, the author recommends group therapy, family casework, and regular medical follow-up for older alcoholics. An emphasis is placed on targeting the stresses associated with aging.

128   Zimberg, S. (1987). Alcohol abuse among the elderly. In L. L. Carstensen & B. A. Edelstein (Eds.), <u>Handbook of clinical gerontology</u> (pp. 57-65). New York: Pergamon Press.

The author of this chapter takes us through seven sections of identification, treatment and the prevention of alcohol abuse in the elderly. Zimberg begins by identifying numerous studies that point to the serious problem of elderly alcohol abuse. The next step is a discussion of the classification of elderly alcohol abusers between the late-onset problem drinkers and the early-onset, adding a new classification of late-onset exacerbation. The third section discusses methods of diagnosing alcohol abuse which includes a scale for measuring abuse ranging in severity from none to extreme. What follows then are the psychosocial factors that contribute to alcohol abuse, including depression, bereavement, retirement, loneliness, marital stress and physical illness. The author hypothesizes that "the sociopsychological stresses of aging can prolong problem drinking in some elderly individuals." The next two sections deal with treatment techniques and Zimberg notes that based on personal experience, psychosocial group therapy is one of the most effective. However, the physician also plays an important role in reducing a variety of psychological problems in the elderly, including alcoholism, by showing interest in the emotional well-being of the elderly patient. The closing section of the chapter discusses prevention techniques, including the need for an effective network of services to assist the elderly through stressful times as an alternative to drinking. Also, Zimberg notes that health professionals need to be more willing to recognize and diagnose this problem within the elderly population.

Empirical Studies

129   Abel, E. L., & Zeidenberg, P. (1985). Age, alcohol and violent
       death: A postmortem study. Journal of Studies on Alcohol,
       46(3), 228-231.
              This article reports on the results of a retrospective analysis of
       all violent deaths reported in the files of the Medical Examiner
       occurring in Erie County, New York from January 1, 1973, to
       December 31, 1983. In each case a toxological examination of blood
       alcohol levels (BALs) and drug levels was performed. Denominator
       populations were derived from the 1980 U.S. Bureau of Census (1983)
       data. The main research question investigated was: what is the
       relationship between age, alcohol, and violent death.
              Alcohol was a factor in deaths from traffic accidents,
       homicides, and suicides. In 48.6% of the traffic accidents the victim
       had been drinking. In 45.2% of the homicides and 35.4% of the
       suicides the victim had been drinking. The percentage of victims
       drinking prior to death was negatively correlated with age, the highest
       involvement occurring among those aged 35-44 and the lowest among
       those 75 and older. The 15-24 age cohort experienced more accidents,
       homicides, and suicides than any other group. Alcohol contributed
       more to traffic accident deaths than to homicides or suicides.

130   Adams, S. L., & Waskel, S. A. (1991). Late onset of alcoholism
       among older midwestern men in treatment. Psychological
       Reports, 68(2), 432-434.
              This article is a very brief report on a study of sixty men
       ranging in age from 61 to 79 years. These men, all of whom were in
       alcoholism treatment centers, were administered a modified Veterans

Alcohol Screening Test to determine age of onset and the Stokes/Gordon Stress Scale to determine the presence of stressors. Data analysis revealed that only 11% met the criteria for late-onset. Many were intermittents, who developed more serious alcohol-related problems in late-life. The stress scores of early- and late-onset drinkers were not significantly different. The authors suggest that we reassess the commonly held assumption that stress causes drinking problems in the elderly.

131   Adams, W. L., Magruder-Habib, K., Trued, S., & Broome, H. L. (1992). Alcohol abuse in elderly emergency department patients. Journal of the American Geriatrics Society, 40(12), 1236-1240.

The cross-sectional prevalence study reported in this article had three objectives: to determine the (1) prevalence of alcohol abuse in elderly emergency department (ED) patients; (2) prevalence of alcohol abuse for various categories of illness and injury among elderly ED patients; and (3) frequency with which physicians in the ED detect alcohol abuse in elderly patients.

Interviews were conducted with persons 65 and older who came to the University of North Carolina Hospital ED in 1990. The following information was collected: quantity of alcohol consumed in the last 24 hours; usual drinking practices including quantity, frequency, and setting; the CAGE Questionnaire; self-report of a past or current "drinking problem;" current medications and medical illnesses; the physical function scale from the Beth/Israel UCLA Functional Status Questionnaire; and the Short Portable Mental Status Questionnaire from the Older Americans Research and Service Center Instrument (OARS). Emergency department records were also reviewed to extract data on blood alcohol levels, medical conditions, demographics, and physician's recording of alcohol problems in all patients 65 and over.

Four criteria were used to identify alcohol abusers and non-abusers: CAGE score, self- report of drinking problems, frequency of drinking in the last six months, and time since last drink.

The final sample consisted of 205 patients 65 and over, 146 of whom could be classified as alcohol abusers or non-abusers. Of these 14% (29 people) were identified as "current alcohol abusers." One hundred seventeen (57%) were classified as "non-abusers." Alcohol abusers were slightly younger than non-abusers, and were more likely to be male (88% versus 37%). The prevalence of lifetime alcohol abuse was 24%. The prevalence of current alcohol abuse was 14%. In the bivariate analysis, alcohol abusers had significantly higher scores on the physical function scale of the Beth/Israel Functional Status

Questionnaire than non-drinkers. Findings revealed high prevalence of alcohol abuse among patients who presented with abdominal problems and low prevalence among trauma patients. Of the 29 alcohol abusers identified by study criteria, physicians correctly identified six (21%).

Authors conclude that "alcohol abuse is a prevalent and important problem among elderly ED patients."

132 Adams, W. L., Yuan, Z., Barboriak, J. J., & Rimm, A. A. (1993). Alcohol-related hospitalizations of elderly people: Prevalence and geographical variation in the United States. Journal of the American Medical Association, 270(10), 1222-1225.

This article is a study to determine the prevalence, geographic variation, and charges to Medicare of alcohol-related hospitalizations among elderly people in the United States. The authors were interested in replicating the findings of the National Hospital Discharge Survey, which found a rate of 65.1 per 10,000 population of alcohol-related diagnoses among hospitalized elderly people. Data were used from the Health Care Financing Administration (HCFA), which maintains a computerized database of all hospital discharges for persons covered by Part A of the Medicare program. Approximately 96% of all those 65 and older in the U.S. are covered by Part A. To test the validity of the data, the authors obtained hospital-compiled discharge diagnoses for all patients 65 years or older admitted to a local teaching hospital in Milwaukee for a 6-month period in 1989.

Results of the study indicate that alcohol-related problems are an issue in the older population: 87,147 elderly Medicare adults, or 1.1% of all hospitalizations in this age group, were hospitalized for alcohol-related problems in 1989. In 33,039 (38%) of these cases an alcohol-related diagnosis was the primary diagnosis listed. Alcohol dependence was the diagnosis most frequently listed, and alcohol liver disease was the most common alcohol-related medical problem. For admissions where the primary diagnosis was alcohol related, the total hospital-associated charges to Medicare were $233,543,500. Median charge per hospitalization was $4,514. There was considerable geographic variation whereby the prevalence ranged by state from 18.9 to 77.0 per 10,000 population. However, the prevalence range by state of hospitalizations for myocardial infarction was slightly lower at 16.9 to 44.1 per 10,000. The authors note that alcohol-related problems in this population have been underaddressed, particularly as there is a higher hospitalization rate for alcohol-related problems than there is for myocardial infarction, which is widely accepted as an important health problem.

133   Alexander, F., & Duff, R. W. (1988). Social interaction and alcohol
use in retirement communities. The Gerontologist, 28(5),
632-636.

The article focuses on alcohol abuse in retirement
communities. A systematic random sample of residents in three
suburban communities was drawn. Two communities were in Southern
California, and one was in Oregon. All residents were middle-class
(N=260). The interview schedule consisted of 143 items covering
demographic characteristics, living arrangements, perceived health, life
satisfaction, patterns and history of alcohol use, attitudes toward
drinking, and perceptions of alcohol use in the community.

Analysis of data revealed that drinking in these communities
was substantially more prevalent than for the rest of the senior
American population. The retirement communities had fewer non-
drinkers than were found in the general community. A relationship
was found between level of drinking and level of social interaction.
Those who were more socially active drank more.

134   Atkinson, R. M., Tolson, R. L., & Turner, J. A. (1990). Late
versus early onset problem drinking in older men.
Alcoholism: Clinical and Experimental Research, 14(4), 574-
579.

This study reports the findings of a research study comparing
early- and late-onset alcoholics. Researchers studied age at onset of
problem drinking in 132 older men (60 and older) admitted to a VA
geriatric alcoholism outpatient treatment program. Age of onset was
determined by asking respondents the earliest age at which they
developed either a social, occupational, or legal problem caused by or
made worse by alcohol. Using this criteria, half of the subjects
developed a problem after age 45. Based on responses, researchers
grouped subjects into three categories: early-onset (at or before age
40, N=50); midlife onset (41 to 59, N=62); and late-onset (at or after
60 years, N=20). Late-onset occurred in 15% of the sample; midlife
onset occurred in 47% of the sample; and early-onset occurred in 38%
of the sample.

Researchers examined the relationship of onset to seven
alcohol-related patient variables, 19 nonalcohol-related patient
variables, and six treatment and treatment compliance variables.
Patient information was collected through structured interviews and
MMPI testing conducted by program counselors. Treatment data were
collected longitudinally. MMPI scales included the three validity or
response tendency scales (L, F, and K), and the standard clinical scales
for hypochondriases, depression, hysteria, psychopathic deviate,
passivity-sensitivity or masculine-feminine, paranoia, anxiety or

psychasthenia, schizophrenia, mania, and social introversion.

In the statistical analysis age of onset was used both as a continuous variable and as a trichotomous variable. The proportion of statistically significant findings in both cases far exceeds chance. Results from analysis of variance revealed that late-onset alcoholism is a milder, more circumscribed disorder than midlife or early-onset alcoholism. Family alcoholism was less common with later-onset. Many of the MMPI scale scores were also lower with later-onset, suggesting secondary, rather than primary alcoholism in later-onset cases. Most (90%) of the later-onset cases were not referred by family or physicians, but rather came to treatment as court supervised drinking drivers. Findings from the analysis of variance also showed that late-onset drinkers had a greater likelihood of completing the 12-month outpatient program and also attended weekly group meetings much more frequently than did early-onset drinkers. Using multiple regression analysis, the researchers did find, however, that special treatment variables such as court supervision, and spouse counseling outperformed all patient variables in predicting completion of outpatient treatment and documented drinking relapses.

135   Atkinson, R. M., Tolson, R. L., & Turner, J. A. (1993). Factors affecting outpatient treatment compliance of older male problem drinkers. Journal of Studies on Alcohol, 54(1), 102-106.

The aim of this study was to identify predictors of outpatient treatment compliance in a group of older male problem drinkers. Two hundred five male military veterans age $\geq$ 55, who had DSM-III alcohol use disorders, agreed to abstain from alcohol and participate in weekly outpatient groups for 12 months. Fifteen patients either died, transferred, or had incomplete data leaving 190 cases for the study. Treatment compliance was measured by the dichotomous variable of completion of the one-year program versus irregular discharge (non-completion), and by a continuous variable of rate of attendance at group meetings. Abstention from alcohol was measured by the dichotomous variable of one or more documented drinking episodes (relapses) during treatment versus none. Program variables such as referral source (courts [drinking drivers] versus other sources, i.e., self, family, friend, social agencies), and patient variables such as marital status, home ownership, depression (MMPI scale), and the number of prior alcohol-related arrests were also gathered. Program counselors collected data through structured interviews and MMPI testing. Breath analysis was used to check sobriety. Treatment data were collected longitudinally.

Results indicated that overall, 5% of the 190 patients

completed one year of treatment. One or more drinking relapses were documented in 27% of the patients. For completion of the program, the multiple regression analysis was significant. Step-wise multiple regression analysis produced a three-step solution in which referral source entered the equation first, followed by spouse participation in counseling and marital status. Court-supervised drinking drivers and patients whose spouse or mate entered counseling were more likely to complete treatment than others. Together these two variables accounted for 13.4% of the variance (adjusted R^2) in program completion. For attendance rate, the result of the multiple regression analysis was also significant. Stepwise regression analysis yielded a two-step solution in which age at onset of the first drinking problem entered first, followed by referral source. Late-onset problem drinkers and court-supervised drinking drivers attended group meetings more than the others. These two variables accounted for 10% of the variance (adjusted R^2) in attendance rate.

136   Atkinson, R. M., Turner, J. A., Kofoed, L. L., & Tolson, R. L. (1985). Early versus late onset alcoholism in older persons: Preliminary findings. Alcoholism: Clinical and Experimental Research, 9(6), 513-515.

Data comparing early-onset (EO) and late-onset (LO) older alcoholics is presented. Thirty-six older problem drinkers (ages 53-76 years) were evaluated for demographics, personal and family alcohol history, and results on the Minnesota Multiphasic Personality Inventory (MMPI) scales prior to entry into an outpatient geriatric alcohol treatment program. Age of onset of drinking was determined by clients' retrospective verbal reports. Fourteen clients reported experiencing problems with alcohol prior to age 40 (EO's); twenty-two experienced the first alcohol problem after age 40 (LO's).

EO's, as opposed to LO's, were significantly more likely to have experienced criminal-legal problems and to report family histories of alcoholism. In addition, EO's showed significant elevations on six of the 10 MMPI clinical scales, although the two groups did not differ significantly on the MMPI MacAndrew alcoholism scale. EO's and LO's were similar for the demographic variables marital status, sex, home ownership, and recent medical hospitalization. Follow-up monitoring of treatment compliance revealed high compliance rates in both groups (over 80% attendance rate with average duration of 9.3 months). The authors emphasize that older alcoholics of both subtypes can be successfully treated using a common social approach.

137   Barnes, G. M. (1979). Alcohol use among older persons: Findings
        from a western New York state general population survey.
        Journal of the American Geriatrics Society, 27(6), 244-250.

A stratified random sample (N = 1,041) of people 18 years and older living in Erie and Niagara counties in Western New York was drawn. Personal interviews were conducted to obtain extensive sociodemographic information and information on drinking history and patterns. Responses were used to establish a Quantity-Frequency-Variability (QFV) index of drinking behavior. Five categories of drinkers were derived: heavy, moderate, light, infrequent drinkers, and abstainers.

Findings revealed a lower proportion of heavy drinkers in the older age group. Heavy drinking was almost nonexistent among older females (1%). About a quarter of the males 60+ were heavy drinkers. About one-third of those 60+ were abstainers, compared to only 8% in the under 50 group and 13% in the 50-59 group. Older adults also reported significantly fewer alcohol-related problems, such as driving while drunk, in the previous year than did those 50 to 59 years of age or those under 50. In those 60 years and older married individuals were more often heavy drinkers (10%), not the widowed (3%). The retired also were less likely to be heavy drinkers (6%) than were those who were employed (12%). These findings do not support the contention that the stress of widowhood and retirement increases the likelihood of heavy drinking in late-life. As the author admits in the discussion section since these data are based on a cross-sectional study, the reported differences in drinking according to age groups may be a function of generational differences (i.e., today's older people drank less in their younger years than do younger people living in today's society). People may, on the other hand, decrease their drinking in later years as a result of health problems, limited financial resources, or changing social pressures. The data could reflect the fact that many heavy drinkers die before they reach age 60.

138   Bikle, D. D., Stesin, A., Halloran, B., Steinbach, L., & Recker, R.
        (1993). Alcohol-induced bone disease: Relationship to age
        and parathyroid hormone levels. Alcoholism: Clinical and
        Experimental Research, 17(3), 690-695.

To examine the interaction of age and alcohol abuse on bone mineral homeostasis, the researchers studied 27 Caucasian males in ambulatory care clinics and an inpatient alcohol unit of a VA, with a history of 10 or more years of alcohol abuse. Subjects ranged in age from 26-68 years. They were evaluated for disordered bone mineral homeostasis by assessing bone density (by quantitative computed tomography of the lumbar spine), histomorphometry of a transcortical biopsy from the iliac crest, serum levels of vitamin D metabolites and parathyroid hormone, and serum and urine levels of bone minerals.

The negative effects of alcohol on bone mineral homeostasis were greater in older subjects. Analyses revealed that the older the subject, the more likely he/she was to have a spinal compression fracture (17 of the 27 had such a fracture). Bone density fell sharply with age. Bone formation and active bone resorption did not correlate with parathyroid hormone levels, but correlated negatively with age. Younger alcoholics tended to have increased bone remodeling out of proportion to the normal decline with age. The researchers conclude that parathyroid hormone may play a role in stimulating bone resorption in younger alcoholics. With time the cumulative effects of alcohol abuse, however, result in reduced bone resorption and bone formation, regardless of the levels of parathyroid hormone. Older alcoholics, who have consumed alcohol over several years, are at increased risk for osteoporosis. Alcohol abuse leads to osteoporosis and fractures in older people.

139   Blankfield, A. (1989). Grief, alcohol dependence and women. Drug and Alcohol Dependence, 24(1), 45-49.

This Australian study examined differences in 37 widows versus 85 non-widows varying in age from 31 to 73 in an alcohol treatment unit. First, the widows reported excess drinking by their late spouses more frequently as compared to the non-widowed subjects. Also widows of alcoholics who had unresolved marital conflict or who were socially isolated showed more susceptibility to abnormal grief reactions. One age-related difference, which is just suggestive since the subject numbers were quite small, showed that 75% of widows under 55 began excess drinking prior to spouse's death, whereas 53% of the older group said they began heavy drinking after the death of spouse. This pilot study offers some interesting questions to be pursued more in-depth in further research.

140   Blum, L., & Rosner, F. (1983). Alcoholism in the elderly: An analysis of 50 patients. Journal of the National Medical Association, 75(5), 489-495.

This is a very early prevalence study from a Queens Alcoholism Clinic, reviewing data from 1974-1979. The study reports behavioral differences between younger and older drinkers during drinking bouts. Loss of appetite, hallucination, and sleeping difficulties were reported as more common in the younger alcoholic. The authors make the argument for the immediate need for doing further systematic research in this area.

141   Booth, B. M., Blow, F. C., Cook, C. A. L., Bunn, J. Y., & Fortney,
        J. C. (1992) Age and ethnicity among hospitalized
        alcoholics: A nationwide study. Alcoholism: Clinical and
        Experimental Research, 16(6), 1029-1034.

        The purpose of this study was to examine issues relative to
age, race/ethnicity, and marital status for alcoholic men in various
types of treatment programs. Data was collected on 62,829 alcoholic
men receiving treatment in VA medical centers between October 1,
1986 and September 30, 1987. The sample was derived from the
Patient Treatment File (PTF), the VA's national hospital discharge data
base. All patients had either a primary or secondary bedsection
diagnosis of alcohol dependence syndrome not coded as "in remission"
(ICD 9-CM codes 303.90, 303.91, or 303.92). Patients were classified
into one of three groups: (1) completed extended inpatient treatment;
(2) brief detoxification or short intervention; (3) no treatment. Chi-
square tests of independence between pairs of variables were used to
test for significant associations.

        Results of analyses revealed that older men were significantly
less likely to receive alcoholism-related services than younger men and
more likely to be hospitalized for primary diagnoses other than
alcoholism, i.e., be in the no treatment group. Two-thirds of men in
their 60's and almost 80% of those at least 70 were in the no treatment
group, compared with only 28.5% and 21% of men in their 30's and
less than 30, respectively. In contrast, two-thirds of alcoholics less
than 30 and just over half of those in their 30's were in the completed
treatment groups, compared with only a quarter of men in their 60's
and only 11.7% of those at least 70. Overall, there were relatively
fewer married men in the completed treatment group and more married
men in the no treatment group. Hispanics and African-Americans were
least likely to have completed treatment, followed by Caucasians.

        In their conclusions the researchers suggest, based on their
large-scale investigation, that older alcoholics and African-Americans
and Hispanics may not be receiving adequate alcoholism treatment
services. These groups should be targeted for such services, which
could reduce the need for later medical hospitalizations related to the
consequences of alcohol abuse.

142   Borgatta, E. F., Montgomery, R. J. V., & Borgatta, M. L. (1982).
        Alcohol use and abuse, life crisis events and the elderly.
        Research on Aging, 4(3), 378-408.

        This study examines the "life crisis events hypothesis" as the
cause for alcohol abuse in the elderly. This paper also carefully
scrutinizes the notion of the existence of Type I and Type II elderly
alcoholics and suggests that this typology is indeed not fact. They state,

"it appears that the belief in the late-onset alcoholism due to life stresses is a belief that has been advanced through repetitive citations of limited clinical research to the status of fact" (p. 386). The authors investigate this assumption using the NORC General Social Survey sample from 1978 and 1980. Of the many life events explored, the only one which had a relationship with drinking was unemployment. The authors caution the reader that this may simply mean that the lack of employment provided more time for drinking or that the drinking behavior may have lead to the unemployment. They conclude that there is little support for the perspective that life events cause late-life drinking. They do include an intriguing discussion on medical services utilization and expenditures among alcoholics.

143   Brennan, P. L., & Moos, R. H. (1990). Life stressors, social resources, and late-life problem drinking. Psychology and Aging, 5(4), 491-501.

This article discusses a research study that compares life stressors and social resources among late-middle-aged problem and non-problem drinkers. Several other major issues were investigated in this study including the differences in the stressors and social resources reported by late-life alcoholics and non-problem drinkers, the difference between stressors and social resources in late-life alcoholic men and women, the relationship between stressors and social resources and how they impact drinking behavior and functioning in the alcoholic and non-problem-drinking groups. The study looked at 501 current problem drinkers and 609 nonproblem drinkers between the ages of 55 and 65 who had recently been to one of two large medical centers.

The results revealed that problem-drinking men and women reported more negative life events and chronic stressors when dealing with home and neighborhood, finances, spouse and friends than did non-problem drinkers. Not surprisingly, problem drinkers also reported fewer social resources than nonproblem drinkers. Problem-drinking men showed more problems with finances, friends and family members compared to problem-drinking women, but the latter had more negative life events, and stressors related to spouse and extended family members. In general, people who experienced more stressors functioned more poorly. Those who experienced more negative life events reported heavier drinking and depression. Across the board, more chronic stressors fueled drinking problems and depression.

Those with fewer social resources consumed more alcohol. Problem drinkers with health, home and financial problems showed less self-confidence. The authors conclude by suggesting that longitudinal studies are needed to clarify the relationship between life-stressors and social resources to show how they both influence late-life drinking behavior. And, more research is needed to determine how this study can be generalized to apply to elderly individuals.

144   Brennan, P. L., Moos, R. H., & Kim, J. Y. (1993). Gender differences in the individual characteristics and life contexts of late-middle-aged and older problem drinkers. Addiction, 88(6), 781-790.

This study focuses on three issues: gender differences in individual characteristics of late-life problem drinkers; patterns of stressors and social resources experienced by these problem drinkers; and how ongoing drinking problems or remission over a one-year interval affects the life contexts of older men and women.

Community residents, between the ages of 55 and 65, who had one or more current drinking problems when assessed at one of two large medical centers, were the focus for the study. The subjects were made up of 476 men and 183 women, with a mean age of 61. A follow up interview was also conducted after a one-year interval.

Results of the study show that on-going drinking problems will have different consequences for men and women. In terms of substance use and depression, women consumed less alcohol and had fewer drinking problems than did men. Women were more likely to be late - onset problem drinkers, with 46% of the women, compared to 28% of the men, stating that their drinking had begun within the past 2 years. However, women used more psychoactive medications and were more depressed than men. Men were more likely to seek help specifically for drinking problems, and reported more chronic stressors in the area of finances and friends. Women experienced less support from spouse and extended family, but more support from children and friends. Most gender differences remained constant at the 1-year interval follow-up. However, remitted women had improved their relationships with extended family members and friends, but reported less support from spouses. Remitted men had more harmonious marital relationships. The authors suggest that longer term follow-ups are needed to study late-life alcohol abuse differences in men and women, and also to determine whether a correlation exists between depression and family adversity, and relapse among remitted women.

145   Bridgewater, R., Leigh, S., James, O., & Potter, J. (1987). Alcohol consumption and dependence in elderly patients in an urban community. British Medical Journal, 6602(295), 884-885.

This is a short report claiming to be the first community-based study in the United Kingdom examining alcohol consumption in the elderly. A subset of 101 patients was drawn from a registry of 828 elderly general medical patients for interview in their homes. Forty-eight men and 53 women (average age=71.3) were ultimately successfully interviewed. The authors report that 23% of the men and 11% of the women were classified as having alcohol problems, as compared to 20% in men and 2% in women as heavy drinkers in a similar New York study. They conclude with remarks on the need for validation of the CAGE with the elderly and also state that "alcohol consumption and alcohol dependence may be a largely unrecognized problem in the elderly" (p. 885).

146   Bristow, M. F., & Clare, A. W. (1992). Prevalence and characteristics of at-risk drinkers among elderly acute medical in-patients. British Journal of Addiction, 87(2), 291-294.

This article reports results from a survey of 327 males and 323 females over age 65 who were admitted to medical and geriatric wards at St. Bartholomew's and Homerton Hospitals in London in 1987/88. All subjects' age, sex, and diagnosis were recorded; all were asked to complete a semi-structured interview dealing with the quantity, frequency, and social circumstance of their alcohol consumption together with a brief account of their drinking history. Subjects who drank more than the Royal College of Psychiatrists' recommended safety limits (21 units/week for men, 14 units/week for women) were given an additional structured interview dealing with sociodemographic information and alcohol-related problems.

Those interviewed were rated as drinking not at all, less than weekly, or at least weekly. Marked gender differences in drinking patterns were revealed. Overall, 4.5% of the sample were found to be drinking "at risk;" all were males. Nine percent of the males interviewed were drinking "at risk." Seventy-five (23%) of the males interviewed had previously drunk more than the recommended safety limits. Reasons given for reducing drinking were medical problems (45%), social reasons (35%), financial reasons (10%) and other reasons (10%). By comparison with the other 293 men in the survey, the 30 "at risk" male drinkers were diagnosed more often with non-malignant respiratory disease. They also had other alcohol-related diagnoses such as gout, peptic ulcers, and cirrhosis. Twenty-five of the thirty "at risk" males agreed to more in-depth interviews. Of these, 12 reported experiencing one of more alcohol-related problems in the past 2 years. Missed meals, tremors, domestic arguments, falls, and drunken driving convictions were some of the problems reported. The "at risk" drinkers were significantly more likely than other males interviewed to be unmarried, not to have a close friend, and to smoke. They were also more likely to be living alone and to have recently experienced a loss. Heavy drinkers were also less mobile than other males surveyed.

147   Brower, K. J., Mudd, S., Blow, F. C., Young, J. P., & Hill, E. M.
        (1994). Severity and treatment of alcohol withdrawal in
        elderly versus younger patients. Alcoholism: Clinical and
        Experimental Research, 18(1), 196-201.

        The present study was conducted to test the following
hypotheses: (1) elderly alcoholics experience a more severe course of
withdrawal; (2) elderly alcoholics are more susceptible than younger
alcoholics to particular types of symptoms during withdrawal; and (3)
elderly alcoholics require higher doses of medication for detoxification
for longer durations than younger alcoholics.

        The researchers conducted a retrospective chart review of
older (N=48, mean age=69) and younger (N=36, mean age=30)
patients who were admitted to residential/inpatient treatment for alcohol
withdrawal and dependence, who were discharged between January,
1987, and April, 1991. Six domains of variables were analyzed:
demographics; drinking history; past history of withdrawal symptoms
and past treatment history; current medical status; withdrawal
symptoms during the reviewed treatment episode; and duration and
dosage of medications for detoxification. Age was the major
independent variable; withdrawal symptoms and treatment received
were the major dependent variables.

        Results revealed that the two age groups did not differ in terms
of recent drinking history; however, the older group had significantly
more withdrawal symptoms for a longer duration than the younger
group. The older group had significantly more symptoms of cognitive
impairment, weakness, high blood pressure, and daytime sleepiness,
whereas the younger group experienced more headaches. Elderly
alcoholics did not require significantly more days of detoxification
medication or higher doses of chlordiazepoxide; however, a nonsignificant trend existed for more days of detoxification medication in
the elderly (3.5 versus 2.3 days). "The study provides support that
alcohol withdrawal may be more severe in the elderly" (p. 200).

148   Brown, B. B., & Chiang, C. (1983-84). Drug and alcohol abuse
        among the elderly: Is being alone the key? International
        Journal of Aging and Human Development, 18(1), 1-12.

        This study examines social background and extent of social
support among 21 elderly clients (age 55 and over) in drug treatment
facilities, 30 older abusers not in treatment, and 155 older non-abusers.
Individuals were selected from three sources in the Madison, Wisconsin
metropolitan area: a 1-month survey of new clients in drug abuse
agencies, a similar 1-month survey of other community agencies, and
a random selection of elderly public housing residents. Determination
of drug-alcohol abuse among respondents not in treatment was made

using a brief structured interview which employed the four-item CAGE instrument and a similar author-created four-item measure of medication abuse.

Demographic social background variables included age, gender, race, and education. Social support measures included marital status, current living arrangements, length of stay at a given residence, geographical nearness of friends and relatives, and frequency of visits with friends and relatives.

Fourteen percent of community elders were classified as abusers. Initial analysis revealed an age-gender bias in those receiving treatment versus those not in treatment. Controlling for age and gender effects, substance abuse appeared more prevalent among single and divorced elderly, and among respondents who lived alone. The authors emphasize the need to concentrate education efforts on agencies that frequently deal with isolated elders. It is suggested that future research should examine the quality of older persons' relationships with immediate others such as spouses and living companions.

149   Buchsbaum, D. G., Buchanan, R. G., Welsh, J., Centor, R. M., & Schnoll, S. H. (1992). Screening for drinking disorders in the elderly using the CAGE questionnaire. Journal of the American Geriatrics Society, 40(7), 662-665.

The primary objective of the study was to assess the adequacy of the CAGE questionnaire in identifying elderly medical outpatients with drinking problems. Participants in this study included all people 18 or older who attended the Medical College of Virginia's ambulatory medicine clinic between October, 1988 and February, 1990. Testers contacted patients as they departed their intake interview with the clinic nursing staff and asked them whether they would agree to participate in a survey of the drinking habits of patients attending the clinic.

Each patient who participated in the study was administered the Composite International Diagnostic Interview-Substance Abuse Module (CIDI-SAM), the CAGE questionnaire, and the alcohol module of the Diagnostic Interview Schedule (DIS). Patients were defined as having a history of alcohol abuse or dependence if they met the DSM-III criteria for these disorders. Patients were further categorized as problem drinkers if they reported at least one symptom on the DIS, but did not meet criteria for history of alcohol abuse or dependence. Researchers compared DSM-III based diagnoses and CAGE scores. Researchers calculated the sensitivity, specificity, and predictive value for CAGE cut-off scores of 0-4, and then constructed a receiver operating characteristic (ROC) curve based upon CAGE performance compared with DSM-III diagnoses. The ROC curve plots the true positive ratio (sensitivity) against the false-positive ratio (1-specificity) as one changes the definition of a positive test. In clinical medicine, the area under the ROC curve represents the test's ability to discriminate between disease and non-disease.

For the analysis CAGE scores and DSM-III diagnoses were reviewed for 323 patients aged 60 or older who met the inclusion criteria. The lifetime prevalence for drinking problems was 63% for men and 22% for women. The ROC curve was .862 with a standard error of .0238, suggesting a very powerful ability of the CAGE to distinguish those patients with a drinking history from those without such a history. The researchers recommend the use of the CAGE questionnaire to screen elderly persons for the presence of drinking problems.

150   Bunn, J. Y., Booth, B. M., Loveland-Cook, C. A., Blow, F. C., & Fortney, J. C. (1994). The relationship between mortality and intensity of inpatient alcoholism treatment. American Journal of Public Health, 84(2), 211-214.

The researchers conducting this study identified men participating in varying intensities of inpatient alcoholism treatment and followed them for three years after discharge. Each alcoholic was placed into one of the three treatment groups: 1) patients who completed extended formal inpatient alcoholism treatment, 2) patients who underwent at least six days of extended formal inpatient alcoholism treatment but did not complete treatment; and 3) patients admitted for short detoxification lasting five days or less. The comparison group received no treatment for alcoholism. Age was measured in 10-year intervals, and age-specific mortality rates were calculated for each racial group. A survival analysis examined the time to death for the three treatment groups, controlling for potential confounding variables. Adjusted mortality rates were computed and survival analysis was performed to assess the risks of death, adjusting for factors that may influence mortality.

Results of the analyses revealed that there was an increasing risk of death with increasing age. Men 70 years of age and older experienced a greater than 10-fold increase in risk of dying during the three year period. The presence of complications of alcoholism, as measured by disease severity, increased the risk of dying by 22% for those whose complications were defined as moderate and by almost 90% for those with more severe complications. Men who were married were less likely to die than those who were not. The adjusted mortality rate for men completing extended formal inpatient alcoholism treatment was twice that of the general population in 1989.

151   Burger, M. C., Botwinick, J., & Storandt, M. (1987). Aging,
        alcoholism, and performance on the Luria-Nebraska
        Neuropsychological Battery. Journal of Gerontology, 42(1),
        69-72.

        The authors examined the premature aging hypothesis of
alcoholism using the Luria-Nebraska Neuropsychological Battery
(LNNB). Sixty alcoholic and 60 non-alcoholic adults ages 30 to 76
participated in the study. Criteria for inclusion as "alcoholic" included:
a previous history of family, legal, or employment problems;
experience of severe withdrawal symptoms; and, report 10 or more
years of excessive drinking. Measures included auditory and visual
acuity determinations, medical and drinking histories, and the LNNB.
All participants were tested individually. Multivariate analysis of
covariance (MANCOVA) was performed with education, occupation,
and acuity measures entered as covariates. Although significant main
effects were found for age and alcoholism on multiple scales of the
LNNB, no interaction effect emerged from the study. In addition,
patterns of effects differed for these two variables.

152   Busby, W. J., Campbell, A. J., Borrie, M. J., & Spears, G. F. S.
        (1988). Alcohol use in a community-based sample of subjects
        aged 70 years and older. Journal of the American Geriatrics
        Society, 36(4), 301-305.

        This study is an epidemiological examination of a rural
population of 774 elderly (70+) in New Zealand. This study reports
the usual decreases in terms of frequency, yet with 7.4% of men and
11.1 % of women saying they took more alcohol with age. The given
reason for the majority of the respondents showing a decrease were
health related and having fewer social opportunities. When the
respondents said they drank more they cited more money and time, and
few said that they drank alcohol to cope with personal problems. The
authors include a discussion of psychotropic drug intake and abstinence
from alcohol.

153   Campbell, J. W., Chumbler, N. R., Danto-Nocton, E., & Flocke, S.
        (1994). Referral of elders for alcohol treatment: Influence of
        gerontological education on medical and nursing students.
        Gerontology and Geriatrics Education, 14(4), 53-66.

        "The primary aim of the present study was to examine the
geriatric educational factors which predict medical and nursing
students' referrals for treatment of older alcohol-dependent patients" (p.
55). Specifically, the researchers hypothesized the following: (1)
respondents (medical students in nursing school and medical students
in medical school) who exhibit more factual knowledge about the

elderly are more likely to refer older alcoholics for treatment; (2) respondents who complete more hours of geriatric alcohol education are more likely to refer older alcoholics for treatment; and (3) medical vis-a-vis nursing students are more likely to complete more hours of alcohol education, possess factual knowledge about the elderly and have a higher propensity to refer older alcoholics for treatment.

To test the three hypotheses, the researchers mailed questionnaires about aging and alcoholism to all first-year and second-year medical students at both a medical and nursing school at the same university. Over 80% of the medical and nursing students returned the questionnaire. To determine the propensity to refer elderly alcoholics to treatment (dependent variable), 8 case vignettes, which contained the age of patient, duration of alcohol use, family willingness to participate in care and other information, were rated on a five point Likert-type scale, where very unlikely to benefit from alcohol treatment $=1$ and very likely to benefit from treatment $=5$. Palmore's Facts on Aging Quiz was administered to determine knowledge about aging. Number of geriatric alcohol education hours was assessed by requesting respondents to list the number of hours participated in during their medical/nursing school training, which pertained to individuals 65 years of age and older.

Zero-order correlations indicate that the propensity to refer older alcoholics for treatment is related to hours of alcohol education $(v=.13)$ and medical students $(v=.22)$. Being a medical student is positively associated with factual knowledge toward the elderly $(v=.23)$ and hours of geriatric alcohol education $(v=.33)$. Multivariate analyses revealed support for two hypotheses. The number of hours of geriatric alcohol education completed by students and being a medical student were significant predictors of referring older alcoholics for treatment. The first hypothesis that factual knowledge about the elderly is a significant predictor of referring older alcoholics for treatment was not supported. The authors recommend that medical and nursing schools structure their curricula to correctly diagnose and refer older alcoholics to treatment. They also note the need for greater awareness of community agencies treating alcoholics being presented to students.

154   Cartensen, L. L., Rychtarik, R., & Prue, D. M. (1985). Behavioral treatment of the geriatric alcohol abuser: A long term follow-up study. Addictive Behaviors, 10(3), 307-311.

This is one of those studies which supports the statement that elderly individuals have a very good chance of recovery and overall have higher remission rates than younger individuals. This study looked at patients two to four years after discharge from a 28-day in-patient alcohol treatment program at a Mississippi VA medical center.

The initial sample consisted of twenty-five 60+ males, with sixteen providing data for the follow-up interview. The results showed that 50% of the subjects were abstaining while 13% were "significantly modifying" their drinking behavior. The remainder were in the "abusive drinkers" category. Though the sample size in this study is clearly small, the article supports the utility of treatment for this older male veteran population.

155   Chaikelson, J. S., Arbuckle, T. Y., Lapidus, S., & Gold, D. P. (1994). Measurement of lifetime alcohol consumption. Journal of Studies on Alcohol, 55(2), 133-140.

The purpose of the study was to develop a measure of lifetime alcohol use that would be appropriate for older adults with an extended drinking history, and to assess the validity and reliability of the instrument. Participants in the study were 72 individuals ranging in age from 61 to 85, who were Canadian army veterans of WWII who earlier had been part of a large scale study in intelligence conducted in 1985 with follow-ups in 1987 and 1990. The 1984 interview included the question, "How many drinks do you have in a week?" Based on the answer to this question, of the 72 participants 40.3% were non-drinkers, 36.1% reported 1 to 7 drinks per week, 9.7% reported 8 to 14 drinks per week, 4.2% reported 15 to 21 drinks per week, 4.2% reported 22 to 28 drinks per week, and 5.6% reported over 28 drinks per week.

For the present study all subjects were tested individually in their own homes in their preferred language, English or French. For those who were married, wives were also tested and interviewed. Demographic data were gathered in a personal interview using a short, structured interview. The Concordia Lifetime Drinking Questionnaire (CLDQ) was administered. The CLDQ includes quantity and frequency questions on current alcohol use and a series of questions about the start of alcohol use. The instrument also requires subjects to collaborate with the interviewer in drawing a graph that represents their lifetime drinking patterns and encourages more accurate recall by use of salient events in the subjects' life history. The Concordia Lifetime Smoking Questionnaire (CLSQ), constructed in the same manner as the CLDQ, except that it quantifies cigarette use, was also administered. The MAST and the Family and Friends Alcohol Use Questionnaire (FAF) were also administered. Two assessments were conducted approximately 33 months apart for each subject.

Lifetime drinking was calculated as the area under the curve defined by the two end-points and all the points of inflection. The graph was also divided at 1963, the approximate midpoint of lifetime drinking for this sample, to provide an estimate of early life (prior to

1963) and later life (since 1963) alcohol consumption. Two separate measures of recent drinking were also available: the amount consumed in the month prior to the most recent drink (last reported month) and the amount consumed in the month prior to testing (current month).

To determine reliability, a comparison of the 1987 and 1990 reports of lifetime drinking were compared using paired-difference t-tests calculated or every fifth year from 1945 to 1985. Reliability coefficients varied from .65 in 1955 to .87 in 1975. An additional measure of reliability was derived by comparing the answers subject gave to the 1984 question about weekly drinking to the amount of weekly drinking they drew on their graphs in 1987 and 1990. The reliability coefficients obtained in this manner were .83 for 1987 and .78 for 1990. Validity was tested by comparing each wife's rating of her husband's drinking at present and at time of marriage with similar points on the husband's graph; the correlations were .878 and .72, respectively. Also, modest correlations were obtained between the MAST and the CLQD. The researchers concluded that the CLDQ is a valid, reliable measure to assess lifetime drinking in older people. As was expected, the researchers found that current drinking levels in an elderly sample were a poor reflection of lifetime alcohol consumption and lifetime drinking problem.

156   Christopherson, V. A., Escher, M. C., & Bainton, B. R. (1984). Reasons for drinking among the elderly in rural Arizona. Journal of Studies on Alcohol, 45(5), 417-423.

This study examined past and present drinking patterns and reasons for drinking among people 65 and older in rural Arizona. An area probability sample derived from the Arizona Census enumeration district was chosen, and interviews were conducted with 444 older adults. Approximately equal numbers of females and males were interviewed. Caucasians were slightly overrepresented and Mexican-Americans were underrepresented in the sample. Drinking behavior was measured in terms of (1) the quantity and frequency of alcohol use (Q-F) using Mulford and Miller's Q-F typology; and (2) the average daily intake of alcohol using Jessor scores. Respondents were presented with 20 reasons to drink and asked whether or not the statement applied to them. Reasons were grouped into six categories: social; food; mood changes; health reasons; coping with personal situations; and coping with social or interpersonal situations.

The results of the statistical analysis indicate that there are four types of older drinkers: abstainers; light drinkers; moderate drinkers; and heavy drinkers. There was strong evidence for either abstaining or drinking as stable, lifelong behaviors. When change in quantity and frequency was identified, it was found that alcohol use diminishes as individuals age. In terms of reasons for drinking, most respondents drank for social reasons or mood reasons. They wanted to fit in socially and have fun; or they wanted to feel better. Analysis of data by age categories revealed that older adults who are in the young-old group (65-74) drink for different reasons than the old-old (75 +). The young-old more often drink for social reasons or to enjoy a meal. The old-old, in contrast, are more likely to drink for personal coping reasons--to feel less bored or lonely, or to feel more satisfied with themselves.

157 Colsher, P. L., & Wallace, R. B. (1990). Elderly men with histories of heavy drinking: Correlates and consequences. Journal of Studies on Alcohol, 51(6), 528-535.

This is a three-year longitudinal study of rural male elderly who were self-reported as heavy drinkers, non-heavy drinkers, or never drinkers and the impact of this categorization on physical and psychological health. As expected the picture is grim for the heavy drinker. Heavy drinkers were more likely to report a history of stroke, stomach or intestinal ulcers, asthma and emphysema or chronic bronchitis, etc. They were also less satisfied with their lives, preferred more solitary activities and were at increased risk of death relative to both other groups.

158 Cook, B. L., Winokur, G., Garvey, M. J., & Beach, V. (1991). Depression and previous alcoholism in the elderly. British Journal of Psychiatry, 158, 72-75.

This prospective study examined the influence of past history of alcoholism upon the clinical presentation, treatment, acute response and outcome in depressed elderly patients. The sample comprised 58 male, non-bipolar depressives over age 55 who were admitted to the Iowa City Veterans Administration Medical Center between 1978 and 1980. All subjects met the Feighner criteria for major depressive episode and none had actively displayed problem drinking during the previous two years. Initial interviews were semi-structured and included questions on subjects' clinical history since discharge and family history of psychiatric illness. Subjects with a history of alcoholism were younger at index admission, had a younger age of onset of depression, and reported more family and occupational dysfunction and suicidal ideation. This group also reported more readmissions to the hospital and more difficulty achieving recovery. Non-alcoholic, depressed elders experienced more delusions and disturbances of motor activity, and were more likely to report a family history of affective disorders as opposed to alcoholism.

159   Curtis, J. R., Geller, G., Stokes, E. J., Levine, D. M., & Moore, R. D. (1989). Characteristics, diagnosis, and treatment of alcoholism in elderly patients. Journal of the American Geriatrics Society, 37(4), 310-316.

The purpose of this study is to examine how well physicians diagnose alcoholism in elderly patients and to define elderly alcoholic patient characteristics. The study was conducted over a three-month period at Johns Hopkins Hospital in Baltimore. All new admissions were screened for alcoholism, using the CAGE questionnaire and Short Michigan Alcohol Screening Test. The authors point out that elderly patients with alcohol problems may be hard to detect because they tend to drink less in terms of quantity and frequency.

The results indicated that 21% of patients 60 years and older screened positive for alcoholism. However, only 37% of the screen-positive older alcoholics were identified through the attending physicians. Doctors were unlikely to diagnose elderly patients who were white, female or had completed high school. And even in those who were diagnosed as alcoholic, physicians initiated intervention in only 24% of the elderly, compared to 50% of the nonelderly.

Concluding remarks note that elderly patients with alcoholism are less likely to be detected and treated because certain stereotypes of patients with alcoholism still exist and interfere with diagnosis in elderly patients.

160   Douglass, R. L., Schuster, E. O., & McClelland, S. C. (1988). Drinking patterns and abstinence among the elderly. The International Journal of the Addictions, 23(4), 399-415.

This is a study examining the drinking patterns of elderly in a community sample (N=207) versus a sample of low-income housing residents (N=71). The major findings were that higher-income respondents were three times more likely to drink (2-6 times per week) than low-income subjects. In the community, the likelihood of being an abstainer increased with age, and most interestingly, no relationships were found that connected living alone to alcohol consumption. This article includes an informative discussion of sample comparability and cohort effect.

161   Dunham, R. G. (1981). Aging and changing patterns of alcohol use. Journal of Psychoactive Drugs, 13(2), 143-151.

This study attempts to describe changing patterns of alcohol use over the life span. Data were collected from interviews with 310 persons 60 years of age and older who were living in government-funded, low-income housing for the elderly in Dade County (Miami), Florida. A self-reported retrospective measure was used to assess lifetime drinking patterns. Respondents were interviewed in their apartments.

Data analysis revealed seven drinking patterns: life-long abstainers (N=210); rise and fall pattern (N=21); rise and sustained pattern (N=24); light throughout life (N=18); light with a late rise (N=6); late starters (N=9); and a highly variable pattern (N=7). Each pattern is described in detail. The most frequent reason cited for a decrease in drinking was a specific health problem. Males and females differed in their drinking patterns. Males are over-represented in the patterns that conclude in continued heavy drinking or a late rise to heavy drinking; females are over-represented in the patterns which conclude with a high rate of return to abstinence or very light drinking. Blacks were over-represented in the highly variable pattern.

162   Dupree, L. W. (1989). Comparison of three case-finding strategies relative to elderly alcohol abusers. The Journal of Applied Gerontology, 8(4), 502-511.

This article reports on the effectiveness of three case-finding strategies for locating elderly alcohol abusers and linking them with the Gerontology Alcohol Project (GAP), a treatment program designed to address late-life onset elderly alcohol abusers in the Tampa Bay area. The three case-finding strategies included the creation of a Community Agency Referral Network (CARN), a Public Awareness Campaign (PAC), and a Community-Based Outreach (CBO). CARN involved the initiation of communications with local formal caregivers and was designed to inform and assist them in identifying elderly alcohol abusers, as well as processing referrals of elderly abusers to the GAP project. PAC used the mass media to inform the general public of GAP and to encourage potential clients and their families to seek treatment for their alcohol-related problems. Written publicity, television, and radio were all used. CBO consisted of 148 on-site visits, 10 educational seminars for staff, and screening of 115 potential alcohol clients, 740 telephone contacts with clients, and 66 follow-up visits to clinics and clients.

Results revealed that CARN generated 247 referrals, PAC yielded 106 referrals, and CBO resulted in 34 referrals. Cost analyses revealed that the lowest costs per appropriate referral were incurred by CARN. PAC incurred the highest cost.

163   Dupree, L. W., Broskowski, H., & Schonfeld, L. (1984). The Gerontology Alcohol Project: A behavioral treatment program for elderly alcohol abusers. The Gerontologist, 24(5), 510-516.

This study examined the effects of a treatment program on

later-life onset alcohol abusers age 55 and over. The research was implemented through the Gerontology Alcohol Project (GAP), a pilot day treatment program. The program emphasized the functional analysis of drinking behavior, acquisition of self-management skills, and reestablishment of viable social support networks. Twenty-four subjects with a mean age of 65.9 successfully completed the 12 month treatment phase. In addition to quantity and frequency of alcohol consumption, GAP assessed five other areas of life affected by alcohol abuse: physical health, mental health, family and social adjustment, financial stability and legal status.

Results of the program were measured at different assessment intervals of 1-month, 3-months, 6-months and after 12-months. Seventeen clients had elected abstinence and all but 3 had met that goal after a year. Seven others had elected a goal of responsible, limited drinking. Less than half were able to maintain that goal after a year, although one client died after the 3-month follow-up. In the areas of quality of life, most areas of concern were found with physical health and social/interpersonal problems. Physical symptoms reported most often in connection with alcohol, were hand tremors, restlessness, blackouts and severe "inner" shakes.

Not surprisingly, the clients had relatively poor social networks, with an average size of 7.20 people. Daily basis contact averaged 0.88 and the average number of relatives was 1.30. The authors felt that GAP is a promising treatment program for later-life onset alcohol abusers. GAP now includes all categories of elderly alcohol abusers.

164   Dupree, L. W., & Schonfeld, L. (1984). Treatment of late-life onset alcohol abuse. Journal of the Florida Medical Association, 71(4), 267-269.

This "short report" paper is the published version of a presentation given by the authors the same year. As in the presentation summary, this paper gives an overview of the NIAAA-funded Gerontology Alcohol Project (GAP). This project focused on late-life drinkers, with onset of drinking after 50. Four treatment strategies were covered: breaking down drinking behavior into antecedents, behavior, and consequences; dealing with the antecedents such as anxiety, anger, depression; problem solving skills development; and an alcohol education group. Interestingly the study had a 50% drop-out rate. The researchers found that at admission the dropouts had a lower estimate of their being successful in the program, higher depression scores, greater internal locus of control, and had tended to consume more alcohol than those who completed the program. Success at one-year was based on whether the client had maintained his individual drinking goal. At 12 months, the success rate was reported as 74%. Despite relapse in the 26%, the authors report "none returned to an abusive drinking pattern throughout the entire 12 months of follow-up" (p. 269).

165   Ellis, R. J. (1990). Dichotic symmetries in aging and alcoholic subjects. Alcoholism: Clinical and Experimental Research, 14(6), 863-871.

This article reports the results of a study designed to test the "right hemisphere hypothesis" using dichotic listening measures of functional asymmetry. The right hemisphere hypothesis predicts a greater loss of right hemisphere functions such as visuospatial and other nonverbal skills, as compared to verbal abilities or left hemisphere functions, as a function of alcoholism and of aging. Another position referred to as the "diffuse generalized hypothesis," on the other hand, suggests that alcoholism is associated with a parallel deterioration in functioning of both cerebral hemispheres.

Forty seven right-handed men (22 abstinent alcoholics; 22 normal non-alcoholics; and 3 with RH lesions due to cerebrovascular disease) from the Boston area were used as subjects. Subjects ranged in age from 25 to over 45 years. Most participants possessed at least a high school education and were of working class background. All alcoholics had at least 7 years of heavy drinking. They were recruited from local halfway houses. The diagnosis of alcoholism was based on information derived from the NIMH Diagnostic Interview Schedule (DIS), a structured psychiatric interview, and from the CAGE questionnaire.

Dichotic testing entailed the administration of two separate listening tasks, one employing "verbal" and the other "nonverbal" stimuli. For the verbal half the Fused Dichotic Words Test (FDWT) was used. For the nonverbal part an adaptation of the Dichotic Piano Notes Test (DPNT) was administered. All dichotic stimuli were delivered through calibrated stereo headphones. Telephonics (TDH-39) at a presentation level of 75 ($\pm$5) dB for each ear. The WAIS-R and WMS tests were also administered in their entirety to estimate verbal and performance IQ's and memory quotients (MQ's).

Multiple regression techniques were used to statistically evaluate the relationships between alcoholism, aging, and measures of laterality. All variables were coded continuously. An interaction factor, age times duration, was included. The overall multiple regression models for both dichotic listening tests yielded nonsignificant F values. For the FDWT, F was 0.93 (df=3,40; p>0.25); and for the DPNT, F was 0.09 (df= 3,40; p>0.50). Partial Fs for each of the separate terms were also examined. Neither age, nor alcohol, nor the interaction term approached significance (p > 0.25) in any of these models.

The study did find clear evidence of a statistically significant association between advancing age and declining nonverbal cognitive performance as measured by the WAIS-R. The study also demonstrated a statistically significant negative association between prolonged, heavy alcohol consumption and nonverbal cognitive skills. For age the partial F (1,41) was 6.22 (p < 0.02). For alcohol the partial F (1,41) was 5.87 (p < 0.02). The interaction term was nonsignificant. Subjects with right hemisphere damage performed at subnormal levels on the tests, confirming the reliability of the dichotic measures as indexes of hemispheric function. The results of this study support the hypothesis that both cerebral hemispheres are equally affected by the decline that occurs with aging and with chronic alcohol abuse.

166   Fillmore, K. M. (1987). Prevalence, incidence and chronicity of drinking patterns and problems among men as a function of age: A longitudinal and cohort analysis. British Journal of Addiction, 82(1), 77-83.

This definitive longitudinal study skillfully examines the often asked question, "Does the prevalence of drinking problems and behavior decrease with age or are these findings merely artifacts of cohort membership in which drinking behavior was greatly discouraged by unique historical events, such as prohibition?"

Two samples were used: a sample of 725 males aged 21-59 first interviewed in 1969 and then interviewed in 1974; and a sample of 482 males reinterviewed in 1974 and first interviewed in 1967. Two national samples and one follow-up sample were used in the cohort analysis. Data were analyzed examining prevalence, incidence and chronicity of drinking. The overall finding was: "incidence of heavy drinking and alcohol problems decrease with age and chronicity of alcohol problems is highest in the middle years of life. It did not confirm the hypothesis that heavy consumption is more likely to be chronic in the middle years of life" (p. 81). The cohort analysis supported the longitudinal findings, with two slight historical effects. The article includes some excellent methodological discussions.

167   Fillmore, K. M. (1987). Women's drinking across the adult life course as compared to men's. British Journal of Addiction, 82(7), 801-811.

This is a thorough longitudinal study of drinking patterns among the female population (N=408). This study examines the prevalence, incidence and duration of multiple drinking patterns across the adult life span. The interval between measurements was approximately 7 years. The author draws several conclusions bearing in mind that the prevalence of reporting decreases with age. There is a sharp decrease in incidence at age 50 and a sharp increase in remission after age 40. For the heavier drinker the incidence is highest in mid-life and almost non-existent after age 60. In the intriguing comparison of men versus women drinkers the following patterns are found: overall compared to women, men are more likely to show higher rates of heavy-frequent drinking; there are also clear episodic changes over the life course when the rates converge in the 30's and again in the 50's. In the cohort analysis, the author concludes that her data do not suggest that there is an alcoholic epidemic among younger generations of women. The author offers an interesting discussion of cultural influences on drinking patterns which is essential reading.

168   Fillmore, K. M., Golding, J. M., Leino, E. V., Ager, C. R., & Ferrer, H. P. (1994). Societal-level predictors of groups' drinking patterns: A research synthesis from the Collaborative Alcohol-Related Longitudinal Project. American Journal of Public Health, 84(2), 247-253.

This meta-analysis investigates the effects of per capita alcohol consumption and divorce rates as predictors of change in quantity and frequency of drinking among various age groups of men and women in multiple longitudinal studies. The analysis includes 25 studies of quantity and 29 studies of frequency from a total of 15 nations. Studies range in length from 1 to 21 years. Weighted least squares regression procedures were employed with effect sizes (standardized mean differences of frequency and quantity between initial and final measurements) as dependent variables. In addition to age and gender, independent societal-level variables included per capita consumption and divorce rates at Time 1, differences in these rates between Time 1 and final measurement, and interactions between rates and demographic variables. When both the period effects of per capita consumption and the divorce rates were considered, the divorce rate was found to be a significant predictor of change in quantity and frequency. Furthermore, increases in divorce rate were found to be associated with decreases in frequency among men, particularly in younger age groups. However, an increasing divorce rate was found to be associated with increased quantity per occasion for all groups. Period effects of changing per capita consumption on quantity and frequency were significant only when the divorce rate was not included in the model. The authors suggest that societal stress in the form of increasing divorce rate may be accompanied by "drier" social contexts, characterized by drinking patterns of a more "volitive" nature (heavier quantity per occasion).

It is further concluded that multiple societal-level factors as opposed to simple per capita consumption must be considered in designing interventions to affect drinking patterns of demographic groups.

169   Fillmore, K. M., & Midanik, L. (1984). Chronicity of drinking problems among men: A longitudinal study. Journal of Studies on Alcohol, 45(3), 228-236.

Researchers tested the hypothesis that the chronicity of alcohol problems among men is a function of age. They designed their study to determine if men in their 40's (older men) who demonstrated alcohol problems at one point in time are much more likely than men in their 20's (younger men) to demonstrate alcohol problems at a later point in time. To test their hypothesis, two independent probability samples of the general adult population were used. The first consisted of 786 White male residents of San Francisco, aged 21-59, who were interviewed in 1967-'68. In 1972, 615 (78%) of these men were followed-up by interview or mail questionnaire. The analyses is based on 186 men 21-29 and 110 men aged 40-49 at Time 1, who were contacted at both measurement times and who reported drinking during each year of measurement. Various problem drinking scales developed were used to obtain data on intake of alcohol and frequency of binge drinking and symptomatic drinking. Scales were also constructed to determine coping, health, social complications, loss of control, and overall problems related to drinking.

Results of the study revealed far less relational distance between alcohol problems for those in the older age group from Time 1 to Time 2 and far more relational distance for those in the younger age group between Time 1 and Time 2. Older men also reported higher levels of a given alcohol-related problem at both points in time, and they reported more alcohol-related problems than did younger men at both Time 1 and Time 2. The data thus demonstrated that the chronicity of alcohol problems is stronger in the older cohort than in the younger as measured across time. The strength of the correlations was tested by multiple stepwise regressions for the San Francisco sample. For most problem areas, the explained variance was at least twice that among the older men than among the younger men. The authors conclude that the chronicity of alcohol problems among men is a function of age. They note that their findings are not necessarily generalizable to women.

170   Finlayson, R. E., Hurt, R. D., Davis, L. J., & Morse, R. M. (1988). Alcoholism in elderly persons: A study of the psychiatric and psychosocial features of 216 inpatients. Mayo Clinic Proceedings, 63(8), 761-768.

This is a companion article to the medical study of 216 inpatient alcoholics, 65 to 83 years old, conducted between 1972 and 1983 at the Mayo Clinic with 50% percent of the patients defined as early-onset and 41% diagnosed as late-onset alcoholics. Three questions were addressed in this study: 1) what is the frequency of psychiatric disorders in this alcoholic group?; 2) do these disorders affect treatment outcome?; 3) are there psychiatric and psychosocial tests that can help distinguish between patients with early- and late-onset alcoholism?

In this study, 30 of the alcoholics also had a diagnosis of drug abuse or dependence. These drugs had been legally prescribed. The most common organic mental disorder present was dementia associated with alcoholism, found in 49 patients. Affective disorders included 18 with major depression, and 5 with bipolar disorder. Early-onset alcoholics cited health, job, legal or economic problems as reasons for admission to the program, while the late-onset alcoholics were more motivated by the concern of friends and families. Also, the late-onset patients reported a higher frequency of life events associated with problem drinking, including retirement, boredom and lack of responsibilities. The authors concluded that while psychiatric disorders other then alcoholism were common in this study, more information was needed to learn how mental disorders affect alcohol treatment in the elderly. Tests used to distinguish between the early- and late-onset alcoholics were less helpful than physician's observation of the patient's style of coping, social circumstances and history of alcohol use.

171   Fulop, G., Reinhardt, J., Strain, J. J., Paris, B., Miller, M., & Fillit, H. (1993). Identification of alcoholism and depression in a geriatric medicine outpatient clinic. Journal of the American Geriatrics Society, 41(7), 737-741.

This study took place at the Coffey Geriatric Outpatient Clinic of the Mount Sinai School of Medicine in New York City. The purpose of the study was to test the effectiveness of the Michigan Alcohol Screening Test (MAST), the CAGE questionnaire, and the Geriatric Depression Scale (GDS) in identifying older adults who are alcoholic and/or depressed. Alcoholism and depression are associated with significant suicide rates, and among older adults, 20% of women and 5% of men alcoholics report suicide attempts.

The sample consisted of 84 males and females over 62 years old. In terms of alcohol screening, results of the study showed that 5% of the subjects scored positive on the MAST, compared to only 1.4% identified through the Cage questionnaire. The geriatric clinic staff had also identified the alcoholic patients. However, only one-third of the geriatric team had previously identified the 32% of elderly patients who tested positive for depression on the GDS. The authors reported that the

GDS was easily administered, well received and demonstrated its ability to identify depression in a frail, predominantly minority geriatric medicine population. In contrast, the MAST and the CAGE had marginal impact on the identification of alcoholism.

172   Glatt, M. M. (1978). Experiences with elderly alcoholics in England. Alcoholism: Clinical and Experimental Research, 2(1), 23-26.

The author presents observations based on results of two earlier studies in England. The first study used 103 problem drinkers aged 65 years and older seen between 1960 and 1966. The other sample consisted of 92 elderly alcoholics seen in an alcohol unit in a hospital between 1967 and 1976. In both studies women outnumbered men. Two types of older drinkers were found. Group I consisted of long-standing excessive drinkers and alcoholics whose drinking habits persisted into old age. Group II consisted of previously moderate drinkers in whom the effects of the aging process--physical, mental, social, and environmental--had led to heavy drinking in their mid 60's or later. Personality factors and experiences such as retirement or bereavement precipitated heavy drinking. Patients showed self-neglect, falls, and confusion. The author recommends that treatment include: group therapy, social support, a therapeutic community, and pharmacotherapy.

173   Glatt, M. M., Rosin, A. J., & Jauhar, P. (1978). Alcoholic problems in the elderly. Age and Ageing, 7(Suppl.), 64-71.

This article reports the findings of two studies conducted in the Greater London area. The first study was conducted using 103 patients, 36 of whom were in a geriatric unit, 67 during psychiatric consultations or at the Alcoholism Unit of a large hospital. The second study used 92 patients referred because of alcoholism and seen in an alcoholism unit of a large hospital. Two types of older drinkers were identified: long-standing heavy drinkers whose drinking habits persisted in old age; and previously moderate drinkers who began drinking heavily in late-life. Factors which precipitated heavy drinking were personality factors (e.g., worrying, anxious personalities) and reactive factors, largely bereavement or retirement. Older alcoholics experienced falls and confusion and demonstrated self-neglect. Many older alcoholic patients were women.

174   Glynn, R. J., Bouchard, G. R., LoCastro, J. S., & Laird, N. M. (1985). Aging and generational effects on drinking behaviors in men: Results from the normative aging study. American Journal of Public Health, 75(12), 1413-1419.

This report looks at data on alcohol consumption obtained from the Normative Aging Study begun in 1963 at the Boston VA Outpatient Clinic. As it applies to the area of alcohol consumption, it yields some informative data. A 15-page survey was returned by 1,897 of the 2,025 men canvassed in 1973 and a follow-up survey in 1982 yielded a return of 1,570. This is a systematic study of the effects of birth cohort on drinking behavior. Six nine-year birth cohorts are examined with the first cohort born in 1892-1900. The overall findings of this report are that the effects of generation and period are far greater than age on drinking behavior. The authors also suggest that this finding has significant public health implications in that their data suggests that the trend is for an increase in drinking for each succeeding cohort; the implications for increased health problems as these cohorts reach old age are serious.

175   Gold, D. P., Andres, D., Chaikelson, J., Schwartzman, A. E., & Arbuckle, T. (1991). A longitudinal study of competence in elderly veterans: The role of alcohol and education. Psychiatry, 54(3), 238-250.

This study was done in Canada following veterans of WWII in terms of the impact on general functioning of post-war alcohol consumption and post-service education. Veterans (N+326) were divided into three groups: alcoholics, nonalcoholics who had obtained post-service education, and nonalcoholic men with no post-service education. Due to the small sample of alcoholics, the researchers reported that they were unable to add a group which would have contained alcoholics with post-service education. Differences were examined for performance on standard intelligence and personality tests, including the Life Complexity Interview (Gribbin, Schaie, & Parham, 1980). The first finding was that number of months of education obtained was indicative of better functioning overall. In decreasing order of general functioning were: nonalcoholics with education, nonalcoholics without further education and alcoholics. One interesting finding was that the nonalcoholic with education group was less likely to use emotion-focused coping mechanisms than their counterparts and were less likely to use avoidance to cope with stress.

176   Goldman, M. S., Williams, D. L., & Klisz, D. K. (1983). Recoverability of psychological functioning following alcohol abuse: Prolonged visual-spatial dysfunction in older alcoholics. Journal of Consulting and Clinical Psychology, 51(3), 370-378.

This study examined the effects of age on vulnerability to the toxic effects of alcohol on neurological function. Thirty-one alcoholics who met DSM-III criteria for Alcohol Dependence were selected from the Salvation Army Harbor Light Alcoholism Treatment Center in Detroit. Participants were classified into three age groups: 20-29 years of age; 30-39 years of age; and 40 and older. Each subject completed 3 months of testing using tests from the Rennick's Repeatable Cognitive-Perceptual Motor Battery (RCPM) to assess visuo-spatial and psychomotor functioning. Tests were administered by experimenters who were thoroughly trained in testing procedures. Data were also gathered on quantity, frequency, and duration of alcohol consumption and drug abuse using multiple measures. Two control samples were chosen to provide data on practice effects and normative test performance. The first control group was comprised of 15 male career army personnel over age 40 tested at the Detroit Artillery Armory.

The eight neuropsychological test scores for each of the three alcoholic and two control groups at each of 14 testing points were subjected to a 5 x 4 repeated measures multivariate analysis of variance (MANOVA). An omnibus MANOVA of these scores revealed significant overall differences among groups. The three alcoholic groups were significantly more impaired than the controls, $F(8, 43) = 4.26$, $p < .001$. The oldest alcoholics were significantly more impaired than the two younger groups of alcoholics, $F(8,43) = 3.28$, $p < .005$.

To examine recovery in each age group, one-way univariate ANOVAs with Newman-Keuls follow-up tests compared the mean test scores for the three age groupings at 4 different time periods of testing. Three-month curves measuring recoverability of visuo-spatial and psychomotor functioning were constructed for each group. Results from statistical analysis showed that alcoholics who were 40 and older failed to recover on most tasks over 3 months, compared to younger alcoholics (under age 40) who recovered completely from functional impairment by 2 to 3 weeks after drinking ceased. Results were not a function of drinking history or demographic variables. The researchers conclude that after age 40, adults experience an increase in vulnerability to the toxic effects of alcohol or are less able to compensate for neurological impairment.

177   Goodwin, J. S., Sanchez, C. J., Thomas, P., Hunt, C., Garry, P. J., & Goodwin, J. M. (1987). Alcohol intake in a healthy elderly population. American Journal of Public Health, 77(2), 173-177.

This study addressed the following questions: (1) What are the drinking patterns in healthy older people, and how are they associated with age, gender, income, and level of education? and (2) is moderate or heavy alcohol intake in this population associated with changes in emotional status, social integration, or cognitive function? The sample consisted or 2,770 healthy people between the ages of 65 and 89, who lived independently in an urban community in the southwestern United States. The group was predominantly Caucasian and middle-class. Forty percent were men. Health status was determined by a complete medical history and physical examination. Alcohol consumption was assessed during a three-day period using a detailed diet record and subsequent computer analysis. The participants weighed and measured alcohol consumed in the three days. Questionnaires were also used to obtain data on current and past alcohol intake.

Cognitive abilities were assessed with a 30-item mental status questionnaire administered verbally by an interviewer. The Halstead Category Test and Wechsler Memory Scale were also administered. Social interaction was evaluated with a revised form of the Interview Schedule for Social Interaction. Subjects gave fasting blood samples for determination of vitamin B_{12} and folic acid, riboflavin, thiamine, pyridoxine, and vitamin C. Blood lipid values were also obtained. To assess emotional status, subjects completed a 92-item symptom checklist.

Findings revealed that alcohol consumption was higher in males, higher income groups and among those with higher levels of education. Alcohol intake decreased with age. Alcohol intake was not associated with any changes in social or psychological state, but was positively associated with several measures of cognitive status, although the correlations were weak. Researchers concluded that old age per se is not a contraindication to alcohol consumption. They did note several important limitations of their study, which may have influenced their findings including: (1) there were no institutionalized or severely ill elders in the study; (2) measurements of alcohol intake may have been insensitive or inaccurate; (3) no heavy drinkers were included in the study; (4) three-day diet records may underestimate the average consumption of alcohol for the entire week and miss "binge" drinkers; and (5) all those studied had volunteered for the study so the sample may be very biased.

178   Graham, K., Zeidman, A., Flower, M. C., Saunders, S. J., & White-Campbell, M. (1992). A typology of elderly persons with alcohol problems. Alcoholism Treatment Quarterly, 9(3-4), 79-95.

Based upon the case study method, 24 cases of elderly persons with alcohol problems were classified into four types. The case typology was then sent to experts in the field of geriatric alcoholism for review. The final typology consisted of four types: chronic alcohol abuser; reactive problem drinker; problem drinkers whose drinking seemed to be interrelated with psychiatric or cognitive problems; and problem or heavy drinkers whose drinking seemed to be interrelated with a heavy drinking abusive spouse/partner. The first three types were described in detail, and brief cases were used for illustrative purposes. Treatment appropriate for each case was discussed.

179   Gurnack, A. M., & Hoffman, N. G. (1992). Elderly alcohol misuse. The International Journal of the Addictions, 27(7), 869-878.
        This study analyzes the records of 869 patients in order to identify issues related to elderly problem drinking. Demographics reveal that three-quarters of the patients were between 60 and 70, mainly male and almost exclusively Caucasian, over half were married, retired and living primarily on a pension, and over half had received a high school education. All had been admitted to a treatment center in 15 states during the period 1983-1985. Each treatment center contracted with the Chemical Abuse-Addiction Treatment Outcome Registry to monitor patient outcomes.
        In the second part of the study the authors determine which factors are related to early versus late problem drinking. The dependent variable, "age of use" is broken down into three categories: 1) use before age 31, 2) use between 31-45, and 3) use after age 45. Distinct differences between men and women are evident when controlled for sex. There are over 80 independent variables used including sociodemographic characteristics, symptoms, usage patterns and medical history. The authors' findings suggest that alcohol use throughout life may simply be carried into old age; that emotional distress and employment status do have an association with the initial use of alcohol, although they do not know the reasons why; and that there are considerable differences between the drinking patterns of older females and males. Future endeavors are needed particularly as related to the life course of alcohol use.

180   Guttmann, D. (1978). Patterns of legal drug use by older Americans. Addictive Diseases: An International Journal, 3(3), 337-356.
        Using a stratified sampling procedure, 447 noninstitutionalized elderly persons were interviewed in the Washington, D.C. SMSA. A questionnaire was used to collect data on socioeconomic background and decision-making patterns of the subjects and information on use of legally available drugs, including alcohol. Results reported on prescriptions drug use, use of over-the-counter (OTC) drugs, and alcohol use.
        Findings on alcohol use revealed that the majority of respondents (56.2%) reported little or no use of alcohol. Less than 20 percent were frequent users. The reasons most frequently given for using alcohol were to have fun (27%), to be accepted by friends (22%),

and to forget about some personal problems (29.9%). Only one variable predicted extent of usage: income. The higher the income, the more frequently respondents tended to use alcohol. Those who used alcohol were also more likely to live with spouse and children or with friends, than with children only.

181   Hurt, R. D., Finlayson, R. E., Morse, R. M., & Davis, L. J. (1988). Alcoholism in elderly persons: Medical aspects and prognosis of 216 inpatients. Mayo Clinic Proceedings, 63(8), 753-760.

This article reviews the medical aspects of a study conducted between 1972 and 1983. Two hundred sixteen elderly patients with alcoholism between 65 and 83 years old, 70% men and 30% women, were admitted to the Alcoholism and Drug Dependence Unit (ADDU) of the Mayo Clinic and Rochester Methodist Hospital. Early-onset alcoholism was present in 59% of the men and 51% of the women, and late-onset alcoholism was present in 39% of the men and 46% of the women. Comprehensive medical exams were given to all patients, which revealed a number of medical diagnoses. Thirty-two of the 216 subjects had a current or past diagnosis of cancer, with colon cancer in men being the most prevalent. The most frequent disease was alcohol liver disease in 83 patients. In addition, fatty liver was diagnosed in 18, alcoholic hepatitis in 11, and cirrhosis in 17. On the other hand, hypertension was less frequent in the alcoholic patients (33.8%) than in the general elderly population (41%). Chronic obstructive pulmonary disease, present in 4.6% of the elderly, was found to be in 30.6% of the alcoholic patients. The authors report that the outcome of their study was less successful than other reported treatment programs and state a number of reasons to explain differences in their results. The article defends the traditionally-oriented inpatient treatment program, and believes that the less intensive programs will not suffice for elderly alcoholics.

182   Hyer, L., Carson, M., & Tamkin, A. (1987). Personality styles in the treatment of older alcoholics. Clinical Gerontologist, 7(2), 15-29.

This paper cites a dearth of studies dealing with personality and older alcoholics and describes a study of 50 patients in the alcohol treatment unit using the MMPI, Beck Depression Inventory (BDI), and the Millon Clinical Multiaxial Inventory. The first major finding is the predominance of dependent personality style in 42% of the cases. Other more complicated interaction data are reported. The authors point out the effect personality has on treatment and convincingly demonstrate this with an overview of four thorough case histories showing how certain aspects of dependency, depression, anxiety, and so forth affect how the client interacts in treatment and beyond in the community.

183   Iliffe, S., Haines, A., Booroff, A., Goldenberg, E., Morgan, P., &
            Gallivan, S. (1991). Alcohol consumption by elderly people:
            A general practice survey. Age and Ageing, 20(2), 120-123.

This study interviewed 241 patients from nine general practitioners in the London area. All were 75 years of age or older, with 83 male participants and 156 female. The subjects were interviewed about their use of alcohol within the previous three months, and studied to see if there was any relationship between alcohol consumption and depression, falls and use of outpatient services or inpatient care.

Researchers found that only three men and five women from this sample needed further detailed assessment of their alcohol use. The authors concluded that in this particular sample, alcohol consumption did not cause an increased number of falls or contribute to increased medical services. There was no association found in this group between alcohol and depression.

184   Janik, S. W., & Dunham, R. G. (1983). A nationwide examination
            of the need for specific alcoholism treatment programs for the
            elderly. Journal of Studies on Alcohol, 44(2), 307-317.

This study addresses the question of whether or not age-specific treatment for alcoholism is more effective for older alcoholics than age-integrated treatment. Data were acquired from the National Alcoholism Program Information System (NAPIS), a national data base developed and operated by NIAAA. Data were collected on initial contact with the agency, on intake into a program, and each month thereafter. Follow-up interviews were conducted with 22.5% of the subjects 180 days after intake. All of the patients 60 and older who had been selected for a 180-day follow-up interview (N=3,163) and 8% of patients 21 to 59 who had been selected for follow-up (N=3,190) comprised the sample.

Age was the independent variable. Dependent variables were divided into three groups: drinking-related characteristics before entering treatment; treatment received; and initial outcome measures (assessed at 180 days after the initiation of treatment).

Analysis revealed no significant differences between age groups for any treatment or outcome variable. Researchers conclude that their data provide little support for age-segregated treatment for alcoholic elders.

185   Jennison, K. M. (1992). The impact of stressful life events and social
            support on drinking among older adults: A general population

survey. International Journal of Aging and Human Development, 35(2), 99-123.

This article reports the results of analysis of stressful life events and alcohol use in a national sample of 1,418 respondents 60 years of age and over. The study tested the "buffering hypothesis," which suggests that older people who suffer major losses in life will be protected from responding by increased drinking if they have sufficient support from various social groups to buffer the stress.

Data utilized in the study consist of a general population sample of 1,418 people 60 and older in four pooled surveys drawn from the National Opinion Research Center (NORC) General Social Surveys (1978, 1980, 1983, and 1984). Stressful role loss included events such as divorce, job loss, family deaths, and hospitalization happening to the respondent during the last year and within five years. Social support measures included objective measures of marital status, family size, and church attendance. Subjective assessments of quality of life or life satisfaction were defined as the degree to which respondents were satisfied with friendships, family life, finances, and job situation. Basic data were cross-sectional baseline prevalence drinking patterns derived from survey questions on self-reported use of or experience with alcoholic beverages (liquor, wine, or beer) and the respondent's subjective evaluation of these experiences. Measures of drinking behavior were continuous.

Analysis of variance and multiple regression techniques were used to test the proposition that social support relations will intervene between role loss and drinking measures. Results indicated that excessive drinking is much more common among older males than among older females. A higher proportion of drinkers was found among groups with higher levels of education and among professionals and those with higher incomes. Results also showed that older adults who experienced stressful life event losses were significantly more likely to drink excessively than were those who did not experience such loses or who experienced them to a lesser extent. Multiple regression was used to assess the mediating effects of support buffers on stressful personal events for older people. The support variables which most significantly reduced the effects of stressful life events on overindulgence drinking were sibling support, church attendance, the quality of the marriage, kinship network support, friendship and the quality of employment or job satisfaction. Results from this study confirm the buffering hypothesis.

186   Jensen, G. D., & Bellecci, P. (1987). Alcohol and the elderly: Relationships to illness and smoking. Alcohol & Alcoholism, 22(2), 193-198.

This is a study that focuses on two elderly groups, one between the ages of 65 and 75, and the other on those older than 90. The researchers were investigating the relationships between past and present alcohol use to a range of physical and mental health variables and some lifestyle issues including smoking. The subjects were all residents of the California Veterans' Home in Napa Valley. All males over 90 living in independent or semi-independent facilities were asked to participate, whereas the other 32 younger men were randomly selected.

The research results revealed that the history of alcohol abuse and current alcohol intake varied significantly between the two groups with 44% of the younger elderly having a history of alcoholism versus 15% of the very old. Over 25% of the younger residents were currently heavy drinkers, and none of the very old currently drank. There was no significant alcohol effect for the amount of cigarette smoking, although past or current drinking in the young elderly revealed heavier smoking, more major medical illness and greater use of medications. The fact that none of the very old are now heavy drinkers supports other research that suggests a declining trend of alcohol abuse between those who are 45-64 and 65+ years of age.

187   Jinks, M. J., & Raschko, R. R. (1990). A profile of alcohol and prescription drug abuse in a high-risk community-based elderly population. DICP, The Annals of Pharmacotherapy, 24, 971-975.

This article gives a thorough overview of alcohol and drug abuse among the elderly clients of Elderly Services of Spokane, a component of the Spokane Community Mental Health Center. The authors describe this unique gatekeeper program using community-based workers such as postal service workers, pharmacists, meter readers, law enforcement personnel, bank personnel, etc. to identify and refer high risk elders. Following assessment and diagnosis, a complete care plan is developed for all aspects of the patient's life including treatment for chemical dependency if necessary. Treatment is monitored weekly (or more often) with home visitation. This article shows that of the available 1,668 ESS cases available for review, 161 were diagnosed with alcohol abuse and fifty clients were diagnosed with prescription drug abuse. Importantly, in the case of prescription drug abusers, 92% of the clients were abusers for more than five years; 32% ranged in the 5 to 10 year category, 36% in the 11-20 year slot and a significant 24% were abusers for 21+ years. Many of these clients exhibited chronic physical illness, 71%; social isolation, 69%, depression, 56%, etc. The need for strong intervention via the ESS team management program is convincingly detailed.

188   Kashner, T. M., Rodell, D. E., Ogden, S. R., Guggenheim, F. G., & Karson, C. N. (1992). Outcomes and costs of two VA inpatient treatment programs for older alcoholic patients. Hospital and Community Psychiatry, 43(10), 985-989.

This article examines the outcomes and costs of a treatment program for older alcoholics called the Older Alcoholic Rehabilitation (OAR) program at the VA Medical Center in Little Rock, Arkansas. Outcomes and costs of this specialized treatment program are compared to outcomes and costs of a traditional alcohol treatment program in a controlled trial.

Study subjects were 137 male alcoholic patients, who were age 45 years or older discharged from detoxification at the VA Medical Center in Little Rock between November 1, 1987 and June 1, 1989. Sixty-five patients were randomly assigned to traditional care and 72 were randomly assigned to the OAR program. The 137 patients were mostly white, poor, unmarried, and had a high school education or less.

Both treatment groups provided 2-7 days of inpatient detoxification, 3-4 weeks of inpatient treatment, and 1 year of outpatient aftercare. Compared to those in traditional treatment, OAR participants received more peer group sessions, Addiction Resource Advisor (ARA) training to help them to understand their drinking, and relaxation therapy. They received less physical therapy. OAR patients also received reminiscence therapy, lived on a special unit in which staff focused specifically on the problems of aging and older alcoholics, and OAR staff were supportive, tolerant, and respectful.

Data on drinking were gathered through questionnaires administered face-to-face on admission and 6 and 12 months after discharge. Extent of alcohol consumption was inferred from questions derived from associates. Information about use of VA hospital services and costs was obtained from VA hospital records and computerized files. Program costs were calculated as 1989 expenditures. Logistical regression analyses were performed.

Results indicated that OAR patients were 2.9 times more likely at 6 months and 2.1 times more likely at 12 months to report abstinence than their counterparts who received traditional treatment. These figures increased significantly for each 10 years of age, so that oldest OAR participants were even more likely to abstain after 6 months and 1 year than were older patients who participated in traditional treatment. Data analyses also revealed that the OAR program was more productive (had a greater effect per unit of input) than the traditional program at 6 month and 1 year follow-up. These result provide support for age-specific treatment for older alcoholics.

189   Kirkpatrick, J. B., & Pearson, J. (1978). Fatal cerebral injury in the
       elderly. Journal of the American Geriatrics Society, 26(11),
       489-497.

       Seventy-one cases of fatal cerebral injuries, which occurred
between 1973 and 1977, were drawn from the medical examiner's
records in Dallas County, Texas. The brain specimen was sliced in
autopsy, and photographs and microsections were obtained. The study
of the circumstances of death included police reports and past medical
records, as well as the report of an assigned field investigator, who
viewed the scene of death and interviewed relatives and witnesses.
Complete toxicologic examination of the blood and other body fluids
was also performed.

       Based on data studied for individuals 60 and older (59 cases),
the authors concluded that males were more likely to suffer accidental
injury, and the majority of accidents (63%) were falls. Household
accidents accounted for 18 cases of falls, most involving ladders or
stairs. Falls were often precipitated by physical illness or ingestion of
alcohol. Consumption of alcohol was also a major factor in the fatal
assault cases. The authors presented two case illustrations in the
article.

190   Kola, L. A., Kosberg, J. I., & Joyce, K. (1984). The alcoholic
       elderly client: Assessment of policies and practices of service
       providers. The Gerontologist, 24(5), 517-521.

       To explore program gaps and deficiencies that may prevent
staff of social service agencies from effectively serving elderly persons
with alcohol problems, a survey was conducted in 47 nutrition and/or
social service programs in or near Cleveland, Ohio. Questionnaires
completed by program coordinators requested information about (1)
perception of the extent of alcohol problems among clients; (2) record
keeping and client identification; (3) formal and informal policies; (4)
treatment philosophy and practices; (5) interaction with community
resources; and (6) staff skills and training needs.

       Analysis of responses revealed a drastic underreporting of
alcohol problems in elderly clients. Less than 1% of the 11,000 clients
served were identified as having an alcohol problem. Nearly three-
quarters of the agencies lacked formal assessment techniques to identify
elderly alcoholics and had no systematic recordkeeping system to track
these clients. They also did not have any formal written policy
regarding the admission and utilization of services by elderly
alcoholics. A quarter of the coordinators felt that alcoholism was a
result of moral weakness, rather than a health or social problem. The
staff of most agencies were not knowledgeable about the treatment of
alcoholism or the elderly's need for alcoholism treatment services.

Forty-two percent of the agencies had provided in-services related to alcoholism, indicating that they recognized their deficiency in this area. Few of the agencies surveyed had any formal agreements with alcoholism agencies to assist them in serving their older clients who abuse alcohol. The researchers concluded their discussion by noting the need for agencies serving older adults to develop adequate programming or treatment facilities to help their clients who are having problems with alcohol. Otherwise, older alcoholics will remain underserved or served ineffectively.

191   Kosberg, J. I., & McCarthy, E. J. (1985). Problem drinking participants in programs for the elderly: Programmatic considerations. Journal of Applied Gerontology, 4(2), 20-29.
        Fifty Florida nutrition, daycare or service programs were surveyed regarding "perception of the extent of alcohol problems among clients, client identification and record-keeping, formal and informal policies, treatment philosophy and practices, community resource linkages, and staff skills and training" (p. 23). The findings showed that 82% of the site managers found fewer than five problem drinkers in their program. Only 44% of the agencies had records which could be used to identify problem drinkers and only four sites have a systematic method of tracking. For the third area of interest, only 24% of the agencies had formal policies regarding service utilization by problem drinkers. There was evidence of staff negative bias toward the problem drinker and few formal linkages were available for consultation and referral needs in this area. The findings in the area of staff skills and training were mixed. While only 24% of the agencies had provided staff training in the area, 36% said that they were aware of resources to provide such training and 22% stated that one of their staff had special knowledge about the treatment of elderly drinkers. The authors conclude with this: "It is imperative that agencies serving the elderly either provide these services directly, or take a liaison or ombudsman-type position in the community to facilitate the obtaining of necessary services" (Carruth, et al., 173, p. 27).

192   Krach, P. (1990). Discovering the secret: Nursing assessment of elderly alcoholics in the home. Journal of Gerontological Nursing, 16(11), 32-38.
        The study reported upon in this article was conducted with fifteen subjects selected from the files of a mental health center, who were aged 55 or older and had a primary or secondary diagnosis of alcoholism for at least 5 years. Assessments of these people were conducted in their homes to provide data on five dimensions of functioning: physical, mental, social, economic, and self-care capacity.

The instruments used were the Older American Resources Survey (OARS) and a mental health inventory from the MMPI.

Findings from each dimension are systematically discussed and presented in table form. Some of the major findings include the following: 97% of the subjects were diagnosed primarily as depressed with alcoholism as the secondary diagnosis. Ninety percent were taking antidepressants or anti-anxiety agents. Over half those interviewed were taking numerous drugs and having some drug-related problems. Some could not read labels or open containers. All subjects had at least one major physical problem. Cardiac and respiratory disease and arthritis were the most common problems. All participants were rated by the investigator as having moderate to severe impairment of mental health. Fifty percent of the subjects were depressed and 20% had been previously hospitalized for a suicide attempt. Only two of those questioned admitted that their drinking was related to their physical or mental health problems. Three quarters of the subjects had weekly phone contact and visits from friends or relatives. Yet 30% said they felt lonely most of the time. The majority (90%) perceived themselves as being severely financially stressed. In the area of self-care, all subjects felt they could eat and dress by themselves, but half of them felt they needed some assistance with shopping and meal preparation.

In the last section the author lists seven books for older adults to read. She also discusses the important role of nurses in assessment, identification, and intervention. She discusses special considerations with elders such as using a much less aggressive confronting style and very carefully probing for drinking history. She concludes with advice to nurses and others working with older clients to assess their own attitudes about alcoholism and to develop a thorough knowledge and understanding of alcoholism and of aging. She offers twenty suggestions for interventions that are effective when working with older alcoholics in a home setting. One suggestion is to contact the person's physician and pharmacist if there are medication-related problems. Another is to encourage participation in AA.

193   Kua, E. H. (1990). Drinking habits of elderly Chinese. British Journal of Addiction, 85(4), 571-573.

This study examines drinking habits of 612 randomly selected Chinese elderly (65+) living in Singapore. The prevalence of alcohol dependence was 0.6%, with the reported frequency for of those who drank at least once a week 3.2% of the sample. This study reported no regular drinking in their female subjects. This brief paper includes a discussion of cultural norms and expectations to explain the low frequency, but also observes that other studies are showing that younger more affluent generations of Chinese are increasing overall alcohol consumption.

194   La Greca, A. J., Akers, R. L., & Dwyer, J. W. (1988). Life events and alcohol behavior among older adults. The Gerontologist, 28(4), 552-558.

This article focuses on the hypothesis that alcohol abuse is related to life events. The relationship between life events and alcohol behavior was investigated among individuals 60 years of age and older. Data were gathered in face-to-face interviews in the homes of 1,410 adults. Subjects lived in two retirement communities and two age-integrated communities.

The dependent variable, alcohol consumption, was operationalized to cover the continuum of alcohol behavior ranging from abstinence to heavy drinking. Frequency of alcohol consumption in the past year was measured on a 9-point scale ranging from a low of no drinking to a high of daily drinking. Four categories were created from responses: abstainers; less than once a month or 2 to 3 times per month; once or twice a week to 3 to 4 times per week; and nearly daily or daily. Frequency of alcohol consumption in the past month included seven response categories, collapsed into the following four groups: abstainers; 1 to 3 times; 1 to 4 times; and daily. Alcohol-related problems covered physiological, psychological, and social consequences related to problem drinking (e.g., liver disease). "Typical" quantity of alcohol consumption referred to the quantity of beer, wine, or liquor consumed on a typical day, measured by the number of cans or bottles of beer, glasses of wine, or drinks of 1 ounce of liquor. Number of life events experienced in the past year were also noted: death of family or close friend, family health problems, own health problems, change of residence, financial difficulty, death of spouse, family separation, retirement, marriage, divorce or fired from job. A measure of social support and a measure of individual coping resources were also included. Socio-demographic variables were age, sex, race, and income.

Findings revealed that among respondents, although many were abstainers, 20% reported drinking nearly daily or daily. Nearly three-fourths experienced at least one significant life event. The researchers found no correlation between the occurrence of life events and the frequency, quantity, or problems of drinking behavior among older adults in the sample. Personal coping resources and levels of social support did not have any effect on the relationship between drinking behavior and life events. This study did not find that social support networks were mediators for the impact of life events on alcohol use among older adults.

195   Lichtenberg, P. A., Gibbons, T. A., Nanna, M. J., & Blumenthal, F.
        (1993). The effects of age and gender on the prevalence and
        detection of alcohol abuse in elderly medical inpatients.
        Clinical Gerontologist, 13(3), 17-27.

        This study was conducted in a 155 bed comprehensive
rehabilitation center that each year treats over 500 stroke patients and
an additional 200 geriatric patients. One hundred eighty consecutive
admissions of patients 60 years or older were seen in 1991. Thirty had
severe language or cognitive impairments and could not participate in
the study. The remaining 150 patients were grouped by age (60-74 and
75 +) and gender (male and female). Each patient was administered the
CAGE questionnaire to assess alcohol use. Physician detection was
assessed by a blind chart review at least one week prior to admission.
        The overall prevalence rate for alcohol abuse was 17%, but
there were striking age and gender differences. Young-old men (60-74)
who had an extremely high rate of alcohol abuse were compared to old-
old men (75 +). Almost 50% of the young-old men reported alcohol
abuse compared to only 15% of the old-old men. Seventeen percent of
young-old women reported alcohol abuse, whereas only 3% of old-old
women did so. Men exhibited much higher prevalence rates than did
women. Young-old men reported a rate of alcohol abuse that was three
times greater than that reported by young-old women. Old-old men
reported a prevalence rate that was five times greater than that reported
by old-old women. Physicians detected alcohol abuse relatively well
in men, but no women alcohol abusers were detected.

196   Linn, M. W. (1978). Attrition of older alcoholics from treatment.
        Addictive Diseases: An International Journal, 3(3), 437-447.

        The problem of alcoholism in the elderly may be more serious
than in younger individuals because alcoholism may be accompanied by
other physical, mental, and social disabilities related to the aging
process. This article reports on a study of the effect of age on attrition
in an inpatient alcoholism treatment unit. All male patients admitted
with a diagnosis of alcoholism to an inpatient substance abuse treatment
unit in a Veterans Administration hospital during 1975 and 1976 were
studied. Patients completed a 90-item questionnaire providing
demographic data; educational, marital, work, legal, and drinking
histories; current drinking patterns; and all prior treatments for
alcoholism. They also completed the Hopkins Symptom Checklist, six
semantic differentials to measure attitudes, and a Ward Atmosphere
Scale.
        Analysis of data revealed that older adults (55 +) were more
likely than younger adults (under age 50) to stay in treatment. For
both younger and older subjects those who were more depressed were

less likely to stay in treatment. Older adults who felt fatigued were more likely to stay in treatment; however, younger subjects who felt fatigued were more likely to drop out. Personal relationships on the ward between staff and patients and between patients were particularly important factors. Older adults who did not feel involved and included dropped out significantly more. Those who did not feel encouraged to be more self-sufficient and independent also dropped out.

197   Magruder-Habib, K., Saltz, C. C., & Barron, P. M. (1986). Age-related patterns of alcoholism among veterans in ambulatory care. Hospital and Community Psychiatry, 37(12), 1251-1255.

Researchers report on results of a study designed to estimate the prevalence of alcoholism among VA outpatients by obtaining age-specific alcoholism prevalence estimates. Patients attending any ambulatory care clinic of two large urban VA medical centers during a one-week period in November of 1979 were randomly sampled. All subjects were screened using an alcoholism screening test and a survey instrument designed to obtain sociodemographic information and to determine whether the patient had been treated for alcoholism within the previous 30 days. The screening test used was the Veterans Alcoholism Screening Test (VAST), a revision of the Michigan Alcoholism Screening Test (MAST). The VAST was completed by 432 patients. Of those 432, age was not recorded for 90. The remaining 342 comprised the sample studied. Sixty-three and one-third percent of these were categorized as never alcoholic; 17.8% as presently alcoholic; and 18.9% as formerly alcoholic. All but nine were male.

Findings revealed that the 65 and older age group had the lowest proportion of former alcoholics. The 65-and-over age group also had the lowest scores on the VAST. In the sample 10.2 of the 65-and-over group were alcoholic. The younger age groups (under age 35, 35-44, and 45-54) were two and a half to three times more likely to be alcoholic that the 65-and-over group. Half of the 65-and-over alcoholics were longstanding alcoholics. Researchers conclude that VA outpatients under age 55 should be the prime targets for alcoholism screening and intervention. They also conclude that we cannot dismiss the problem of alcoholism in older adults and point out that as the population continues to age the problem will be ever greater in the future.

198   Makkai, T., & McAllister, I. (1990). Alcohol consumption across the lifecycle in Australia, 1985-1988. Drug and Alcohol Dependence, 25(3), 305-313.

The researchers analyzed national population survey data collected in Australia in 1985 and 1988 to examine alcohol consumption patterns by age and gender. Results showed a dramatic drop in consumption rates for males and females, with females showing an even greater decline than males. Analyzing data by age and gender showed a pattern of consistent decline across the lifecycle for all age and gender groups, with the partial exception of females in 1988, who showed two small increases during the 30's and 50's. The greatest decline in heavy drinking was found in males in their 50's and 60's. Authors attribute the drops to the influence of the National Campaign Against Drug Abuse.

199   Malcolm, M. T. (1984). Alcohol and drug use in the elderly visited at home. The International Journal of the Addictions, 19(4), 411-418.

This study was done by an English physician hoping to get a clearer picture of alcohol and drug use and abuse through a home visit survey of 223 patients referred for a psychiatric opinion. He found that the mean consumption was 2.9 drugs daily and that one-third took 4 or more drugs. He also found that 10% of the patients visited exhibited a severe alcohol-related problem. Though this was not a rigorous scientific study, the observations and ending discussion are excellent.

200   Mangion, D. M., Platt, J. S., & Syam, V. (1992). Alcohol and acute medical admission of elderly people, Age and Ageing, 21(5), 362-367.

This article reports the results of a prospective study of prevalence and determinants of alcohol abuse and alcohol-related medical admissions in 539 patients 65 and older admitted to the departments of medicine in two separate Health Districts in the United Kingdom. A combination of alcohol-intake history, CAGE questionnaire and laboratory tests (GGT and MCV) were used to determine alcohol abuse. Data were also obtained from patients and/or informants on current admission principal diagnosis, age, sex, marital status, living status, social group, use of sedative drugs, cigarette smoking, ongoing chronic illness and independent mobility.

Alcohol abuse was defined as: alcohol intake greater than 21 units/week for men and 14 units/week for women, a positive CAGE response, and/or elevated GGT (>41 IU/1) or MCV (>98 fl). Of the forty-two patients classified as alcohol abusers, 41 were identified by alcohol intake history and one by a positive CAGE response. The reported alcohol intake among abusers was significantly higher in men than in women. Of the rest of the sample, 337 were abstainers or occasional drinkers, while 160 drank regularly but within defined safe limits. Sixty-seven reported enough heavier drinking in the past to be classified as alcohol abusers (men=63; women=4). The major reasons for reduction of intake with age were onset of illness (36%), loss of social contact (28%), financial difficulty (19%) and a feeling that alcohol was impairing health (4%).

The prevalence of alcohol abuse in patients was 7.8%. Thirteen of the admissions were due to alcohol intoxication. In alcohol abusers, 24% of admission were alcohol-related. Only one death was alcohol-related. Comparing alcohol abusers and non-alcohol abusers, it was found that alcohol abusers were significantly more likely to smoke and were more physically mobile than those who did not abuse alcohol. No late-onset drinkers were found.

201   McInnes, E., & Powell, J. (1994). Drug and alcohol referrals: Are elderly substance abuse diagnoses and referrals being missed? British Medical Journal, 6926(308), 444-446.

The study was part of a larger survey of use of tobacco, alcohol, and drugs by hospital inpatients 65 years and over in three hospitals in New South Wales, Australia. "The major aim of the study was to assess identification rates by medical staff of problem substance use among elderly inpatients, and to assess whether those identified as problem users were considered for referral to the hospital drug and alcohol service" (p. 444).

Medical staff caring for 263 older inpatients, who had been identified through face to face interviews as patients with problem substance use, were interviewed by phone or face to face using a standardized questionnaire. Results revealed that overall, hospital medical staff diagnosed only 25% of problem users and considered referring only 10% to drug and alcohol services. Of the 99 identified patients who were problem users of alcohol, only 33 were correctly identified by medical staff, and only 19 were considered in need of referral to drug and alcohol services. Men aged 65-74 were more likely to be considered for referral. The researchers concluded, based on these findings, that a high percentage of elderly substance users were missed and intervention was unlikely.

The researchers discuss several reasons for the lack of identification of older substance abusers including: a belief that older people should not be asked to give up established habits; poor history taking regarding drug use; lack of education about drug use; and lack of available drug and alcohol treatment services to refer to. The authors call for more education about drug and alcohol use in older people, and recommend a hospital based drug and alcohol counselor to work specifically with older adults at each hospital.

202   Mears, H. J., & Spice, C. (1993). Screening for problem drinking in
        the elderly: A study in the elderly mentally ill. International
        Journal of Geriatric Psychiatry, 8(4), 319-326.

        Subjects studied were all admissions to an acute unit for the
elderly mentally ill, who completed a questionnaire about problem
drinking, drinking habits, attitudes to alcohol, and possible sequelae of
alcohol use. Recent alcohol consumption was recorded, and the CAGE
was also administered. Patients already identified in the case notes as
having an alcohol problem were assigned to the group of problem
drinkers. These individuals were compared to non-problem drinkers.
        Results of the study are based on data obtained from 78
subjects ranging in age from 65 to 96 years (mean age = 77), who
completed the questionnaires. A highly significant difference in
consumption of alcohol was found between problem drinkers and the
remainder of the group, with consumption of 14 or more units of
alcohol per week being associated with high risk of adverse
consequences such as falls, medical illness, incontinence, and sleep
problems. Of the patients with a drinking problem, one-third were not
detected by the assessing physician. Problem drinkers were
significantly more likely to have been bereaved in the previous year
than were those who did not have drinking problems.

203   Meyers, A. R., Goldman, E., Hingson, R., & Scotch, N. (1981-82).
        Evidence for cohort or generational differences in the drinking
        behavior of older adults. International Journal of Aging and
        Human Development, 14(1), 31-45.

        This study, part of a larger, longitudinal study of alcohol use
among people 18 and older, reported upon alcohol use in a sample of
928 non-institutionalized individuals aged 60 years or older in the
Boston Metropolitan area. Data were gathered in 1977 through a 30-
minute personal interview.
        Researchers compared drinking behavior of young old (60-74)
and old-old (75+) respondents. Results indicate that the old-old are
much less likely to drink than are the young-old. Nearly two-thirds
(62%) of those 75 and older claim to be abstainers, compared to about
half of their younger counterparts. Researchers also found a consistent
negative relationship between relatively high levels of alcohol
consumption (2 or more drinks per day) and old age. Eleven percent
of the young-old claim to drink at least two drinks a day, compared to
1% of those who are 75 and older. Among octogenarians, no one
reported having more than two drinks daily. The young-old were more
likely to report that they were liquor drinkers, while most old-old
respondents drank wine. The zero-order partial correlation between
age and average daily volume is negative and statistically significant;

the relationship persists independent of the effects of gender, marital status, and education.

Several explanations for the findings are offered. One explanation is that heavy drinkers are underrepresented in the old-old group because heavy drinkers die earlier in life and do not survive into their seventies. Another possible explanation is that people drink less as they age due to a decreased tolerance for alcohol associated with aging. The final explanation, and the one the researchers accept as the most likely, is a cohort or generational one that posits that present cohorts of older people have always drunk less than their younger counterparts. The old-old were the cohort of Prohibition. They were children between 1900 and the enactment of Prohibition, a period when temperance education was mandatory in every state and abstinence was the norm. The young-old, on the other hand, matured during the Prohibition period. They witnessed widespread dissatisfaction with Prohibition and massive disobedience to the prohibitionist laws. Repeal of Prohibition and the Depression are likely also to have played important roles in differences in beliefs about alcohol and patterns of alcohol use in the young-old.

204   Meyers, A. R., Hingson, R., Mucatel, M., Heeren, T., & Goldman, E. (1985-86). The social epidemiology of alcohol use by urban older adults. International Journal of Aging and Human Development, 21(1), 49-59.

This study, based on an analysis of cross-sectional data, looked at two components related to older adults and alcoholism: prevalence of alcoholism in older adults and whether there is a correlation between alcohol-related problems and lower levels of life satisfaction. Noninstitutional residents of Boston, aged 60 or older (N=928), were interviewed for 30 minutes to gather information about their social and demographic characteristics.

The Boston data indicated that older people drink alcohol infrequently and in small quantities with 53% as abstainers, twice as high as younger adults interviewed. Four percent of the older adults said that they had some kind of alcohol-related problem while 10% of the younger adults had drinking problems. However, this study found no evidence that alcohol substitutes for the loss of jobs, income or companionship. While problem drinkers did express lower levels of satisfaction with their marriages, friends and families, the relationship between satisfaction and alcohol-related problems in this study is not clear. Also, the authors did not find any evidence to suggest that widowhood, retirement, or social isolation is associated with higher risks of problem drinking. This particular finding poses some interesting questions about prevailing theories of late-onset alcoholism which bears further investigation.

205   Midanik, L. T., Soghikian, K., Ransom, L. J., & Polen, M. R.
        (1992).   Alcohol problems and sense of coherence among
        older adults. Social Science Medicine, 34(1), 43-48.
        In this study researchers investigated the relationship between
alcohol problems and sense of coherence (SOC), a salutogenic model
developed by Antonovsky. SOC focuses on individuals who do not
have a particular disease and on their reaction and subsequent ability to
manage stressors, which in others may cause illness. Nine hundred
fifty-two older members of a health maintenance organization were
mailed questionnaires. Included in the questionnaire were: a 5-item
Alcohol Problem Index derived from national drinking practices
surveys; a quantity/frequency scale of alcohol consumption; a frequency
of drunkenness measure; and a 9-item shortened version of the original
SOC scale. Demographic data was also collected. Three groups of
drinkers were identified: lighter drinkers (< .022 oz. of absolute
alcohol/day), moderate drinkers (0.22 - 0.99 oz. of absolute
alcohol/day), and heavier drinkers (> 0.99 oz. of absolute
alcohol/day). Data were analyzed using correlational analyses, t-tests
and linear multiple regression. Data were presented for the entire
sample and for men and women separately.
        Multiple regression analyses revealed that SOC was a
significant negative predictor of alcohol problems while controlling for
alcohol consumption levels and frequency of drunkenness, for men and
women. SOC scores were significantly higher for lighter drinkers than
for heavier drinkers.

206   Molgaard, C. A., Nakamura, C. M., Stanford, E. P., Peddecord, K.
        M., & Morton, D. J.   (1990).   Prevalence of alcohol
        consumption among older persons. Journal of Community
        Health, 15(4), 239-251.
        This cross-sectional study of alcohol consumption among
individuals 45 years or older in the San Diego area compared drinking
percent prevalences among Whites (N=819), Blacks (N=629), and
Mexican-Americans (N=657). Several instruments were administered
in interviews including: Older Americans Resource and Services
(OARS) questionnaire, Center for Epidemiological Studies Depression
Scale (CES-D), Wolinsky Nutritional Risk Assessment (NRA) and
Second National Health and Nutrition Examination Survey (NHANES
II). Self-reported weekly consumption of beer, wine, and hard liquor
were scaled as minimal, mild, moderate or severe drinking.
        Findings revealed that Whites reported the highest overall
percent prevalence of drinking after age 40 at 78.9%, followed by

Blacks at 59.1%, and Mexican-Americans at 50.1%. For those 64 or older, Whites also had the highest overall percent prevalence of drinking, followed by Blacks and Mexican-Americans. Mexican-Americans drank moderately, while mild drinking characterized Blacks. Males had significantly higher percent prevalences of mild, moderate, and severe drinking than did females. Findings also support the literature that alcohol consumption decreases with age. Total drinking decreased from 70.2% in the youngest age category (45-54 years) to 49.6% in the oldest age range (75 years and over). Regardless of ethnicity, alcohol consumption declined with age.

207   Moos, R., Brennan, P., Fondacaro, M., & Moos, B. (1990). Approach and avoidance coping responses among older problem and nonproblem drinkers. Psychology and Aging, 5(1), 31-40.

This research report examined coping responses of older problem drinkers versus non-problem drinkers. They reported that problem drinkers were more likely to rely on cognitive avoidance, resigned acceptance and emotional discharge. Problem drinking men were found to be less likely seekers of support and problem drinking women were more likely to use positive reappraisal and seek alternative rewards. The authors conclude that "we found no support for the idea that older problem drinkers use avoidance coping because they have more difficult stressors to manage or because they appraise their stressors differently than nonproblem drinkers do" (p. 37). The results are many and complex and of interest to readers wishing to understand more completely coping among the problem versus non-problem drinker.

208   Moos, R. H., Brennan, P. L., & Mertens, J. R. (1994). Diagnostic subgroups and predictors of one-year re-admission among late-middle-aged and older substance abuse patients. Journal of Studies on Alcohol, 55(2), 173-183.

This naturalistic study uses data based on clinical records to examine treatment utilization and 1-year re-admission rates among three diagnostic subgroups of late-middle-aged and older substance abuse inpatients in Department of Veterans Affairs (VA) Medical Centers. 21,139 patients were divided into three groups based on their ICD-9CM (Commission on Professional and Hospital Activities, 1986) diagnoses: patients with alcohol and/or drug dependence and no other substance abuse or psychiatric diagnosis (N=11,652); patients with a diagnosis of alcohol or drug psychosis (N=3,510); and patients with alcohol or drug dependence and/or alcohol or drug psychoses, who also had one or more concomitant psychiatric diagnoses (N=5,977). In all three groups, 98% or more were men; more than 80% were white; the average age was 62 years.

Four sets of variables were examined for each group: characteristics of the index episode of inpatient care such as type of treatment unit, length of stay, and so forth; prior inpatient and outpatient care; postdischarge outpatient care for the year after the index episode of inpatient care; and re-admission rates for substance abuse or psychiatric disorders for a one-year interval after discharge from the index episode of inpatient care.

Overall, in the 2- to 3-year interval 21,000 patients in the three groups received a total of more than 1.5 million days of inpatient care. Results of one-way analyses of variance (ANOVA) and Student-Newman-Keuls (SNK) tests for the continuous variables, and chi-square tests for the categorical variables revealed interesting differences among diagnostic groups. As expected, results revealed that patients with an alcohol or drug psychosis and patients with an alcohol or drug disorder and a concomitant psychiatric disorder received more treatment before, during, and following an index episode of care than did patients with only an alcohol or drug dependence diagnosis. Patients in the more severe diagnostic groups were also significantly more likely to be re-admitted for care than patients with only an alcohol or drug dependence diagnosis. Relatively few older substance abuse patients received substance abuse or psychiatric aftercare.

As expected, re-admission rates were higher for patients with alcohol or drug psychosis and those with concomitant psychiatric disorders. Results of analyses revealed the following as predictors of re-admission: unmarried status; need as indicated by prior treatment; more prior outpatient visits for medical care; a psychiatric diagnosis; and discharge against medical advice and dropping out of treatment.

209   Moos, R. H., Brennan, P. L., & Mertens, J. R. (1994). Mortality rates and predictors of mortality among late-middle-aged and older substance abuse patients. Alcoholism: Clinical and Experimental Research, 18(1), 187-195.

In this study researchers examined the death rate in a group of over 21,000 late-middle-aged and older substance abuse patients relative to the death rate in an age-, sex-, and race-matched group in the general population. Patients' treatment is traced back over four years before the index episode and followed four years after discharge. They also describe how death rates vary by specific diagnostic and treatment factors. Three sets of factors, which may contribute to the prediction of time-to-death among older substance abuse patients, were examined. These included: demographic factors; patients' substance abuse, psychiatric, and medical diagnoses; and proxy indicators of illness severity.

Researchers calculated standardized mortality ratios (SMRs) which are ratios of observed to expected deaths in a sample, given general population death rates. They found that 5,073 of the 21,139 patients died during the four-year follow-up interval. The expected death rate for an age-, sex-, race-matched general population group is 9.1%, thus the excess mortality or SMR is 2.64. The SMR was higher among nonmarried than among married, and among Caucasian than among Black or Hispanic patients. The SMR declined with age. The SMR was also elevated among patients with alcohol psychosis, organic brain disorder, and several medical diagnoses including neoplasms, liver cirrhosis, respiratory, endocrine, metabolic, and blood disorders. As expected, patients who had prior episodes of inpatient care for medical disorders had higher excess mortality rates, as did patients who had prior episodes of inpatient care for substance abuse disorders. The SMR rose to 3.86 among patients with three or more prior medical episodes. Also, patients who had more outpatient medical care had higher mortality rates.

Researchers also found that the rate of mortality was significantly higher for patients who received little or no outpatient care in the year after the index episode during the three subsequent years following discharge. They conclude that "mental health aftercare may delay mortality" (p. 194).

Authors suggest that it is important to learn more about how much of the premature mortality identified among alcoholics is due to alcohol-related causes. Future research is needed that combines information about individuals' diagnostic and treatment history with information from death certificates and the probable alcohol involvement in different disorders.

210   Moos, R. H., Brennan, P. L., & Moos, B. S. (1991). Short-term processes of remission and nonremission among late-life problem drinkers. Alcoholism: Clinical and Experimental Research, 15(6), 948-955.

In this study researchers examine the short-term process of remission among late-life problem drinkers. The study is prospective and compares alcohol use, functioning, life stressors, social resources, and help-seeking among three groups of older people: remitted problem drinkers; nonremitted problem drinkers; and nonproblem drinkers. To obtain their sample, researchers used a screening survey to obtain initial information on drinking problems and health from men and women between the ages of 55 and 65, who had recent contact with one of two large medical centers. Time 1 data collection was completed by 1,884 participants.

Classification into problem and nonproblem drinking groups was based on responses to alcohol-related problem items on the screening survey and to a 17-item Drinking Problems Index which covers general problems due to drinking such as: intoxication; adverse consequences or life problems that result from excessive drinking; and alcohol dependence or withdrawal symptoms. One year later the researchers followed over 96% of the problem drinkers who were still alive and categorized them into two groups: (1) remitted problem drinkers (N=192 or 29% of drinkers) who reported at follow-up that they had experienced no drinking problems during the last 12 months, and (2) nonremitted problem drinkers (N=467 or 71% of drinkers) who indicated at follow-up that they had experienced one or more drinking problems during the past year. They also followed 95% of the nonproblem drinkers (N=574). Respondents were also classified as early-onset or late-onset problem drinkers on the basis of their drinking history.

Indices of health-related and social functioning, life stressors and social resources, and help-seeking were drawn from the Health and Daily Living Form (HDL), the Life Stressors and Social Resources Inventory (LISRES), and the Coping Responses Inventory (CRI). Multivariate Analyses of Covariance (MANCOVA) controlling for sex and marital status were used to compare to-be-remitted and to-be-nonremitted problem drinkers with nonproblem drinkers at Time 1 and again at 1-year follow-up. Paired-sample t-tests were used to examine changes between Time 1 and Time 2. Partial correlations and multiple regression analyses were used to identify predictors of remission and abstinence among early- and late-onset problem drinkers.

Results indicated that at initial assessment, to-be-remitted problem drinkers consumed less alcohol, reported fewer drinking problems, had friends who approved less of drinking, and were more likely to seek help from mental health practitioners than were those who would continue to have drinking problems. Nonproblem drinkers had higher levels of functioning and more social resources than either group of problem drinkers. At Time 2 remitted problem drinkers continued to consume less alcohol and had better social resources and fewer stressors than those who continued to drink. Compared with early-onset alcoholics, late-onset problem drinkers were more likely to remit over the year.

211   Moos, R. H., Mertens, J. R., & Brennan, P. L. (1993). Patterns of diagnosis and treatment among late-middle-aged and older substance abuse patients. Journal of Studies on Alcohol, 54(4), 479-487.
This naturalistic study uses data based on clinical records to

examine treatment utilization and 1-year re-admission rates among three diagnostic subgroups of late middle-aged and older substance abuse inpatients in Department of Veterans Affairs (VA) Medical Centers. 21,139 patients were divided into three groups based on their ICD-9CM (Commission on Professional and Hospital Activities, 1986) diagnoses: patients with alcohol and/or drug dependence and no other substance abuse or psychiatric diagnosis (n = 11,652); patients with a diagnosis of alcohol or drug psychosis (n = 3510); and patients with alcohol or drug dependence and/or alcohol or drug psychoses, who also had one or more concomitant psychiatric diagnoses (n = 5977). In all three groups, 98% or more were men; more than 80% were white; the average age was 62 years.

Four sets of variables were examined for each group: characteristics of the index episode of inpatient care such as type of treatment unit, length of stay, etc.; prior inpatient and outpatient care; postdischarge outpatient care for the year after the index episode of inpatient care; and re-admission rates for substance abuse or psychiatric disorders for a one-year interval after discharge from the index episode of inpatient care.

Overall, in the 2- to 3-year interval 21,000 patients in the three groups received a total of more than 1.5 million days of inpatient care. Results of one-way analyses of variance (ANOVAS) and Student-Newman-Keuls (SNK) tests for the continuous variables and chi-square tests for the categorical variables among diagnostic groups revealed interesting differences. As expected, results revealed that patients with an alcohol or drug psychosis and patients with an alcohol or drug disorder and a concomitant psychiatric disorder received more treatment before, during, and following an index episode of care than did patients with only an alcohol or drug dependence diagnosis. Patients in the more severe diagnostic groups were also significantly more likely to be re-admitted for care than patients with only an alcohol or drug dependence diagnosis. Relatively few older substance abuse patients received substance abuse or psychiatric aftercare.

As expected, re-admission rates were higher for patients with alcohol or drug psychosis and those with concomitant psychiatric disorders. Results of analyses revealed the following as predictors of re-admission: unmarried status; need as indicated by prior treatment; more prior outpatient visits for medical care; a psychiatric diagnosis; and discharge against medical advice and dropping out of treatment.

212   Moran, M. B., & Naughton, B. J. (1991). Performance of an alcoholism screening test in elderly men. Clinical Gerontologist, 11(1), 86-88.
      Moran and Naughton review the performance of a screening

test (Cyr & Wartman, 1988) as part of a cross-sectional study of 96 male veterans, 70-93 years of age. The purpose of the screening is to measure its results against the Michigan Alcoholism Screening Test (MAST) (Selzer, 1971). In the brief screening test, a positive response to one or both of the questions: "Have you ever had a drinking problem?" and "When was your last drink?" is considered a positive test for alcoholism. The prevalence of alcoholism as indicated by a MAST score greater than or equal to 5 was 26.0%, much lower than previously tested. Neither the MAST nor the brief screening test distinguish between active and recovering alcoholics. An explanation for differences in test results may lie in birth cohort differences between the two study samples. The article concludes by stating that while a validated screening test for older alcoholics remains illusive, clinicians should include questions about alcohol use in the routine medical history.

213   Moran, M. B., Naughton, B. J., & Hughes, S. L. (1990). Screening elderly veterans for alcoholism. Journal of General Internal Medicine, 5, 361-364.

This study was done to determine the usefulness of an alcohol screening test (Cyr and Wartman alcoholism screening questions) with an older population. This instrument had been used successfully with young adults. The authors found a sensitivity of .52, and a specificity of .76 for this sample and discuss these findings in terms of age-related differences in attitude and drinking behavior. Methodological constraints are also discussed such as the possible impact of the sex of the respondent on the outcome.

214   Mulford, H. A., & Fitzgerald, J. L. (1992). Elderly versus younger problem drinker profiles: Do they indicate a need for special programs for the elderly? Journal of Studies on Alcohol, 53(6), 601-610.

The research reported in this study was designed to answer the question, do elderly problem drinkers differ from younger ones and need special treatment? The study population consisted of adults 18 and older, who lived in or near Iowa and who had their driver's licenses revoked by the Iowa Department of Transportation after they had been arrested for "operating a motor vehicle while intoxicated." Subjects were contacted by phone or mail (age 18-30, N=319; 31-54, N=326; 55-64, N=542; 65+, N=243). To obtain the subjects descriptive profile, researchers administered a slightly modified version of the Iowa Alcoholic Intake Schedule (IAIS), designed to obtain a comprehensive self-report picture of the role of alcohol in one's life. Younger persons (18-54 years) were compared with two overlapping elderly age groups (55 and over and 65 and over). Chi-square tests were used to determine statistically significant differences. Subjects were also dichotomized as "early-onset" (at least one problem-drinking indicator occurred prior to age 55) and "late-onset" (all problem drinking indicators occurred at age 55 or later). When younger problem drinkers and older problem drinkers were compared, their profiles were much more alike than different. There were some statistically significant differences, but most were relatively small. One significant difference was noted. Elderly problem drinkers, early- and late-onset, were much more likely than younger problem drinkers to be taking prescription drugs. The early-, but not late-, onset elderly problem drinkers were also much more likely to be taking a prescribed depressant. Early-onset elderly drinkers reported more deviant drinking than late-onset elderly drinkers. Early-onset elderly problem drinkers had not progressed as far in the alcoholic process as either the early-onset elderly drinkers or the younger problem drinkers. Late-onset elderly problem drinkers were less likely to believe their drinking impaired their driving than were late- onset elderly drinkers and younger drinkers. Researchers found significant differences between early-onset elderly problem drinkers and late-onset elderly problem drinkers. The late-onset elderly problem drinkers were more likely to be lighter drinkers and less advanced in the alcoholic process than early-onset elderly problem drinkers. Because they found few statistically significant differences between younger and older problem drinkers, the authors conclude that special treatment programs for older problem drinkers are not justified or necessary.

215   Naik, P. C., & Jones, R. G. (1994). Alcohol histories taken from elderly people on admission. British Medical Journal, 6923(308), 248.

This study reports on a random sample of elderly people (65 + years) admitted to a hospital with an acute medical condition over a six month period. The interviewer obtained sociodemographic data and alcohol history. Alcohol histories recorded by admitting doctors were examined.

Results revealed that of the 80 patients identified, 22 were excluded leaving 26 men and 32 women aged 66-94. Twenty-four admitted to drinking alcohol, but when asked if they put alcohol in their tea or coffee, an additional 10 admitted to using alcohol. The prevalence rate of excessive drinking was 10%. Excessive drinking was not related to age, sex, or social class.

The admitting doctor had recorded a qualitative alcohol history for 28 patients and a quantitative history for 2 and had not recorded a history for 28 (including one who drank excessively). An alcohol history was significantly less likely to be recorded with increasing age ($x^2 = 6.026$, df=2, P<0.04) and higher social class ($x^2 = 6.304$, df = 2, p<0.04). The researchers conclude that doctors are less likely to record an alcohol history in older patients. They recommend that a quantitative alcohol history be taken routinely, from all elderly people admitted to the hospital, and that it include a question about use of alcohol in tea or coffee.

216   Nakamura, C. M., Molgaard, C. A., Stanford, E. P., Peddecord, K. M., Morton, D. J., Lockery, S. A., Zuniga, M., & Gardner, L. D. (1990). A discriminant analysis of severe alcohol consumption among older persons. Alcohol and Alcoholism, 25(1), 75-80.

Researchers report the results of a study of variables that predict severe versus non-severe drinking among older adults. Respondents, were randomly selected (N=1,034), noninstitutionalized residents of San Diego between 45 and 99 years of age. They were interviewed by trained interviewers. Interviews were conducted in the respondent's home and lasted about 1.5 hours. Instruments used included the Older Americans Resource and Services (OARS) questionnaire, portions of the Second National Health and Nutrition Examination Survey (NHANES II), the Center for Epidemiological Studies Depression Scale (CES-D), the Wolinsky Nutrition Risk Assessment (NRA) scale, and the Activities of Daily Living (ADL) Scale. Demographic information and self-reported weekly consumption levels were also gathered. Self-reported weekly consumption of beer, wine, and hard liquor were scaled into one of four categories: minimal drinking; mild drinking; moderate drinking; or severe drinking. Severe drinking referred to the intake (weekly) of 2 or more six-packs of beer and/or greater than 8 glasses of wine and/or liquor.

For the multivariate stepwise discriminant analysis a total of 34 independent variables were entered in the model. The discriminant function analysis used the Wilks' stepwise procedure with a minimum tolerance level of 0.001 and an F to enter or remove of 1.0. Severe alcohol consumption was the dependent variable. Minimal, mild, and moderate drinking were combined to correspond to non-severe drinking.

Variables that best discriminated severe from non-severe drinking in individuals 45 and older included: age 64 and under; no military service; not married; physical summary rating (not impaired accounting for 82% of severe drinkers); ADL ratings (not impaired accounting for 79% of severe drinkers); male gender; smoked after age 40; and heavy alcohol intake before age 40. The sample was stratified into two groups; those 65 years of age and older, and those 64 years of age and younger. For those 65 and older the best discriminator for predicting membership in the non-severe versus the severe group was the ADL objective summary rating (not impaired accounting for 68% of severe drinkers). Two other discriminators which predicted membership in the non-severe versus severe group were smoking after age 40 and drinking before age 40.

217   Nelson, D. E., Sattin, R. W., Langlois, J. A., DeVito, C. A., & Stevens, J. A. (1992). Alcohol as a risk factor for fall injury events among elderly persons living in the community. Journal of the American Geriatrics Society, 40(7), 658-661.

The present study was designed to determine if alcohol use is a risk factor for fall injury events among older people. The study was a case-control study which utilized a subset of data from a larger population-based case-control study in south Florida.

For the present study, cases were persons aged 65 or older in South Miami Beach, Florida, who fell in the home or in its associated environs, and who sought treatment at a hospital with a newly diagnosed serious injury due to a fall (IDC-9-CM Code E880-888). Three hundred twenty cases were interviewed within six months of their fall injury event. Controls were people 65 years or older who resided in homes in the study area, who were randomly selected from Medicare files (n=609). They were also interviewed. Based on interview data on alcohol intake, the researchers calculated current weekly alcohol consumption, and categorized subjects as: none; light (1-3 drinks); moderate (4-13 drinks); and heavy (14 or more drinks) drinkers. To establish relative risk, the Mantel-Haenszel method was used to calculate odds ratios for each level of alcohol use, as well as to calculate the summary odds ratios.

Results revealed that in general, cases were more likely to be older, non-Hispanic, and have more limitations of ADL than were controls. Alcohol users were slightly less likely than non-users to have sustained a fall injury event. Authors conclude, since there was no significant association between alcohol use and fall injuries in older people, further efforts at reducing injuries to older people from falls should concentrate on other modifiable risk factors.

218   Oscar-Berman, M., Hancock, M., Mildworf, B., Hutner, N., & Weber, D. A. (1990). Emotional perception and memory in alcoholism and aging. Alcoholism: Clinical and Experimental Research, 14(3), 383-393.

The study reported on was designed to investigate the relationship between emotion and memory in alcoholism and aging. Sixty-eight males ranging in age from 23-77 were divided into five groups based on alcohol history (with or without Korsakoff's syndrome) and age (49 and younger, or 50 and older). The five groups were: 12 Young Normals; 15 Older Normals; 14 Young Alcoholics; 17 Older Alcoholics; and 10 Alcoholic Korsakoff's patients.

Individuals were given several tasks to measure their perception of emotional stimuli and memory. The visual task presented them with a set of photographs of six faces with six emotional expressions: happy, sad, angry, surprised, disgusted, or neutral. Subjects were asked to match facial expressions with a written label. The auditory task presented 32 tape-recorded sentences. The emotional intonation of the sentences expressed the same emotions as the photographs. Subjects were asked to identify the emotional expressions of the speaker's tone of voice. To test memory, subjects were later given a new set of photographs and asked to identify whether or not each photo had been in the first set of photographs viewed. Similarly, they listened to a new set of sentences and were asked to identify those sentences they had previously heard.

ANOVAs or multiple regression analysis were performed separately on results of each experimental procedure of the visual and auditory tasks. Results showed consistently severe deficits in emotional functions and memory in the Korsakoff patients, but only minor alterations in non-Korsakoff alcoholics. Older subjects, whether they had a history of alcoholism or not, exhibited significant deficits on most of the tests. Based on their results the researchers reject the commonly accepted premature aging hypothesis, which posits that alcoholism accelerates aging.

219   Oscar-Berman, M., Hutner, N., & Bonner, R. T. (1992). Visual and auditory spatial and nonspatial delayed-response performance by Korsakoff and non-Korsakoff alcoholic and aging individuals. Behavioral Neuroscience, 106(4), 613-622.

The purpose of the study reported on in this article was to assess the degree to which frontal lobe dysfunction contributes to cognitive impairments associated with long-term abuse of alcohol. A secondary purpose of the study was to provide evidence for or against the premature aging hypothesis that alcoholism leads to precocious development of behavioral changes typically associated with advancing age.

Subjects were recruited from various outpatient services of the Department of Veterans Affairs (VA) Medical Center, Boston, and from other VA hospitals, after-care programs, nursing homes, and half-way houses in Boston. Thirty-six male alcoholics and 24 controls were divided into five groups based on age (49 years and younger or 50 years and older) and alcohol history (with or without clinical evidence of Korsakoff's syndrome). The five groups were: (1) young alcoholics (mean age = 36.2 years, N=11); (2) young nonalcoholic controls (mean age = 37.2, N=13); (3) older alcoholics (mean age = 56.8, N=12); (4) older nonalcoholic controls (mean age = 61.2, N=11); and (5) Korsakoff patients (mean age = 60.4, N=13). The alcoholics met DSM-III-R criteria for alcohol abuse and alcohol dependence and had a drinking history of at least 5 years. The Korsakoff patients were diagnosed by the psychology and neurology services of the participating medical centers. Polydrug abusers and patients with major psychiatric disorders were excluded from the study.

Each subject was tested in four delayed-response conditions: visual-spatial; visual-nonspatial; auditory-spatial; and auditory-nonspatial. A custom-made human test apparatus was equipped with speakers, light panels, response bars, and a coin dispenser. Visual stimuli were two different colored lights and the auditory stimuli were tones of two different frequencies.

Results indicated that on all tests Korsakoff patients were consistently impaired relative to other subjects. Under the most difficult experimental conditions, controls and non-Korsakoff alcoholics who were over 50 years old performed worse compared with those 27-49 years old. Age-linked deficits were mild, however, compared to Korsakoff deficits and disappeared on easier tasks. The authors conclude that "the results implicate cortical pathology in alcoholism and normal chronological aging and suggest that prefrontal damage accompanies alcoholic Korsakoff's syndrome."

220   Parker, E. S., & Noble, E. P. (1980). Alcohol and the aging process in social drinkers. Journal of Studies on Alcohol, 41(1), 170-178.

This article reports the results of an empirical investigation of the effects of social drinking on cognitive performance in older adults. Questionnaires concerning drinking history were mailed to a random sample of men living in a suburban California community (N=450). After careful screening of responses by a physician 102 subjects who completed questionnaires were chosen to complete a battery of tests which included the Shipley Institute of Living Scale (SILS) for measuring intellectual impairment, the Category Test of the Halstead-Reitan neuropsychological test battery, the Wisconsin Card Sorting Test and a multitrial free-recall learning test. Subjects were asked to refrain from drinking or taking psychoactive medicines for 24 hours prior to testing.

Results reported confirmed the alcohol accelerated-aging hypothesis. All significant correlations were in the direction of decreasing cognitive performance with increasing drinking and increasing age. Drinking was strongly related to decreased cognitive performance, as was age. Comparison of slopes of the regression of quantity of drinking on cognitive performance of the young (28-42) and the old (43-63) support the notion that the old are more affected by drinking than the young and suffer greater deleterious effects of alcohol consumption on conceptual formation and shifting as measured by the Wisconsin Sorting Test (p= < .01).

221 Peppers, L. G., & Stover, R. G. (1979). The elderly abuser: A challenge for the future. Journal of Drug Issues, 9(1), 73-83.
        Findings are presented on 5,500 adults aged 55 and older who entered any form of drug treatment program administered by the South Carolina Commission on Alcohol and Drug Abuse (SCCADA) in 1976. Responses provided on an intake form administered to each client was the source of data for the study. Four questions were addressed: Who abuses drugs? What are the principal drugs abused? By what means is the substance abuser identified? How does the SCCADA respond to problems of the elderly abuser?
        Analysis of data revealed that elderly white males, especially those who are not employed, are the ones most likely to abuse drugs. The most frequently abused drug, and in many cases the only drug abused, was alcohol. The vast majority of drug abusers are referred to treatment by themselves, concerned others, usually family or friends, social control agencies, and other drug and alcohol programs. Approximately one-half of those in the system received treatment by the designated state agency (SCCADA). Many were referred to medical facilities or other alcohol and drug programs.

222 Prescott, C. A., Hewitt, J. K., Truett, K. R., Heath, A. C., Neale, M. C., & Eaves, L. J. (1994). Genetic and environmental influences on lifetime alcohol-related problems in a volunteer sample of older twins. Journal of Studies on Alcohol, 55(2), 184-202.
        This very extensive study examines correlates and possible underlying mechanisms of alcohol abuse and alcohol-related problems among elder adults in a sample of over 4,000 male and female twins. The sample was community-based and included both same- and opposite-sex dizygotic (DZ) pairs in addition to monozygotic (MZ) pairs. Subjects were administered questionnaires covering general health, alcohol use, history of neurological symptoms, cigarette smoking, social attitudes, and self-report measures of personality. Measures of current and lifetime alcohol use and alcohol-related problems were developed specifically for the study and were based on CAGE items and adapted from Feighner and DSM-III-R criteria. Validity and reliability of these measures were examined by comparison

with self-report of alcohol consumption, previous diagnosis and treatment for alcoholism, and by comparison with a report from the co-twin.

The authors report significant gender and age effects for measures of current and lifetime alcohol-related problems. Specifically, severity of alcohol abuse was linked to age of drinking onset, family history of alcoholism, lower SES, male gender, and more recent birth cohorts. Structural modeling techniques suggested substantial familiality for a variety of definitions of alcohol abuse. Median estimate of genetic variance across five alternative definitions was 32%, while that for common environmental factors was 16%. The authors discuss their results in the light of recent published reports and emphasize the utility of behavior genetic approaches.

223   Rains, V. S., & Ditzler, T. F. (1993). Alcohol use disorders in cognitively impaired patients referred for geriatric assessment. Journal of Addictive Diseases, 12(1), 55-64.

The purpose of this study is to describe the alcohol consumption characteristics and determine the presence of alcohol abuse and dependence, known as Alcohol Use Disorder (AUD), in patients presenting for outpatient geriatric assessment. A retrospective medical review was performed on all patients referred for evaluation by the Geriatric and Family Consultation Service (CFCS) elderly patients with cognitive impairment and multiple medical problems.

Of the 383 patients evaluated, current consumption of alcohol was reported in 109 (29%) patients and 75 (69%) of these were cognitively impaired. All those patients who drank regularly (12%) were cognitively impaired. AUD was a contributing factor to medical problems in 40 (10%) cases, with an almost even split between men and women. The 10% prevalence of alcohol-related cognitive impairment suggests to the authors that "the contributing role of alcohol in the presentation of these patients may be much higher than previously recognized." Elderly patients with AUD may present characteristics of dementia rather than the more classical symptoms of intoxication, dependence, and withdrawal. The authors state that patients with AUD have the potential for significant recovery, contrary to other studies done. Further research on alcohol and dementia is suggested.

224   Rhoades, V. R., Marshall, M., Attneave, C., Echohawk, M., Bjork, J., & Beiser, M. (1980). Impact of mental disorders upon elderly American Indians as reflected in visits to ambulatory care facilities. Journal of the American Geriatrics Society, 28(1), 33-39.

Data obtained from the Indian Health Service (IHS) allowed researchers to compare disease patterns, mental health problems, and social problems of older and younger Indians. A study of utilization patterns of ambulatory care facilities by various age groups of Indians revealed that, compared to other age groups, older Indians (65+) are the least likely to visit such facilities and most visits for elder Indians concerned "social" problems rather than mental disorders.

Data from the Albuquerque area of the IHS revealed alcohol abuse as the most frequent cause of referral (20%) for those 45 to 64 years of age. For those 65 and older alcohol abuse ranked ninth in the 10 top psycho-social problems (5%).

225   Rix, K. J. B. (1982). Elderly alcoholics in the Edinburgh psychiatric services. Journal of the Royal Society of Medicine, 75(3), 177-180.

This study examines an elderly (31) versus a younger (30) population of alcoholics identified from an Edinburgh psychiatric service. The study found the two groups quite similar except for the complication of "organic brain disease" in the elderly. They suggest that the elderly and younger alcoholics be treated together with the exception of those with cognitive impairment being treated in a psychogeriatric service.

226   Robbins, C. A. (1991). Social roles and alcohol abuse among older men and women. Family Community Health, 13(4), 37-48.

In the first sections of this article the author reviews demographic trends (increases in aging population); biomedical correlations and age-related changes in drug metabolism, absorption, and excretion; and role loss as a factor in alcoholism in late-life.

The last part of the article presents data comparing older men and women with each other and with younger adults in their drinking behavior and problems. The data for the study are from the 1985 National Household Survey on Drug Abuse (NHSDA) sponsored by the National Institute in Alcohol Abuse and Alcoholism (NIAAA). A total of 8,038 interviews were completed with individuals 55 years or older. Three alcohol abuse measures were administered: a question on use of alcohol and drugs in the last 12 months; a list of 18 problem symptoms of drinking including morning drinking, blackouts, sneaking drinks, and other symptoms; and questions about personal life consequences subjects attributed to their alcohol or drug use in the past year including driving unsafely, money problems, trouble with the police, skipping meals regularly, and requiring emergency help.

Analyses revealed differences by age and gender on all measures of alcohol abuse. Abuse declines with age, and men abuse alcohol more than women. Intoxication is much more frequent among younger women than among women 55 and over. Among men, intoxication is more frequent in the 18-25 age group and declines thereafter. One exception is apparent. There is a rise in levels of intoxication in males 65 and older, who report being intoxicated almost as frequently as young men. Nearly 17% of adults reported using drugs and alcohol on the same occasion at least once in the last 12 months; however, this phenomenon was quite rare among those 55 and older. Only 4% of the older women report any symptoms of problem drinking. About 20% of the men 55-64 and 17% of the men 65 and older report one or more of the problem drinking symptoms. The occurrence of personal consequences from drinking is greater among men than women for each age group. For men there is a steady decline in personal consequences of drinking with age until the 55-64 age group (from 17% down to 2%), but a slight increase in personal consequences in those 65 and older (3%). No relationship exists for marital status or employment status and alcohol abuse for older women; however, for men 55 and older, marriage and full-time employment are negatively related to alcohol abuse.

227   Rodgers, H., Aitken, P. D., French, J. M., Curless, R. H., Bates, D., & James, O. F. W. (1993). Alcohol and stroke: A case-control study of drinking habits past and present. Stroke, 24(10), 1473-1477.

This research study was performed in England between August, 1989 and July, 1990. Previous studies have reported a "U-shaped" relation between alcohol consumption and stroke. Rodgers, et al. studied stroke patterns between those subjects who had never consumed alcohol and those who had given up drinking.

Three hundred sixty-four cases of acute stroke and 364 community-based control subjects matched for age, sex, and family practitioner were examined to note current and previous drinking habits. Results of the study determined that lifelong abstainers were at higher risk for stroke than those who had given up alcohol. The Odds Ratio of lifelong abstention from alcohol versus those who have ever drunk regularly was 2.36 (95% CI, 1.67 to 3.37). No relationship was found between stroke and current non-drinkers, but current heavy male drinkers had an increased risk of stroke. Conclusions drawn were that lifelong abstention may be harmful to your health, while moderate alcohol consumption appears to protect against cerebrovascular disease. The level of consumption at which this protective effect is lost and alcohol becomes a risk factor for stroke, are unknown.

228   Runge, C., Prentice-Dunn, S., & Scogin, F. (1993). Protection
       motivation theory and alcohol use attitudes among older
       adults. Psychological Reports, 73(1), 96-98.
           This article investigates the responses from a pilot study of
       elderly persons to an Alcohol Attitude Survey, which focuses on
       preventative health behavior. Using the protection motivation theory,
       a comprehensive model of the social psychological factors that
       influence a person's response to a health threat, 17 elderly
       community-based persons and 20 VA alcoholic inpatients were
       interviewed for the pilot. The six major components of the theory
       (severity, vulnerability, and rewards associated with alcohol abuse;
       response efficacy, self-efficacy and response costs associated with
       moderating one's drinking) were examined through self-reporting.
       Community participants were interviewed by telephone, while VA
       patients were interviewed in person.
           Results compared the community and hospitalized groups on
       each of the protection motivation theory components and on alcohol
       use. Inpatients felt more vulnerable, perceived higher costs in
       moderating drinking, showed lower response efficacy, and consumed
       substantially more alcohol than the community-based elders.

229   Saunders, P. A., Copeland, J. R. M., Dewey, M. E., Davidson, I.
       A., McWilliam, C., Sharma, V. K., Sullivan, C., &
       Voruganti, L. N. P. (1989). Alcohol use and abuse in the
       elderly: Findings from the Liverpool longitudinal study of
       continuing health in the community. International Journal of
       Geriatric Psychiatry, 4, 103-108.
           This study reports on problem drinking and patterns of alcohol
       consumption for a random sample of 1,070 elderly (65+) individuals
       from lists provided by general practitioners in Liverpool. Data were
       gathered in the initial and three-year follow-up phase through interviews
       using the GMSA, a community version of the Geriatric Mental Status
       Examination. In the three year follow-up, the History and Aetiology
       Schedule (HAS) was also administered. Both the GMSA and the HSA
       have sections dealing with alcohol consumption and abuse. The criteria
       for rating an alcohol problem were either the subject's admission of a
       problem or the rater's belief that alcohol is currently damaging the
       individual's social, physical, or emotional wellbeing. An estimate of
       usual weekly consumption was recorded for each subject. Differences
       between subject groups in average alcohol consumption were assessed
       using analysis of variance (ANOVA). The significance of the
       differences in the proportions of each group falling into the various
       categories was assessed using the chi-square test.
           Results indicated the prevalence of current drinking problems

was 9.4/1000 subjects aged 65 and over. Males were two to four times more likely than females to be problem drinkers. Nearly one-fifth of both males and females who drank regularly exceeded recommended sensible limits of alcohol consumption. At follow-up, one-third were drinking moderately. Detailed examinations of drinking patterns revealed a decline with age in the number of subjects drinking regularly.

230   Scherr, P. A., LaCroix, A. Z., Wallace, R. B., Berkman, L., Curb, J. D., Cornoni-Huntley, J., Evans D. A., & Hennekens, C. H. (1992). Light to moderate alcohol consumption and mortality in the elderly. <u>Journal of the American Geriatrics Association</u>, <u>40</u>(7), 651-657.

The main objective of this study was to determine whether there is a relationship between low to moderate consumption of alcohol and cardiovascular mortality in older people. The study design included prospective cohort studies with five-year mortality follow-up using vital statistics on elders from three communities: East Boston, Massachusetts (N=3,808), two rural counties in Iowa (N=3,673), and New Haven, Connecticut (N=2,812).

Each participant was interviewed asking questions about intake of alcohol such as how often they had consumed beer, wine, and/or liquor during the past month and how many drinks they usually had at one time. Information from these questions was used to calculate an average daily intake of alcohol by assigning weights to each beverage type according to the Farmingham classification. To determine cause of death, all death certificates for participants who had died were reviewed by a single certified nosologist, who applied uniform criteria to code cause of death according to the Ninth International Classification of Diseases (ICD-9).

Prevalence rates at the baseline of four categories of alcohol consumption were examined by age and gender. For each category of alcohol consumption (none in past year; none in past month; ≤ 1 ounce per day; and ≥ 1 ounce per day), five-year age-standardized mortality rates for each gender were calculated for each of the following age groups: 65-69; 70-74; and ≥ 75 years; and a standard population consisting of the sum of the East Boston, Iowa, and New Haven populations. Standardized relative risks, risk differences, and corresponding 95% confidence intervals were also calculated using the group that consumed no alcohol in the past year as the reference group.

Results of the analyses revealed that women were more likely than men to have not consumed alcohol in the past year, as were older subjects regardless of gender. The proportions not consuming any alcohol in the past year were higher in Iowa men and women than in

East Boston and New Haven men and women. Sex and age-adjusted five-year mortality rates were lowest in the Iowa cohort, as were cardiovascular and cancer mortality rates. In East Boston and New Haven, alcohol consumption was associated with a statistically significant 40%-50% decreased risk of total mortality, and a similar pattern was observed for cardiovascular mortality. In East Boston the pattern was similar, with rates of cardiovascular and total mortality being lowest in low to moderate alcohol consumers (< 1 ounce per day), with relative risks compared to non-drinkers in the past year of .06 in East Boston and .05 in New Haven (95% confidence intervals exclude 1.0). In Iowa, on the other hand, rates of cardiovascular mortality were significantly higher for those who had consumed alcohol in the past year, but not in the past month, compared to non-drinkers in the past year. The researchers cautiously conclude that "despite the limitations of the study, the findings from this investigation suggest that consumption of small to moderate amounts of alcohol may confer a protective effect on both total and cardiovascular mortality among the elderly in some populations" (p. 656).

231   Schonfeld, L., & Dupree, L. W. (1991). Antecedents of drinking for early- and late-onset elderly alcohol abusers. Journal of Studies on Alcohol, 52(6), 587-592.

The authors of this study compare antecedents (emotional states, thoughts or events) that precede recent drinking in early and late-onset elderly alcoholics. Subjects are chosen from 170 clients who had been previously admitted to a treatment program during the past 10 years. Individuals selected are those who could be readily categorized as early- or late-onset abusers and then matched according to both age and sex. Criteria is then applied to select the final subjects for the present study, which includes two groups of fifteen men and eight women.

The study utilizes a variety of instruments, including the Gerontology Alcohol Project Drinking Profile, the Social Support Inventory, the Brief Psychiatric Rating Scale and three self-administered inventories. Using chi-square tests, demographic descriptions of the two groups show similarities in terms of education, monthly income, living alone, marital status and employment status. Early-onset subjects were more likely to have changed residence. Mean ages for evidence of drinking problems were 40.0 for the early-onset subject, and 61.5 for the late-onset group. As expected, the early-onset drinkers experienced greater delirium tremens, inner shakes and severe sweating. The pre-admission drinking patterns revealed that the early-onset abusers were intoxicated twice as often as the late-onset subjects. There are also differences noted in expectations and program completion with the late-onset alcoholics anticipating greater success and completion of treatment. However, both groups had similar feelings of loneliness and depression (antecedents) prior to recent drinking. The authors suggest that similar antecedents may be due to diminished social support for both groups albeit different reasons, and conclude by noting that a non-conformative approach to treatment is appropriate for the older alcoholic.

232   Smart, R. G., & Adlaf, E. M. (1988). Alcohol and drug use among the elderly: Trends in use and characteristics of users. Canadian Journal of Public Health, 79(4), 236-242.

This is a Canadian study using data from four cross-sectional surveys to examine trends in alcohol and tranquilizer use among men and women in their older adult years (60+). Differences were observed with males reporting higher alcohol intake and females more likely to take sleeping pills. Age was negatively correlated with frequency for both alcohol use and tranquilizer use. This study also reports that the overall frequency data reported in Canada was 9.6% males and 1.6% females aged 65+ reported consuming 14 or more drinks during the past week, compared with 12% of the total adult sample.

233   Solomon, K., & Stark, S. (1993). Comparison of older and younger alcoholics and prescription drug abusers: History and clinical presentation. Clinical Gerontologist, 12(3), 41-56.

Solomon and Stark compare data from a study that was conducted on 26 patients aged 60 and over and 33 patients aged 59 and younger diagnosed with substance abuse. All subjects were inpatients on the Alcohol/Drug Dependent Treatment Unit of the Geriatric Psychiatric Unit of the St. Louis Department of Veterans Affairs Medical Center. The study was implemented through a structured questionnaire that researched demographic, medical, psychiatric and social factors.

Results indicate that alcohol was the drug most frequently used by all patients, although both groups were also likely to be "poly-drug" abusers. While older addicts were more likely to be married than younger addicts, older addicts demonstrated greater overall problems: Older addicts had greater numbers of psychiatric disorders, and were more likely to abuse prescription directions than younger addicts. They were more likely to have problems with personal hygiene and activities of daily living, to display cognitive and psychiatric effects of their addiction, and to be in non-compliance with medical care. In addition, nearly five-sixths of the elderly abusers had dual diagnoses compared to one-third of the younger patients. Concluding remarks raise the issue of whether age-peer and other tailored treatment programs are more effective in treating the elderly. While the literature both supports and negates the need for specific elder treatment programs, the authors write that "Treatment will prevent significant secondary morbidity in elderly patients and improve the quality of life for those who maintain abstinence."

234   Speckens, A. E. M., Heeren, T. J., & Rooijmans, H. G. M. (1991).
       Alcohol abuse among elderly patients in a general hospital as
       identified by the Munich Alcoholism Test. Acta Psychiatrica
       Scandinavia, 83(6), 460-462.
       This is a hospital-based prevalence study of elderly alcoholism in the Netherlands. A sample of 132 patients, 55 men and 77 women were studied, with mean ages of 73, and 75, respectively. Nine percent were classified as alcohol dependent. In only four of the 12 cases did the physician know about the problem and fewer overall were diagnosed as such. The researchers noted the usual finding of higher usage of psychotropic drugs by the alcoholic group and warned of the necessity to look beyond the vague presenting symptoms found often in the alcohol-dependent patient.

235   Stott, D. J., Dutton, M., Murray, G. D., Williams, B. O., &
       McInnes, G. T. (1991). Hemodynamic effects of a single
       moderate dose of alcohol in elderly subjects. Journal of
       Studies on Alcohol, 52(4), 377-379.
       Eight subjects ranging in age from 70-96 (6 male, 2 female) participated in this study. In a randomized, balanced crossover study design, the effects of 0.5 g of alcohol per kg body weight in the form of vodka made up of 200 mls with unsweetened orange juice, were compared with the effects of 200 mls of orange juice alone, each consumed over 15 minutes. Recordings of blood pressure and heart rate were made at baseline and four times following the ingestion of fluids. Venous hematocrit was measured as an indirect assessment of plasma volume. Changes in blood sugar and plasma sodium and potassium were also measured.
       Data were analyzed using repeated measures analyses of variance (ANOVA). Results revealed that compared to control, alcohol increased mean sitting and standing heart rates by 3.4 ± 1.3 (p=.08) and 5.4 ± 1.9 (p= <.05) beats/minute respectively. Mean venous hematocrit rose by $3.9 \pm 1.3\%$ (p= <.05). There were no significant changes in systolic or diastolic blood pressure. Blood sugar was not significantly different after alcohol compared to controls. There were no symptoms suggestive of hypotension.

236   Tabisz, E. M., Badger, M., Meatherall, R., Jacyk, W. R., Fuchs, D.,
       & Grymonpre, R. (1991). Identification of chemical abuse
       in the elderly admitted to emergency. Clinical Gerontologist,
       11(2), 27-38.

This article examines the results of a study used to detect
chemical abuse in older adults. The research was done in conjunction
with the Elders Health Program which was designed to include
identification, intervention and treatment. Based on previous studies
that have been found to be reliable and valid in detecting alcoholism,
the authors used the brief Michigan Alcoholism Screening Test
(BMAST) and the CAGE questionnaire to identify alcohol dependent
elderly patients (aged 65 and over). The "Manitoba Drug Dependency
Screen" test and a urine drug screen was used to detect the presence of
benzodiazepines and opiates. In addition, a clinical assessment was
made based on the physician's clinical evaluation to identify patients "at
risk." The study was conducted between November, 1988 and
November, 1989 and clinical evaluations were performed in the
Emergency Room on 493 elderly persons.

Results indicated that 22.7% of the subjects needed further
evaluation and were consequently assigned to the Elders Health
Program or another chemical abuse program. 66.5% were free of
opiates and benzodiazapines, 16.8% used the drugs but were not
considered abusers and 16.8% were evaluated as having a problem with
an opiate and/or benzodiazepine. Analysis was done to determine if
some of the tools used to screen for chemical dependency could be
eliminated to keep the screening process simple and quick. The authors
concluded that the BMAST and the clinical assessment could be
eliminated without sacrificing sensitivity to the screening procedures.
Further research would determine the value of the urine drug test.

237   Tabisz, E. M., Jacyk, W. R., Fuchs, D., & Grymonpre, R. (1993).
       Chemical dependency in the elderly: The enabling factor.
       Canadian Journal on Aging, 12(1), 78-88.

This article takes an in-depth look at the enabling factor in
chemical dependency. A Canadian project entitled The Elders Health
Program (EHP), was developed as a model project for others needing
to provide services to chemically dependent older adults. The Elders
Health Program was designed to include three phases: identification of
chemical abuse problems in the elderly, intervention to confront the
older adult, as well as the enablers and codependents, and treatment.
This particular study compares the chemically dependent seniors in the
EHP with identified enablers, to those in the program without identified
enablers. The intervention process was intended to have the elderly
abusers adopt healthier lifestyles and to change the attitudes and

behaviors of the enablers through education.

Of the 68 participants in the Elders Health Program, it was determined that 22 chemically dependent elderly had active and visible enablers, while 46 did not. Enablers were defined as individuals whom "actively interfered with the intervention process and in some ways supported the elder's use of the substance." The EHP identified four categories of enablers: family, professional, physician and others. The 22 participants had enablers who were 47% family members, 26% professionals, 21% physicians and 6% others. Females were twice as likely to have enablers as males. No difference in type of substance use was found between those with and without enablers. Also very little difference appeared in the outcomes. What was different appeared in the level of intensity required and the length of the intervention. Many interventions were blocked because of family interference. Results indicate a need to develop a screening tool to detect enabling and testing of the patient's network prior to treatment. It is necessary to deal openly with active enablers in order to treat the chemically dependent elderly.

238   Tucker, J. A., Vuchinich, R. E., Harris, C. V., Gavornik, M. G., & Rudd, E. J. (1991). Agreement between subject and collateral verbal reports of alcohol consumption in older adults. Journal of Studies on Alcohol, 52(2), 148-155.

This study investigated the accuracy of self-report data in the natural community setting by using matched collaterals to verify drinking behavior reported by the elderly person. A total of 83 subjects were included, 47 males and 36 females. Most of the collaterals lived in the same residence (78.75%) and the majority were spouses (62.65%). The findings support strongly the accuracy of self-report data, but the authors point out several caveats that may have contributed to the high quality data obtained here. One of these is the minimization of negative consequences for reported drinking, thus the data may not have been of such high quality were the subjects heavier drinkers or alcohol abusers. This study is important for its methodological content and discussion.

239   Vogel-Sprott, M., & Barrett, P. (1984). Age, drinking habits and the effects of alcohol. Journal of Studies on Alcohol, 45(6), 517-521.

This article reports the results of a study of 41 male volunteers between the ages of 19 and 63 conducted to determine blood alcohol levels (BALs) and task performance after drinking alcohol. Blood alcohol level was measured from breath samples using an Atalmeter. The performance task employed a balance beam, which subjects were asked to stand on the center of, arms folded, heel to toe, for 90 seconds or until they lifted a foot or touched the handrails. A bead-string task, obtained from the Stanford-Binet IQ test was the second performance task. Each subject received 0.72 ml absolute alcohol/kg body weight, divided equally into two drinks presented 20 minutes apart. BAL was measured just before the second drink was served, and at 20 minute intervals thereafter until the end of the session. Task performance on the balance beam and bead-string task were measured for each subject. Quetelet's Index, the Ponderal Index, and the Leanness Index were used to estimate the proportion of body water in body weight for each subject.

Results of multiple regression analyses revealed that alcohol absorption and elimination rates were not significantly related to age. The Ponderal Index was negatively correlated with age. Older subjects had proportionately less body water. Older subjects also obtained higher BAL's. The amount of alcohol-induced impairment in task performance was also shown to increase significantly with age. The authors conclude that the major reason older adults choose to drink less in late life is to compensate for the increased effect of alcohol and the decreased level of performance related to drinking.

240   Wattis, J. P. (1981). Alcohol problems in the elderly. Journal of the American Geriatrics Society, 29(3), 131-134.

In this article the author presents seven cases of older alcoholics. All cases were seen in a new psychiatric service for the elderly in England. Three cases began abusing alcohol for the first time late in life; four were life long alcohol abusers. None of the cases initially presented as alcohol abusers. Three were first seen because of repeated falls. Four were referred for dementia, confusion, or self neglect. All the elderly females were widows. In three cases alcohol-abusing family members enabled the older adult to continue abusing alcohol.

241   Wells-Parker, E., Miles, S., & Spencer, B. (1983). Stress experiences and drinking histories of elderly drunken-driving offenders. Journal of Studies on Alcohol, 44(3), 429-437.

The present study was part of a larger project designed to assess the effectiveness of several treatment modalities in reducing the incidence of rearrest for drunken driving (DUI/DWI) in Mississippi. Analysis of a subsample of elderly drivers was performed. The purpose of the study was to determine whether elderly first-time DWI offenders differed, prior to their arrest, from a sample of comparable nonoffenders in terms of the occurrence of stressful life events.

Ninety-two offenders and 68 non-offender men over age 60

were interviewed by trained interviewers. Fifty-two questions related to drinking problems were adapted from existing instruments, particularly the Mortimer-Filkins Interview Schedule. Subjects were also asked whether the problem had first occurred before or after age 55 and whether the problem had occurred during the past five years. The measure of psychosocial stress history was developed from two existing scales of stressful events: The Social Readjustment Rating Scale developed by Holmes and Rahe and a modified version of the Holmes and Rahe scale developed by Dohrenwend and colleagues. In addition to data obtained in interviews, extensive demographic and psychometric data on all DWI offenders were examined; driving histories were also available for controls.

Three groups of older DWI offenders were identified. One group had at least one DWI arrest prior to age 55. One group had no arrests prior to age 55 with one arrest occurring during the preceding five years. One group had no arrests prior to age 55, but had an arrest prior to the five-year period covered by the interview. The first group were long term offenders, whereas the other two groups clearly had late-onset DWI problems. Problem-drinking indices and self-reported drinking patterns were compared between long-term and late-onset groups, and also between DWI offenders and controls. Results of the analysis revealed that the long-term offenders had significantly more drinking problems than did the late-onset group ($t = 3.140$, $p < .01$); and the long-term group had significantly more DWI arrests in the preceding five years than did the late-onset group ($x^2 = 4.108$, $p < .05$). There were no significant differences in the number of drinking problems experienced by control subjects and DWI offenders after age 55. These findings suggest that while the late-onset group had less severe drinking and DWI histories, they had experienced drinking problems earlier in life. The researchers suggest that these individuals have probably experienced movement in and out of problem drinking. Multivariate analysis of variance revealed that the DWI offenders reported significantly more stressful life events within the one year interval prior to arrest than did the control group. Five of the 29 offenders in the late-onset group of DWI offenders experienced at least one death of a significant person within the interval of arrest, compared to only one of the 64 controls ($x^2 = 5.165$, $p < .025$). These results suggest that the occurrence of a first-time DWI offense at an older age is related to the occurrence of potentially stressful events, particularly losses of significant others.

Suggestions for treatment are offered in the last section of the article. Authors recommend therapy that focuses on coping with severe losses such as deaths of significant others. They note that many first time offenders have a history of drinking problems earlier in life and should also receive therapy that deals with the alcohol problem.

242   Wiens, A. N., Menustik, C. E., Miller, S. I., & Schmitz, R. E.
        (1982/83). Medical-behavioral treatment of the older alcoholic
        patient. American Journal of Drug Alcohol Abuse, 9(4), 461-
        475.
           The purpose of this study was to assess the treatment
        effectiveness of a multi-modality alcoholism treatment program at
        Raleigh Hills Portland Hospital, which uses aversive conditioning in
        which the patient learns to associate the sight, smell, taste, and thought
        of alcohol with an unpleasant reaction.   Each patient has an
        individualized treatment plan and aftercare plan developed and overseen
        by a team consisting of physician, psychologist, nurse, aftercare
        coordinator, and alcoholism counselor.
           Treatment outcome is considered successful if the patient is
        abstinent for a lifetime.   For the research the treatment success
        criterion was sobriety for one year after treatment.   Sobriety was
        defined as total abstinence.   Data sources included: self-report,
        observation when in the hospital for aftercare visits, collateral sources
        of information, and information about each patient documented in the
        chart.   Patients first admitted to the hospital in 1978 and 1979 (N=87,
        treated N=78) were included in the study.   Their abstinence percentage
        combined for the two treatment years was 65.4% continuous sobriety
        over a 12-month follow-up period.   The majority of patients began
        drinking in their 20s but reported their drinking got "out of control" in
        their 60s.   The elderly patient group with the least amount of formal
        education reported the highest percentage of sobriety on one-year
        follow-up.

243   Willenbring, M. L., Christensen, K. J., Spring, W. D., & Rasmussen,
        R. (1987). Alcoholism screening in the elderly. Journal of
        the American Geriatrics Society, 35(9), 864-869.
           The researchers studied the validity of the Michigan
        Alcoholism Screening Test (MAST), UMAST (unit scoring of the
        MAST), the Brief MAST (BMAST) and Short MAST (SMAST) in 52
        male alcoholic patients 60 years of age or older and 33 older male
        controls, who were not alcoholics.   Subjects were recruited from
        patients admitted to the Alcohol/Drug Dependency Treatment Program
        of the Minneapolis Veterans Administration Medical Center (VAMC).
        All subjects met criteria for Alcohol Abuse for Dependence of the
        DSM-III.   Thirty-three male controls 60 years of age and older were
        recruited from two sources: patients hospitalized at the Minneapolis
        VAMC for nonalcohol-related reasons (N=28) and patients seen for
        general health care at a community health center (N=5).   Controls

were carefully screened for possible indications of alcoholism.

As expected, scores were significantly higher among Cases as compared to Controls on all four versions of the MAST. The MAST was found to have excellent sensitivity and specificity. Using a cutting score of 6+ (with weighted scores), it correctly classified all of the Cases and 90% of the Controls. Using unit-scoring the MAST had a sensitivity of 96% and a specificity of 86% with a cutting score of 3+, and 93 and 96%, respectively, with a cutting score of 5+. The SMAST correctly identified 98% of the Cases. The BMAST had acceptable sensitivity and specificity when a lower cutting score of 4 was used. Factor structure of the two brief versions was similar to that found in younger alcoholics. The authors recommend the use of the MAST and UMAST for screening for alcoholism in the elderly. The study did not address the validity of these instruments with elderly women. The authors also recommend caution in using these instruments with acutely disturbed psychiatric patients.

Miscellaneous Works

244   Abrams, R. C., & Alexopoulos, G. S. (1987). Substance abuse in the
        elderly: Alcohol and prescription drugs.   Hospital and
        Community Psychiatry, 38(12), 1285-1287.
        The literature on alcohol and prescription drug problems in
older adults is briefly reviewed. In the first half of the article, the
authors cite reasons for the "apparent" decline in alcohol use with age:
increased mortality rate in chronic drinkers, cohort effects, and, in
particular, difficulty in detecting alcoholism in older adults. It is
emphasized that alcohol abuse must be considered in elderly patients
with depression, cognitive impairment, or both.
        The second half of the article discusses factors in prescription
drug misuse and abuse, and profiles elders who misuse versus those
who intentionally abuse drugs. The authors recommend that all geriatric
patients, including nursing home residents, be evaluated for drug and
alcohol problems - especially since treatment is generally effective.

245   Amodeo, M. (1990). Treating the late life alcoholic: Guidelines for
        working through denial integrating individual, family, and
        group approaches. Journal of Geriatric Psychiatry,
        23(2), 91-105.
        The purpose of this article is to provide strategies for doing
effective work with elderly alcoholics. After a brief discussion of age-
related physiological changes related to aging, which increase the
negative effects of alcoholism, treatment considerations are discussed.
Stereotypes of the elderly alcoholic as a late-stage drinker, perhaps
disheveled in appearance or homeless, interfere with accurate diagnosis
and appropriate intervention. Another problem which interferes with
effective intervention is overidentification with the children of the

alcoholic and alliance with them against the elderly drinker. It must be kept in mind that the older alcoholic is also a victim.

The problem of denial is a major focus of the article. Guidelines for breaking down denial are offered. One guideline is to view resolution of denial as a lengthy process rather than an event to be undertaken and concluded in one or two sessions. Family and group approaches are highlighted. AA and Al-Anon are recommended for older alcoholics and family members.

246   Berger, H.   (1983).   Alcoholism in the elderly.   Postgraduate
         Medicine, 73(1), 329-332.
         Berger presents his views on why the elderly may be at particular risk for alcoholism and which treatment approaches are the most beneficial. Included is a brief discussion of late-life psychosocial stressors (such as isolation, loss of job, and financial difficulties) and comments on possible physiologic complications of drinking. Acquisition of new employment is considered by the author to be the best treatment for the older alcoholic.

247   Blose, I. L.   (1978).   The relationship of alcohol to aging and the
         elderly.   Alcoholism: Clinical and Experimental Research,
         2(1), 17-21.
         The author points out that older residents of nursing homes suffer from alcoholism just as do older adults living in their own homes. One factor related to late-life alcoholism is self-hatred and a shattered self-image. Many older people are not alcoholics, but do abuse alcohol and are problem drinkers. The author argues that we should consider those with a drinking problem as a group separate from alcoholics, but also at risk. The author defines three types of older drinkers: (1) the person with no history of a drinking problem before retirement or widowhood who begins drinking as a reaction to the loss; (2) the person who has intermittently experienced problems with alcohol but did not develop regular patterns of abuse until late middle age or older age; and (3) the person typically defined as alcoholic, who has had serious problems with alcohol for a long time.

248   Burns, B. R.   (1988).   Treating recovering alcoholics.   Journal of
         Gerontological Nursing, 14(5), 18-22.
         The article describes the Day Treatment Center (DTC), part of the Alcoholism Program located in a Veterans Administration (VA) Medical Center in the northeast. The program focuses on the special needs of older alcoholics, addressing issues of aging and disabilities. The program offers older, recovering alcoholics support, companionship, and fun. The DTC is coordinated by a specialist in

psychiatric-mental health nursing and staffed by students from nursing, occupational therapy, psychology, and allied health disciplines. The DTC is an outpatient clinic that meets daily, Monday through Friday. Lessons in cooking, assertiveness training, and other educational programs are offered at the DTC. Issues of denial, how to maintain sobriety, and other alcoholism issues are addressed in group meetings. Several special groups are described in the article. The Cooking Group, General Education Group, Alcohol Education Group, and Social Meetings are highlighted. Case examples of recovering older alcoholics are included.

249   Champlin, L. (1983). The aging alcoholic: Silent, often invisible - in need of care. Geriatrics, 38(5), 31-44.

This news report focuses on late-life alcoholism as a serious, hidden and underdetected problem. Several authorities in the field of aging and alcoholism are quoted on topics such as physicians' inability to accurately diagnose alcoholism in older patients, incidence of late-life alcoholism, clinical signs of underlying alcohol problems, and efficacy of treatment. Reasons cited for the continued invisibility of the aging alcoholic include: elders' loss of social roles, denial due to the stigma of alcoholism as a moral failing, family indulgence of problem drinking as an acceptable coping mechanism for elders' and physicians' failure to probe into the causes of many accelerated maladies. Epidemiologic data from several of Sheldon Zimberg's early studies are provided, as well as prevalence estimates from the Senior Alcohol Services project in Vancouver, Washington, and the National Council on Alcoholism. Lack of funding for ambulatory alcoholism services is seen as the major barrier to treatment.

250   Cutezo, E., & Dellasega, C. (1992). Substance abuse in the homebound elderly: A casefinding approach. Home Healthcare Nurse, 10(1), 19-23.

This brief article is written by nurses and directed at nurses who come in contact with homebound elderly who may be alcohol abusers. The article focuses on how to recognize and help alcohol abusers who are living in their own homes in the community. In the introduction the authors discuss age-related changes which place older adults at greater risk of suffering from negative effects of alcohol use and abuse. Age-and alcohol-related changes are presented in a table. They include: decline in liver function, decreased glucose tolerance, slowed peristalsis, polypharmacy, and decline in immunological competence. The authors also discuss negative alcohol-drug interactions of homebound elderly, and include a table of medications and alcohol-induced effects. The authors next turn their attention to detection and intervention.

The first step in assisting home health care nurses detect substance abuse is education. The second step is to screen and assess all older clients. It is important to collect data on past and present substance abuse. Signs to look for include: poor personal hygiene, neglect of home, repeated falls, tremors, incontinence, withdrawal from social activities, and frequent automobile accidents. A case history of a 68-year-old alcoholic is presented to illustrate some of the key signs and symptoms of alcohol abuse in homebound older adults.

The last section focuses on treatment and nursing management. The authors stress that the first step in nursing management is to get the alcoholic elder to recognize he/she has a drinking problem. Breaking down denial is essential. They suggest family and friends be involved in treatment. Educating the family about late-life alcoholism is essential. The home health care nurse should refer those with alcohol problems to an alcohol rehabilitation center where detoxification occurs first. The next essential ingredient for effective treatment is client counseling. The authors recommend support groups of AA chapters, day treatment centers, occupational therapy, and the availability of the home health care nurse for support. In conclusion, the authors state that denial of and/or neglect of substance abuse in the elderly is "ageism at its worst form" (p. 23).

251   Dicicco-Bloom, B., Space, S., & Zahourek, R. P. (1986). The homebound alcoholic. American Journal of Nursing, 2(1), 167-169.

The authors begin this article with case examples of older alcoholics. Next, Dicicco-Bloom, Space and Zahourek discuss an alcohol education program developed for staff of the Long Term Home Health Care Program at St. Vincent's Hospital in New York City. The program was planned to include six one-hour sessions scheduled at three-week intervals, plus individual appointments as needed to discuss specific patients. Coordinated by a nurse and a social worker the program had six objectives: to help staff develop more positive attitudes toward working with elderly alcoholics; to educate staff about alcoholism; to stop "enabling" problem drinking; to improve intervention skills; to provide a support group for staff; and to make the staff independent in their management of alcoholic patients.

252   Drew, D. (1990). Home care of the elderly alcoholic. Home Health Care Nurse, 8(5), 26-31.

Written by a home health care nurse who formerly worked in an alcohol treatment unit, this article is directed toward professionals providing home health care for older people. Drew presents her information in the disease framework, arguing that alcoholism, like diabetes, cancer, and other conditions, is a disease with recognizable signs and symptoms and requires accurate diagnosis and appropriate treatment. She identifies the visible stigmata of alcoholism listing common features such as: loss of weight; jaundiced skin; bloated stomach and/or swollen ankles; rum nose; and dilated capillaries on face and hands. Behavioral clues are also discussed. The author suggests home health care workers look for the following kinds of behavioral clues: denial of drinking; disheveled appearance; rationalizations for drinking; evidence of spouse or animal abuse; and empty bottles and other evidence of drinking around the home.

Drew also discusses the dangers of alcohol-drug interactions. She cautions against prescribing drugs to treat depression when the alcoholism is unrecognized and untreated. Two charts are presented for readers. One lists the effects of mixing alcohol with each one of several drugs commonly prescribed for the elderly patient. The other lists the percentage of alcohol found in commonly used OTC preparations.

The primary focus of this article is on assessment of alcoholism. The last section offers suggestions on how to best help the alcoholic elder. Ideas include the premise that the staff must understand their own attitudes toward alcoholism and determine if they can work with alcoholics; staffing should include at least one health care professional with a good background in alcoholism and substance abuse treatment; and the family should be informed and involved. The author also provides a helpful list of names, addresses, and phone numbers of five substance abuse organizations.

253   Dunlop, J., Skorney, B., & Hamilton, J. (1982). Group treatment for elderly alcoholics and their families. Social Work with Groups, 5(1), 87-92.

In this article authors report on the Senior Alcohol Services Project for Elderly Alcoholics, a demonstration project funded by the National Institute of Alcohol Abuse and Alcoholism (NIAAA). One objective of this project is to develop and implement effective treatment modalities to serve older alcoholics. The project treatment team includes a clinical psychologist, an alcoholism counselor, an outreach worker, and a medical social worker. The staff's major involvement with the clients has been in the motivational and aftercare phases of treatment.

Group work for clients and their families has been effective at several points in the treatment continuum--in the motivational phase, in the intensive treatment period, and during aftercare. Family intervention is a powerful treatment tool and involves staff, client, and family members in structured group sessions. Family meetings occur weekly and have a two-fold purpose: to educate the family about alcoholism and to make members aware of the way in which they adjust to the problem drinker. The authors also discuss the effectiveness of the aftercare group, which meets regularly and provides a source of social interaction and emotional expression. The group also encourages reminiscing and discussion of current problems and issues. In addition, staff members have added an educational function to aftercare groups providing education of the twelve steps, family dynamics, nutrition and fitness, depression, and a variety of other topics.

Special characteristics of elders that affect the group process, such as the presence of special physical impairments, hearing difficulties, and preference for day meetings, are also discussed.

254   Dunne, F. J. (1994). Misuse of alcohol or drugs by elderly people. British Medical Journal, 6929(308), 608-609.

Dunne notes that between 5% and 12% of men and 1% and 2% of women in their 60's are problem drinkers, and that older people are less tolerant of the adverse effects of alcohol due to several age-related physiological changes. The editors point out that alcohol and drug problems in older people are easily missed by doctors. Common signs of alcohol misuse in older adults include: poor hygiene, falls, incontinence, self-neglect, hypothermia, loss of libido, insomnia, depression, and anxiety.

Recommendations include use of appropriate alcohol screening measures, taking a full alcohol and drug history, an alcohol and drug counselor to work specifically with older patients at each hospital, and age-based treatment programs for older alcohol abusers.

255   Dupree, L. W., & Schonfeld, L. (1989). Treating late-life alcohol abusers: Demonstration through a case study. Clinical Gerontologist, 9(2), 65-68.

This is a very short article in the Clinical Comments section of the journal, yet it is an excellent case study which provides real insight into the post-treatment activity of an elderly female alcohol abuser. The authors make the clear statement that "treatment fails or succeeds in the long run based upon the appropriateness of the skills acquired..." They go on to explain that this client was taught several concrete skills such as how to reduce anxiety, tension, and depression; how to deal with drinking cues; assertion training for anger and frustration; how to work on negative self statements; how to develop social contacts; and how to deal with relapse. The client was directed to carry a "consequences card" that listed the consequences of her drinking, to be read often and particularly at the point when she felt the urge to drink again. The authors further detail her recovery over the first 3, 6, and 12 months after treatment.

256   Elson, M. R. (1989). Addressing the special needs of the older adult. Counselor, 7(2), 15, 22.
        The author emphasizes the need for treatment professionals to distinguish lifetime "survivors" of chemical dependence from "late-onset" users who accelerate drug use in response to major lifestyle changes. It is further suggested that continuing care and post-treatment follow-up of the chemically dependent elder should include a wide range of social and medical services delivered by professionals with a genuine interest in and acceptance of older adults.

257   Erckenbrack, N. L., & Klug, C. (1989). What's missing from elderly aftercare? Counselor, 7(2), 16-18.
        Discharge planning is discussed as an essential but often excluded component of aftercare of the chemically dependent elder. The authors provide a chart detailing the six areas of discharge planning (transportation, housing, health, social support, finances, and legal issues) along with pertinent questions to ask clients and appropriate agencies to contact.

258   Fredriksen, K. I. (1992). North of market: Older women's alcohol outreach program. The Gerontologist, 32(2), 270-272.
        This article describes an innovative outreach program specifically designed to assist older women with alcohol problems. The program, called the North of Market Older Women's Alcohol Outreach Program, services an impoverished, high crime area of San Francisco and receives funding through the State of California's Department of Drug and Alcohol Program. Its mission is to "provide outreach services to isolated older women alcoholics and to increase their participation in treatment and recovery services." Female clients are 55 and older, live on limited means and generally find housing in residential hotels. The program employs two full-time female staff members, who create programs to increase socialization and encourage the development of support networks in lieu of the more traditional approach of breaking down defense barriers.
        During the 1989/1990 fiscal year, the program spent 72.6% of its time in direct outreach, 12.1% on recreational activities, 10.8% for support and/or alcohol education and 4.5% in case management and service referral. Of the 113 women who participated in program activities, 75% became involved in other alcohol/drug recovery services. Rather than proposing complete abstinence as the treatment

goal, the outreach program stresses less use of alcohol for better health and functioning level. Its success has meant more older women seeking assistance for both alcohol and poly-drug abuse, with limited resources for expansion of services.

259   Friedlander, A. H., & Solomon, D. H. (1988). Dental management of the geriatric alcoholic patient. Gerodontics, 4(1), 23-27.

Following a brief comment on prevalence of geriatric alcoholism and a psychosocial profile of the elderly alcoholic, the authors review both the pharmacokinetics and physiologic effects of alcohol in older adults. It is stressed that the orofacial examination can be very helpful in identifying the alcoholic patient. In particular, dentists are advised to look for facial edema, jaundice, dilation of the blood vessels of the nose, dry mouth, and dysplastic lesions of the oral mucosa. Chronic periodontal disease and high incidences of coronal and root caries are considered common findings in alcoholics. The authors recommend performance of clinical exams at 3-month intervals, avoidance of long-acting benzodiazepines, barbiturates and non-steroidal anti-inflammatory agents, and use of local anesthetics of the ester class.

260   Gerbino, P. P. (1982). Complications of alcohol use combined with drug therapy in the elderly. Journal of the American Geriatrics Society, 30(11, Suppl.), 88-93.

Gerbino states that excessive alcohol use by the elderly, in association with medications, can severely compromise and complicate a well-planned therapeutic program. Many drugs commonly taken by older adults interact with alcohol. These include: CNS depressants, analgesics, anticoagulants and other cardiovascular drugs, and antidiabetic agents. The most dangerous combination is alcohol and CNS depressants, which results in synergistic or additive CNS-depressant effects. A detailed discussion of the interaction between alcohol and various drugs is presented. The author suggests the need for patient counseling to prevent drug-alcohol interactions.

261   Glantz, M. (1981). Predictions of elderly drug abuse. Journal of Psychoactive Drugs, 13(2), 117-126.

This paper was written by a research psychologist at the National Institute of Drug Abuse in 1981 and basically served as a warning that the elderly are overprescribed to, are likely to mix over-the-counter and prescribed drugs, and to mix these with alcohol. He discusses studies that clearly show that they are vulnerable to drug misuse and drug abuse. This is a good review of what the state-of-the-art was at the beginning of the 80's decade; all the questions and issues that were researched during this decade are discussed in this article.

Also included is an interesting comparison between the life transitions that adolescents experience, with accompanying changes in self-esteem, and those experienced by individuals going from middle-age into old age.

262   Graham, K. (1986). Identifying and measuring alcohol abuse among the elderly: Serious problems with existing instrumentation. Journal of Studies on Alcohol, 47(4), 322-326.

In this article Graham argues that existing instrumentation for identifying and measuring alcohol abuse is inappropriate for use with older adults because existing instruments were developed and normed on a younger population, and older adults differ in several respects from younger adults.

Graham discusses five domains used to develop instruments, and the problems of using each with older adults. The first domain, self-report of alcohol consumption, presents problems when used with older adults because self-report requires accurate recent memory of past consumption and requires some mental averaging. Older adults may have difficulty remembering and doing mental averaging. Denial of alcohol abuse is also much greater in older adults and may influence reports. Finally, the same amount of alcohol affects older and younger people differently, and older people may drink the same or less than younger people with greater effects.

The domain, alcohol-related social or legal problems, usually contains questions much more appropriate for younger adults than for older adults. Physical aggression, breaking the law, and driving a car while intoxicated are not appropriate for older retired men who do not drive cars. Questions about problems with a spouse may not pick up alcohol abuse in older people, who are more likely to be widowed and living alone.

Alcohol-related health problems, another domain, is also a problem for older people. Many older people experience health problems as a natural consequence of aging. It may be hard to separate alcohol-related health impairment from chronic illness and medication effects.

Symptoms of drunkenness or dependence is another domain. The major problems of applying dependence measures to the elderly are likely to be based on inaccurate self-report and confounding dependence symptoms with symptoms of aging.

Many diagnostic measures contain questions concerning self-recognition of an alcohol-related problem. Older people may have more difficulty recognizing that they have an alcohol problem due to their denial or many other health problems they have, which they assume may be causing the problems and symptoms related to alcohol abuse.

263   Hinrichsen, J. J. (1990). Alcoholics Anonymous. The heart of treatment for alcoholism. Aging, 361, 13-17.

Hinrichsen describes the Alcoholics Anonymous 12-step recovery program and strongly advocates this type of socially-oriented therapy for older alcoholics. According to the author, advantages of this program for elders include its being offered at no cost, its provision of a strong social network, and its widespread availability. Also included is a list of symptoms associated with long term drinking, an outline of steps in the referral process, and tips on how to overcome client resistance to treatment.

264   Hoffman, N. G., & Harrison, P. A. (1989). Characteristics of the older patient in chemical dependency treatment. Counselor, 7(2), 11.

The authors briefly summarize results from a recent study done by the Chemical Abuse/Addiction Treatment Outcome Registry (CATOR) on a national sample of 127 patients in treatment for chemical dependency. Hoffman and Harrison report that the findings of CATOR suggest that older substance abusers have distinct needs that may challenge current service providers.

265   Horton, A. M., Jr. (1986). Alcohol and the elderly. Maryland Medical Journal, 35(11), 916-918.

Horton very briefly reviews the epidemiology of aging and alcoholism, early- versus late-onset classifications, the potential role of late-life stressors, and specific research issues in the treatment of the older alcoholic. It is emphasized that future research should focus on effective modes of therapy (mainstream versus elder-specific), the role of alcohol in dementia, and the relationship of alcoholism to other psychiatric disorders such as suicide and depression.

266   Kafetz, K., & Cox, M. (1982). Alcohol excess and the senile squalor syndrome. Journal of the American Geriatrics Society, 30(11), 706.

Kafetz and Cox present two very brief cases of older women, who were heavy drinkers, with the senile squalor syndrome. The senile squalor syndrome is a deterioration into squalor and self-neglect by a patient without dementia or a chronic physical illness impeding self-care. The authors argue that many patients suffering from the senile squalor syndrome, defined earlier by Clark and his colleagues, are alcohol abusers.

267   King, G., Altpeter, M., & Spada, M. (1986). Alcoholism and the elderly: A training model. <u>Alcoholism Treatment Quarterly</u>, <u>3</u>(3), 81-94.

This article presents a model training program for counselors in elderly services and alcoholism agencies to better identify, refer and treat elderly clientele. The authors point out that there is great need for programs of this nature as the problem of elderly alcoholism is undertreated and underreported. A discussion follows on the barriers to alcoholism treatment for the elderly. The model program, entitled the "Beneficiary Awareness Program," was implemented to increase the number of elderly alcoholics getting treatment.

The program has three phases of training: an educational workshop for agencies that serve the elderly; a second workshop that provides information on the elderly for alcohol agencies; and an interdisciplinary conference designed to build networking between the two delivery systems. The model was piloted on a regional basis. The authors conclude that the pilot was very effective in educating state agencies and their local providers, as well as providing the essential geographic networking. Ongoing interagency and interdisciplinary cooperation are essential if there are to be adequate services to the elderly.

268   Kola, L. A., & Kosberg, J. I. (1981). Model to assess community services for the elderly alcoholic. <u>Public Health Report</u>, <u>96</u>(5), 458-463.

In this article the authors present a model which addresses prevention of elderly alcoholism, as well as treatment and control. Three types of elderly alcoholics are identified: the person with no history of drinking problems before old age who turns to alcohol to cope with the losses and stresses of aging; the person who has intermittently experienced problems with alcohol, but did not develop patterns of alcohol abuse until old age; and the person typically defined as alcoholic throughout adult life. The model assesses three levels: client, agency, and community.

At the client level, many services are required to meet needs. These include 24-hour emergency services; inpatient services; outpatient services; intermediate care services, such as, drop-in centers and half-way houses; and consultation and educational services.

At the agency level, agencies must demonstrate competence in several areas. These include: policies about alcoholism and elderly alcoholics; treatment philosophy and practices which are appropriate for older alcoholics; continuity of care; recordkeeping that allows for accurate identification of elderly alcoholics; adequate manpower with appropriate knowledge and training to effectively serve older alcoholics;

accessibility of services; and adequate funding.

At the community level, it is important to impart correct information about aging and about alcoholism. The community needs to offer alcohol education. The community must bring health and social services together to most effectively treat the older alcoholic.

269   Lamy, P. P. (1988). Actions of alcohol and drugs in older people. Generations, 12(4), 9-13.

Four topics are discussed: normal age changes in body organ systems that heighten sensitivity to the effects of drugs and alcohol; physiologic effects of chronic alcohol abuse; alcohol-drug interactions; and, alcohol withdrawal. Lamy cites alarming figures on hospital admissions related to alcohol-drug interactions, and warns that alcohol use may drastically alter effects of many commonly prescribed drugs. Specific recommendations for withdrawal treatment include judicious use of parenteral fluids, multivitamin therapy, magnesium sulfate and other electrolytes as needed, diazepam (Valium), and, possibly, phenytoin. The author discourages the use of disulfiram (Antabuse) with older adults.

270   Lindblom, L., Kostyk, D., Tabisz, E., Jacyk, W. R., & Fuchs, D. (1992). Chemical abuse: An intervention program for the elderly. Journal of Gerontological Nursing, 18(4), 6-14.

This article highlights the Elders Health Program (EHP), a program which was developed as a demonstration project to address the problem of providing services to chemically dependent seniors. The EHP was designed to include three phases: identification, intervention and treatment. This article concentrates on the first two phases of the program. Three criteria were used to screen persons aged 65 and over in the emergency department for chemical dependency: screening questionnaires (BMAST,CAGE, and Manitoba Drug Dependency Screen), clinical physician's assessment, and social assessment. After one year, 68 patients from the emergency room and from outside referrals underwent an EHP intervention.

One of the goals of the Elders Health Program was to design intervention strategies currently employed by chemical dependency treatment facilities, and to integrate this process with knowledge and respect for normal aging changes. The authors describe the three intervention strategies that were developed and also give examples of case studies. The first intervention level is intended to voice concern to the patient in a supportive manner to encourage the patient to seek help. The second level involves a more confrontational approach by family members or friends, and level three is employed, with the professional intervention coordinator becoming involved, only if attempts at the first two levels do not produce a change. The authors write that ageism has prevented the development of treatment programs specifically designed for the elderly. Yet, the "Elders Health Program illustrates that all elders have a network that can be employed or created in an effort to move the client into accepting the need to change. The ultimate goal is to improve the well-being of the client."

271   Maddox, G. L. (1988, Summer). Aging, drinking and alcohol abuse. Generations, 12, 14-16.

Maddox warns that evidence from studies on drinking behavior and aging must be interpreted with caution due to the use of diverse sampling techniques and widely divergent definitions of alcoholism. In a brief summary of conclusions about age-related patterns of drinking, the author emphasizes that alcohol use and abuse rates are not high among older adults, that problem drinking is more often found among those of lower socioeconomic status and those seen in health or welfare clinics, and that late-onset problem drinkers constitute a very small proportion of older alcoholics. The NIMH Epidemiologic Catchment Area (ECA) study is cited as an example of a large (N=8,000), multisite study that used standard definitions of abuse and dependency. ECA prevalence rates for elder alcohol abuse/dependency were 1.9-4.6% for males and 0.1-0.7% for females. Maddox concludes that while prevalence rates are relatively low, alcoholism among elders is a problem that warrants attention because of the special risks associated with drug and alcohol use in old age.

272   Merry, J. (1980). Alcoholism in the aged. British Journal on Alcohol and Alcoholism, 15(2), 56-57.

Merry briefly outlines the case histories of nine problem drinkers over age 70, who were admitted to the Epsom District Hospital, Epsom, Surrey, between June and December 1975. Notably, all nine patients were female, and seven were living alone at the time of admission (six widows). Two were diagnosed as Korsakoff's psychosis. The author comments on the need for early diagnosis of problem drinking and more supportive measures for lonely and bereaved older women.

273   Minnis, J. R. (1988). Toward an understanding of alcohol abuse among the elderly: A sociological perspective. Journal of Alcohol and Drug Education, 33(3), 32-40.

This article offers a theoretical approach from the sociology of deviance literature toward understanding alcohol abuse among the elderly. The elderly alcohol abuser is attempting to adjust or cope with external stresses, or with feelings of low status, hopelessness, or a combination of these factors. Alcohol abuse represents a deviant act engaged in by older people reacting to negative social stereotyping and loss of social status. Putting forth a social theory of alcohol abuse, the author suggests that older adults who have a stronger bond to family, community, and society and a greater commitment to conventional goals or aspirations are less likely to abuse alcohol than are the less involved, less socially committed elders. The theory also suggests that the greater the beliefs in the moral validity of conventional norms in society, the less likely the elderly person is to engage in alcohol abuse. The social control perspective of deviance as applied to elderly alcohol abuse does have some limitations which are mentioned in the paper.

274   Newman-Aspel, M.   (1990).   Two cases of late life alcoholism. Journal of Geriatric Psychiatry, 23(2), 107-116.

The author of this article is a clinician who has worked with many alcoholic elders. Newman-Aspel presents two vignettes to illustrate how to deal with denial and other motivational problems in older alcoholics. One case is an individual, the other is a family case. A planned intervention is described in the individual case. Four old friends and the housekeeper were part of a carefully orchestrated confrontation of the older female alcoholic who denied her problem. The steps of the intervention process are discussed, and parts of the actual conversations are also included. The author attributes her success at treatment to several factors, including her ability to break down denial, her ability to use concerned family and friends in the therapeutic process, and her willingness to forego the use of labels and biases which may stress older patients.

275   Osgood, N. J.   (1987).   The alcohol-suicide connection in late life. Postgraduate Medicine, 81(4), 379-384.

The author discusses the relationship between alcoholism and suicide, and warns that both are serious and underdetected problems among older adults. Factors contributing to alcoholism and suicide are considered within a stress and "learned helplessness" framework. The elderly are said to experience a variety of losses and a contracting social world. Use of alcohol provides a coping mechanism to relieve depression, loneliness, feelings of hopelessness, and loss of control. In turn, overuse of alcohol may allow destructive impulses to surface, as well as cause deterioration of needed social relationships, factors in suicidal behavior.

Three case reports that illustrate the connection between late-life alcohol use and suicidal behavior are provided. Osgood stresses the need for early recognition of the symptoms of late-life depression and alcoholism, and includes a chart of specific warning signs for use with patients. Several approaches to prevention are suggested, such as retirement planning, grief counseling, and creation of employment opportunities for older adults.

276   Osgood, N. J. (1988). Identifying and treating the geriatric alcoholic. Geriatric Medicine Today, 7(8), 53-57.

Osgood discusses barriers to the recognition of alcoholism in older adults and offers tips for accurate diagnosis. Elders who are at high risk for problem drinking include males, widowed and socially isolated persons, and persons with a history of mental illness. Successful treatment strategies include socially oriented therapies, involvement of family members, treatment of concomitant depression, and stress management. The author suggests that the physician treating elderly patients can play a crucial role in early identification of geriatric alcoholism.

277   Parette, H. P., Jr., Hourcade, J. J., & Parette, P. C. (1990). Nursing attitudes toward geriatric alcoholism. Journal of Gerontological Nursing, 16(1), 26-31.

After presenting figures on the scope of the problem of geriatric alcoholism (2-10%), the authors address the need for educating the public about this problem and the appropriate role that nurses can play. Education about the medical sequelae of alcoholism and alcohol abuse is advised. Liver problems, cardiac problems, and other conditions caused by or exacerbated by alcohol abuse are briefly mentioned. The need for accurate assessment of late-life alcoholism is discussed.

The authors argue that maintaining a positive attitude toward alcoholism is the foundation for all services provided by nurses who work with older patients. This attitude affects the quality of assessments, diagnosis, and treatment strategies employed. The authors offer brief self quizzes contained in boxed figures for nurses to take to determine their own attitudes toward alcoholics, and to explore their reasons for rejecting older patients with alcoholism. Case examples of older alcoholics are presented. Several suggestions of ways to help improve attitudes of nurses are made. These include a call for more in-service education on the subject and staff support groups.

278   Peck, D. G. (1979). Alcohol abuse and the elderly: Social control and conformity. Journal of Drug Issues, 9(1), 63-71.

In this article Peck presents a demographic overview highlighting the dramatic growth in the older population since 1900. He reviews the problem of alcohol abuse by presenting rates of alcoholism and highlighting differences in risks between various groups including males and females. The main body of the article discusses late-life alcoholism in the sociological framework of modernization theory. Peck notes that as societies modernize, older adults lose valued roles and status, and are less socially integrated and more socially isolated. Alcohol abuse is a coping mechanism chosen by older adults in such a society.

Using Hirschi's social control theory of deviance, Peck further argues that alcoholism (the deviant act) results when an older individual's bond to society is weak or broken. Older adults are not as controlled by socially accepted norms and are not as involved in conversational activities as are younger adults. They are also less likely to be committed to the generally accepted moral values in the society. Older adults are therefore more likely to engage in deviance in the form of alcoholism.

279   Perez, V. S. (1989). Dual diagnosis of the older adult: Diagnosis and treatment issues. Counselor, 7(2), 12-13.

The dual diagnosis of depression and alcoholism in the older adult is discussed relative to late life stressors such as physical illness and loss of loved ones. Perez comments on popular misconceptions about aging and drug use and about the atypical presentation of the depressed elderly alcoholic which may act as barriers to diagnosis and treatment. Also included is a list of frequently prescribed medications which may cause severe depression.

280   Petersen, D. M. (1978). Introduction: Drug use among the aged. Addictive Diseases, 3(3), 305-309.

Society's view of drug-seeking behavior as predominantly a youth phenomenon is misdirected. Adults use proportionately more kinds of all drugs than the rest of the population. Individuals 65 and older buy three times as many prescribed drugs as younger people do. The author summarizes several major studies on illicit drug use, licit drug use, misuse, and abuse, and alcohol use.

281   Powers, J. S., Lichtenstein, M., & Spickard, A. (1984). Elderly alcoholics in a general medicine practice. Journal of the Tennessee Medical Association, 77(7), 397-400.

This report looks at a sub-group of patients in a general medical practice who were followed from diagnosis through recovery. This article written for a physician audience includes case studies and deals systematically with how the physician might detect alcoholism, and how the physician is integral to setting in motion the health care and mental health care mechanisms supportive of recovery. This is a good introduction for the medical practitioner unfamiliar with alcoholism in the elderly.

282   Price, J. H., & Andrews, P. (1982). Alcohol abuse in the elderly. Journal of Gerontological Nursing, 8(1), 16-19.

Written primarily for nurses, this short article presents a brief discussion of early- and late-onset alcoholism and outlines physical health problems associated with alcoholism. Depression, belligerence, anti-social behavior, cancer, osteoporosis, malnutrition, as well as stomach, liver, and pancreatic diseases are all associated with alcoholism. Negative alcohol/drug interactions are also discussed and presented in a figure. Nurses are urged to be non-judgmental and understanding. Education of health care professionals, older adults, and family members is also recommended.

283   Rains, V. S. (1990, October). Alcoholism in the elderly - The hidden addiction. Medical Aspects of Human Sexuality, 24, 44-47.

Several reasons are explored for geriatric alcoholism as a commonly missed diagnosis: physicians lack training in the recognition of early stages of alcohol dependence; elder alcoholics often present with moderate and misleading levels of ingestion; alcoholism in older adults is frequently masked by the normal aging process; alcoholism mimics and contributes to the presentation of many other diseases. Rains offers a brief guide to physical symptoms and behavioral abnormalities that may signal an underlying alcohol problem. The author highly recommends group recovery programs that are based on the principles of Alcoholics Anonymous.

284   Rathbone-McCuan, E., & Triegaardt, J. (1979, Summer). The older alcoholic and the family. Alcohol Health and Research World, 7-12.

A review was conducted of a number of cases of older alcoholics treated in a small inpatient treatment program attached to a private hospital in St. Louis, Missouri. Ten cases were selected, which provided a variety of family dynamics that characterized older alcoholics in treatment. The ten cases are presented.

After each, a brief discussion of family dynamics and family problems follows. Some family problems highlighted include: denial of problem by family members; retirement-related changes in family relationships; and the need for the spouse's cooperation in treatment.

285   Robertson, A. (1989). Treatment issues of the older adult. Counselor, 7(2), 8-9.

Robertson briefly discusses ten treatment issues which distinguish older substance abusers from their younger counterparts.

Among these are grief/loss issues, effects of normal aging, effects of physical illness and medication use, and generation-associated views of drinking and drug use. The need for elder-specific treatment programs is stressed.

286   Rosa, K. D. N. (1989). Serious fun. Counselor, 7(2), 21-22.
Rosa advocates the inclusion of physical rehabilitation in the treatment/recovery process of the chemically dependent elder. Beneficial results from the author's "Serious Fun" exercise and stress management program are discussed.

287   Schonfeld, L., & Dupree, L. W. (1990). Older problem drinkers - Long-term and late-life onset abusers: What triggers their drinking? Aging, 361, 5-8.
Following introductory comments on late-onset drinking, the authors identify several problems with existing alcoholism screening methods and treatment programs which often target young adults. Results from two University of South Florida projects aimed at the older alcoholic are briefly described: the Gerontology Alcohol Project conducted 1979-1981, and the Substance Abuse Program for the Elderly begun in 1986. The authors suggest that older alcoholics, regardless of age of drinking onset, can benefit from specific treatment methods which address late-life losses and focus on rebuilding social support systems. A final comment is made on the expense and lack of funding for such programs.

288   Schuckit, M. A. (1990). Introduction: Assessment and treatment strategies with the late life alcoholic. Journal of Geriatric Psychiatry, 23(2), 83-89.
The author presents alcohol prevalence figures in the first section of this article, and emphasizes the seriousness of the problem of late-life alcoholism. He notes that based on prevalence studies, 20 to 60% of older adults seeking acute medical care are alcoholics. The next section focuses on the identification of the older alcoholic. In order to identify the problem, it is important to ask each patient about his/her life problems and whether or not alcohol has been a problem. Certain medical problems such as cancers of the mouth, esophagus, stomach or liver, high blood pressure, and liver disease should be clues that alcoholism may exist. Depression and mood swings are other clues to look for.
The last section of the article discusses different treatments and highlights detoxification and rehabilitation. Group therapy, family involvement, sharing of feelings and emotions, and socialization therapies are all recommended.

289   Scott, R. B. (1989). Alcohol effects in the elderly. <u>Comprehensive</u>
            <u>Therapy</u>, <u>15</u>(6), 8-12.
                Dr. Scott, of the Medical College of Virginia, has written an
        overview on the metabolic and pathologic effects of alcohol on the
        elderly. The first section describes the extent of alcohol abuse by the
        elderly and why it is challenging for the physician to identify it as a
        problem.   He then defines the origins of early- and late-onset
        alcoholics. Next is a discussion of what accounts for the clinical
        differences in the way older persons are affected by alcohol, and the
        author points out that both social and abusive use of alcohol can
        exaggerate the effects of normal aging or early dementia. Dr. Scott
        states that there is no evidence to suggest that alcohol has a unique
        toxicity in older adults. However, the normal defenses against toxic
        chemicals may decline with age. An area of immediate concern to the
        physician is the interaction of alcohol with prescribed medication, and
        the author describes the physiological ramifications of drug-alcohol
        interactions in the elderly. The article concludes with a summary of
        the major injurious effects of alcoholism in the elderly.

290   Seixas, F. A. (1979). Drug/alcohol interactions: Avert potential
            dangers. <u>Geriatrics</u>, <u>34</u>(10), 89-102.
                Written by a physician and directed primarily toward other
        physicians, this article emphasizes the responsibility of physicians to
        determine the level of alcohol consumed by their patients, and to take
        this information into account when prescribing drugs. The majority of
        the article is devoted to a discussion of the interaction of alcohol with
        particular drugs. The negative effects of using aspirin while drinking
        alcohol are discussed. The author points out that the use of hypnotics
        and sedatives with alcohol can prove fatal. The article includes a very
        comprehensive three-page table of alcohol-drug interactions for ready
        reference.   The last part of the article presents a more general
        discussion of alcoholism and aging. In this section Seixas describes
        three types of late-life alcoholics: those who begin drinking for the
        first time in later life; those who have experienced intermittent
        problems with alcohol over the years, but had no regular pattern of
        alcohol abuse until later in life; and those defined as typical alcoholics
        who have a long history of alcohol problems. He discusses the
        importance of breaking down the belief that alcohol is a good friend
        and one of the remaining pleasures in late life.

291   Serkin, E. (1987, September/October). Elderly alcoholics and their
            adult children: Stereotypes and other obstacles to treatment.
            <u>Focus</u>, (12-13), 23-25, 39.
                This is a lay-oriented overview of late-onset alcoholism. The

article follows the basic theme that "there is probably no group of alcoholics in America as misunderstood, ignored, misdiagnosed, and underserved as the elderly." Serkin includes an explication of the problem in her article and offers insight into the reasons that this group is in such dire need of attention. A major focus is a case study of an elderly married man in his early 70's who is a late-onset alcoholic; through this case study Serkin presents the many warning signs that exhibit themselves long before help is found. She notes how many of the psychological and physical symptoms of this disease are masked by the normal aging process and in many cases ignored as "just being part of the normal aging process." She ends her article with a section entitled, "work to be done" in which she strongly argues for the need for education (of the public as well as practitioners), early intervention programs, and especially for appropriate screening instruments and treatment services.

292   Shanahan, P. M. (1978). The elderly alcoholic. Issues in Mental
       Health Nursing, 1(1), 12-24.
              The nurse/educator who authored this article attempts to place alcoholism in a disease context, and reviews past and recent literature on elderly alcoholism. She defines alcoholism as a primary, progressive, chronic disease; a community illness which affects individuals of all ages and walks of life. In addition to the victims of the disease, the community includes two other groups: family, friends and others intimately associated with the alcoholic, who suffer as a result of his/her drinking; and members of the larger community who are potentially in positions to help the alcoholic, but who because of denial and concealment fail to intervene. Older adults are found in all three groups.
              The article presents extensive findings from the author's review of literature on alcoholism and aging. Based on a review of past and current literature, Shanahan notes first that there is a notable lack of attention to elderly alcoholics or a blatant conclusion that alcoholism is not a serious problem for older adults. Some widely used books on alcoholism omit mention of the elderly alcoholic specifically. The author also found a lot of confusion and disagreement about what constitutes and causes alcoholism. Alcoholism and alcohol abuse were confused as well. Based on her review the author concluded that "up-to-date information about the definition and diagnosis of alcoholism has apparently not found its way into the gerontological literature." Alcoholism is more often presented as a symptom of some other condition or as a defense rather than a primary disease with an underlying biological base.
              The author reviewed the gerontological and geriatric literature

to look for detailed discussion of the long-term physiological effects of alcohol on the heart, liver, brain, and other body systems of older adults. Based on her review, the author concludes that the problem of alcohol abuse and alcoholism in older adults is underrecognized, and much misinformation exists in the literature. Stigma and lack of accurate information are the major problems in recognition and treatment of alcoholism in community elders. The author concludes her article with a plea for health professionals to use and disseminate accurate information.

293   Snyder, P. K., & Way, A. (1979). Alcoholism and the elderly. Aging, 291, 8-11.
This article includes a brief discussion of drinking patterns among older adults, obstacles to the identification of the elderly alcoholic, late-life stressors as precipitating factors in alcoholism, and treatment options. The need for alcoholism education programs that target both medical professionals and senior citizens is highlighted. The authors emphasize that inpatient treatment of older alcoholics should always be followed by supportive outpatient follow-up such as Alcoholics Anonymous, programs for senior citizens, and outreach services for those with reduced mobility. The coordination of alcohol treatment services and existing geriatric social services is highly recommended.

294   Thobaben, M. (1987). Relationships: Dealing with the elderly alcoholic patient. Home Healthcare Nurse, 7(1), 12-13.
This article looks at why home health care nurses are reluctant to assess and treat alcohol abuse. The author claims that this reluctance can be based on nurses', patients' and society's attitudes about the disease; nurses' personal or familial associations with the disease; and nurses' lack of knowledge about the disease of alcoholism. The author ends the article with a series of provocative self-analysis questions: for example, how does your own use influence your attitudes? has abuse been in your family and how has it affected you? what are your beliefs and attitudes about drinking? is alcoholism a moral weakness or a disease? and several questions about knowledge of treatment resources and prior experiences with treatment.

295   Vandeputte, C. W. (1989). Special detox needs of the elderly. Counselor, 7(2), 19, 22.
Differences in drug withdrawal and detoxification between older and younger adults are briefly examined. It is emphasized that, for the geriatric patient, withdrawal is a lengthy, complex process requiring extended monitored detoxification.

296   Wade, M. (1987). Meeting the challenge of alcohol and drug abuse in the older adult. <u>Home HealthCare Nurse</u>, <u>5</u>(5), 19-23.

This is a practitioner-oriented article which deals with the assessment of alcoholism in a very straight forward and pragmatic way. The author gives an overview of the immediate signs and symptoms which the practitioner should attend to. These symptoms include physical, psychological and social. She points out the necessity of looking at nutritional aspects of the patient, especially in terms of prescription and non-prescription drug intake which may exacerbate any alcohol abuse. She includes an important discussion about the effectiveness of treatment with the elderly client and gives an overview of AA and other treatment options.

The author also asks the practitioner to examined her/his own attitudes toward alcoholism and ask if she/he is being moralistic, critical or pessimistic, or is she/he being judgmental or stereotyping. This article is very general but covers the major points for those unfamiliar with the problem.

297   Whittington, F. J. (1988). Making it better: Drinking and drugging in old age. <u>Generations</u>, <u>12</u>, 5-7.

Whittington comments on the current state of research in aging and alcoholism. Two problems facing geriatric alcoholism research are lack of communication between researchers and practitioners, and repetition in the literature of "facts" that have not been critically evaluated. The author suggests that future research directions should include the study of subgroups of elders at risk for alcoholism and translation of data into clear, usable strategies.

298   Willenbring, M., & Spring, W. D. (1988). Evaluating alcohol use in elders. <u>Generations</u>, <u>12</u>(4), 27-31.

The authors explore professional attitudes about drinking that interfere with the proper and timely evaluation of alcohol use in clients. Professionals' reluctance to inquire about clients' drinking habits may stem from a lack of formal education about alcoholism, feelings of inadequacy and hopelessness regarding the effectiveness of treatment, a poor understanding of the denial process, and embarrassment due to the stigma attached to problem drinking.

Approach to the diagnosis of alcoholism in elders should include an awareness that: persons who drink develop a relationship with alcohol; drinking and its effects exist on a continuum; the health risks and medical consequences of alcoholism must be distinguished from the dependence syndrome. Elder alcoholism is complicated by the physiologic changes that accompany aging, prescription drug use, a more intense denial, and, frequently, by grief issues. The authors emphasize the need for routine screening of alcohol use and give an example of a rapidly administered screening device (the "HEAT").

299   Zimberg, S. (1978). Diagnosis and treatment of the elderly alcoholic. Alcoholism: Clinical and Experimental Research, 2(1), 27-29.
       Diagnosis of alcoholism in elders and early- versus late-onset classifications are discussed. The author presents his own Scale of Alcohol Abuse that details six levels of severity ranging from "None" to "Extreme." It is stressed that older problem drinkers exhibit fewer physical signs of alcohol addiction than their younger counterparts. Suggested treatment approaches include group socialization, social and family casework, and use of the "therapeutic community" for management of elder alcoholics in nursing homes. Zimberg advocates delivery of intervention through facilities that serve the aged, such as home-care programs, outpatient geriatric services, and senior citizen programs.

300   Zimberg, S. (1978). Treatment of the elderly alcoholic in the community and in an institutional setting. Addictive Diseases: An International Journal, 3(3), 417-427.
       Three types of alcoholics are described: (1) those with no previous history of drinking who begin drinking later in life as a reaction to loss of a job or spouse (late-onset); (2) those who intermittently experienced problems with alcohol but in old age developed a more severe and persistent problem of alcohol abuse (late-onset exacerbation); and (3) those who have had a long history of alcoholism and continue their problem drinking into old age (early-onset).
       Treatment recommended for older alcoholics include: day hospitals and home visiting, anti-depressant medication, and social therapies such as AA and family therapy. Zimberg recommends delivering treatment through existing organizations and facilities which serve seniors such as senior centers. He also calls for active outreach and case-finding services.

301   Zimberg, S. (1983). Alcoholism in the elderly a serious but solvable problem. Postgraduate Medicine, 74(1), 165-173.
       The author presents a diagnostic tool, the Alcohol Abuse Scale, which he developed. The scale assesses the extent of drinking, social problems, health problems, and legal problems. Older adults can be classified on severity of alcohol abuse in one of six categories ranging from None (1) to Extreme (6). Treatment is also discussed. A case is made for in-home treatment, medical and supportive treatment, and social therapy. Zimberg favors the use of a therapeutic

community in which patient-staff groups are established to discuss problems, and patients are given autonomy and decision-making through a form of patient government. He notes the importance of outreach and case-finding services. He does not recommend referral of elderly alcoholics to alcoholism treatment programs or advocate AA.

Author Index

The following index entries include names of authors and individuals appearing in reference citations as well as in text and annotations. Numbers in *italics* refer to page numbers. All other numbers refer to the number of the annotated references appearing in Chapters 2 through 6 and numbered consecutively from 001 to 301.

Menustik, C.E. *30, 51,* 242
Merry, J. 272
Mertens, J.R. 208, 209, 211
Meyers, A.R. *3, 8, 13, 15, 46,* 103, 203, 204
Mezey, E. *16, 50*
Midanik, L.T. *4, 43,* 169, 205
Mildworf, B. 218
Miles, S. *11, 51,* 241
Miller, M. 171
Miller, M.J. *18, 47,* 104, 171
Miller, N.S. *3, 47,* 032
Miller, R.H. 090
Miller, S.I. *30, 51,* 242
Millhorn, H.T. *25, 31, 46,* 031
Minnis, J.R. 273
Mishara, B.L. *27, 28, 47,* 105, 106
Mittelman, A.P. 107
Molgaard, C.A. *3, 47,* 206, 216
Montgomery, D. *19, 46*
Montgomery, R.J.V. *7, 8, 12, 41,* 142
Moore, R.D. *5, 21, 42,* 159
Moos, B.S. *13, 47,* 207, 210
Moos, R.H. *13, 14, 38, 40, 43, 47, 52,* 079, 143, 144, 207, 208, 209, 210, 211
Moran, M.B. 212, 213
Morgan, P. 183
Moriarty, H.J. *9, 47*
Morrissey, E.R. *8, 49*
Morse, R.M. *5, 8, 12, 21, 43, 45, 47,* 033, 170, 181
Mortel, K.F. 119
Mortimore, G.E. *17, 43*
Morton, D.J. *3, 47,* 206, 216
Moss, G. *17, 47*
Mucatel, M. *3, 8, 13, 15, 46,* 204
Mudd, S. 147
Mulford, H.A. 214
Mulry, J.T. *20, 47*
Mumford, J. *26, 40*

Murphy, G.E. *18, 47*
Murray, G.D. 235
Murray. R.M. *26, 40*
Myers, J.K. *7, 8, 44,* 094
Mysak, P. *9, 41*

Naik, P.C. 215
Nakamura, C.M. *3, 47,* 206, 216
Nanna, M.J. 195
Naughton, B.J. 212, 213
Neale, M.C. 222
Nelson, D.E. 217
Newman-Aspel, M. *32, 47,* 274
Newton, M. *17, 43,* 082
NIAAA *18, 24, 29, 31, 32, 36, 47*
Noble, E.P. *18, 48,* 220
Norris, A.H. *16, 50*
Novak, L.P. *16, 47*
Nowak, C.A. *15, 47*

Ogden, S.R. 188
O'Leary, M.R. *8, 49*
Olsen-Noll, C.G. *24, 47,* 034
Oropilla, T. *9, 50,* 048
Oscar-Berman, M. 218, 219
Osgood, N.J. *23, 29, 32, 47, 48,* 275, 276
Oslin, D.W. 028

Palola, G.E. *18, 48*
Parette, H.P., Jr. *28, 48,* 277
Parette, P.C. *28, 48,* 277
Paris, B. 171
Parker, E.S. *18, 48,* 220
Parsons, O.A. 108
Pary, R. *9, 50,* 048
Pascarelli, E.F. 035
Pashko, S. 074, 098
Pastor, P.A. *9, 34, 49,* 039
Pattee, J.J. 036
Pearson, J. 189
Peck, D.G. 278
Peddecord, K.M. *3, 47,* 206, 216

Subject Index

The numbers appearing in *italics* in this index refer to pages on which the topic was mentioned. All other numbers refer to annotation numbers. Some topics were mentioned in almost every work. For that reason, only citations for which there was major coverage or emphasis on topics are listed.

About the Compilers

NANCY J. OSGOOD, Professor of Gerontology and Sociology at Virginia Commonwealth University/Medical College of Virginia, Richmond, has authored and co-authored books, book chapters, and numerous journal articles on the topics of substance abuse and aging, suicide in the elderly, and creative arts and aging. Her books include *The Science and Practice of Gerontology: A Multidisciplinary Guide (*Greenwood, 1989*), Suicide and the Elderly* (Greenwood, 1986), and *Suicide in Later Life: Recognizing the Warning Signs* (1992). Dr. Osgood has also directed an AoA-funded statewide model detection and prevention program for geriatric alcoholism in Virginia.

HELEN E. WOOD, a student in the clinical psychology doctoral program at Virginia Commonwealth University, played a major role in the Virginia geriatric alcoholism program and has contributed articles to professional journals.

IRIS A. PARHAM, Professor of Gerontology, Psychology, and Geriatric Medicine, chairs the Department of Gerontology and serves as Executive Director of the Virginia Geriatric Education Center at Virginia Commonwealth University. She is the author of *Gerontological Social Work: An Annotated Bibliography* (Greenwood, 1993), *Fundamentals in Geriatrics for Health Professionals: An Annotated Bibliography* (Greenwood, 1990), co-authored *Crisis Intervention with the Elderly: Theory, Practical Issues, and Training Procedures (*1988*),* and edited *ACCESS: Aging Curriculum Content for Education in the Social-Behavioral Sciences* (1990). She has also been a member of the Governor's Advisory Board on Alzheimer's Disease and Related Disorders.

ISBN 0-313-28398-2

90000>

9 780313 283987

HARDCOVER BAR CODE